THE NEW COMPLETE
ALASKAN MALAMUTE

Ch. Kougarok, a Best in Show winner in his native Alaska, once named the greatest dog in Alaska. He is owned by Kay and Linton Moustakis.

THE NEW COMPLETE
ALASKAN MALAMUTE

Maxwell Riddle
and
Beth J. Harris

HOWELL
BOOK HOUSE
New York

Macmillan General Reference
A Simon & Schuster Macmillan Company
1633 Broadway
New York, NY 10019-6785

Library of Congress Cataloging-in-Publication Data
Riddle, Maxwell.
    The new Complete Alaskan Malamute / Maxwell Riddle and Beth J. Harris.
        p. cm.
        Rev. ed. of: The complete Alaskan Malamute / by Maxwell Riddle and Eva B. Seeley. 1976.
        ISBN 0-87605-008-9
        1. Alaskan Malamute. I. Harris, Beth J. II. Riddle, Maxwell. Complete Alaskan Malamute. III. Title.
  SF429.A67R5   1990
   636.7'3—dc20   89-29796   CIP

10 9 8 7

Printed in the United States of America

Contents

The Authors

Maxwell **Riddle** still lives on the farm where he was born at Ravenna, Ohio. His father, H. Warner Riddle, was a breeder of bloodhounds. Maxwell's first dogs were two foxhounds and a Great Dane. After college he became a pioneer in Ohio Field Trials for springer spaniels and retrievers. He was an organizer of the Ravenna Field Trial Club and the Ravenna Kennel Club and has been president of both. He was show chairman at Ravenna for thirty-eight years. He has also been president and show chairman of Western Reserve Kennel Club of Cleveland, and is an honorary life member.

Mr. Riddle began judging in 1933 and became an all-breed judge about thirty years later. He has been writing a dog column for the *Cleveland Press* for thirty-eight years, and he wrote a separate column for other papers and magazines in the United States and Canada. He has won every writing award for which he has been eligible many times, and has served as president and vice president of the Dog Writers Association of America. He is associate editor of *Dog World*, and writes for English *Dog World* and *Review Chien 2000* in France.

His books include *The Springer Spaniel, The Loveable Mongrel, This Is the Chihuahua, The Complete Book of Puppy Training and Care, Dog People Are Crazy, Your Show Dog, A Quick Guide to Standards for Show Dogs, The New Shetland Sheepdog,* and *The New Complete Brittany.* He was a contributor to the *World Book Encyclopedia, Encyclopedia Americana,* the *Hunter's Encyclopedia,* and was the major contributor to *Modern Dog Encyclopedia.* He also contributed to *Champion Dogs of the World* and the *International Dog Encyclopedia.* He revised the second edition of the latter.

As a dog show judge, Mr. Riddle has officiated in South Africa, England, Japan, Hong Kong, Ceylon, Cuba, Australia, New Zealand, and twenty-seven times in South America, plus a number of times each in the Caribbean Islands, and in Canada from Vancouver and the Yukon Territory to Nova Scotia and Newfoundland. He has twice been named "Dog Writer of the Year" in the Gaines national poll; twice "Dog Journalist of the Year" in the *Kennel Review* annual poll; and "Dogdom's Man of the Year" in the Gaines poll. He was honored in Cleveland when Mayor Carl Stokes proclaimed December 14, 1968, to be Maxwell Riddle Day, a most fitting tribute for a man whose accomplishments as an authority on dogs are unparalleled among his contemporaries in the field.

Beth J. (Finder) Harris is one of dogdom's distinguished ladies, also one of its most active. From infancy, her interest in purebred dogs was fostered by her family. The dogs of Ms. Harris's Beowulf's Hilltop are renowned for their outstanding temperament and quality, both in the show ring and in obedience competition.

As a small child in New Hampshire, she was introduced to Arctic dogs through Lorna Demidoff's Siberian Huskies of Monadnock Kennels. During the mid-fifties, Ms. Harris had the opportunity to meet the famous dog driver Stuart Mace of Snowmass, Colorado, and his approximately two hundred dogs when she moved for a brief time to nearby Carbondale. Undeniably, her life changed at the very moment Stuart confronted his dogs, raised his arms, and said, "Sing boys!" Two hundred sled dogs raised their muzzles to the sky as a deafening "Arctic choir." Having suddenly "fallen in love," she knew that sled dogs had to be a part of her life. It was not until 1962, however, that she was able to purchase her first Alaskan Malamute puppy, which grew up to be Ch. Beowulf Thor, C.D.

Beth Harris has been very active as an exhibitor, a professional handler, an all-breed obedience trainer, a breed club founder and officer, in addition to belonging to many single and all-breed clubs at national and local levels. She has been a featured writer for virtually all magazines devoted to Arctic dogs, and particularly Alaskan Malamutes. Ms. Harris has been a featured columnist for the breed, and has written articles of general interest to all fanciers for both *Dog World* and the *American Kennel Gazette* in addition to writing for numerous other publications.

While en route to her B.A. in psychology, Ms. Harris gained the highest scholastic honor, an invitation to join Phi Beta Kappa. She has also earned California certification for drug counseling and is currently studying for her master's degree in psychology. Beth Harris and her dogs make their home in Sacramento, California.

Acknowledgments

Many people have helped to make this book possible. We list a few of them, though by no means all of them: Keith Hurrell, Ilene J. Mulry, Jeff and Michele Loucks, Linda Dowdy, Dr. T. K. L. Bourns, Ed Dixon, Jeanne Olbrich, Nancy Russell, Virginia Devaney, Henry W. Dodd, J. Linton Moustakis, Cindy Adams, and all those who helped on the first edition of this book.

THE NEW COMPLETE
ALASKAN
MALAMUTE

Captain Ross (later Rear Admiral Sir John) is shown meeting Eskimos on his first trip to the Arctic in 1818. Note the harness on the dogs.

1

The Eskimo People
and Their Dogs

IF WE ARE TO APPRECIATE the remarkable qualities of the Alaskan Malamute, we ought to know something about the remarkable people who owned and developed them. The Alaskan Malamute is an Eskimo dog. It gets its name from a particular group of Eskimos known as the Malemutes. The partnership between man and dog was a vital factor in making life possible in a land generally considered too inhospitable for human beings.

The Eskimos are a fairly homogeneous race of people who occupy nearly all the Arctic Coast from the Bering Sea north to Point Barrow, then all the way across the continent, and across the sea to Greenland. It is an inhospitable land, desired by no one until the white man found it a rich source of fur, minerals, and now oil. It is a land without trees and with very little vegetation except lichens. There are long periods of darkness for six months of the year, and for six to nine months each year the land is covered with snow and ice.

The radiation theory proposes that successive waves of people crossed the Bering Strait when it was dry, perhaps even by boat when the strait was under water, and were forced to move south or north by succeeding migrations. Some did, of course, but it is now believed that our Plains states were also occupied about 15,000 years ago, and that the people may have come originally by sea and from both coasts.

Carbon-14-dating indicates that rock cave painters were at São Raimundo Nonato deep within Brazil 32,000 years ago. People of an advanced culture built row houses at Orente, 800 miles south of Santiago, Chile, 32,000 years ago. The remains of a charcoal cave fire near the tip of South America have been carbon-14-dated to be 29,000 years old.

The theory that radiation from the Bering Strait and human settlement of South America were unconnected, and possibly well separated in time, is supported by the following facts. Except for cats, no North American animals ever made it to South America. The horse originally developed in North America, then disappeared, not to return until the conquistadors brought them from Spain. But the cave painters of São Raimundo Nonato had them thousands of years before. A somewhat similar history is postulated for the dog.

The radiation theory presumes that the Eskimos came from Asia. If so, they turned north into a land which could only support a people of their hardihood and their genius. All others, with one possible exception, turned south into the fertile forests below the tree line.

It is true that Eskimos have certain features which could indicate Mongol origin. Attempts to link their language with any of the Asiatic tongues, however, have not generally been accepted by linguists. Blood type is a fairly stable genetic characteristic. The Eskimo blood type is B, and this type was unknown among the Indians, who are also supposed to have come from Asia. Apparently there was never any mixture of the two until quite modern times. And there is probably more mixture of Indian and white blood than of Eskimo and Indian blood.

Eskimos have some remarkable distinguishing features. For example, they have unusually small hands and feet. One could hardly expect this in a race forced to live under such difficult conditions. Their dentition is slightly different from that of Asians, Indians, and Caucasians. They have "shovel-shaped" incisors, and such strong jaws and teeth that they use them for tasks which those of other races could not do without destroying the teeth. They have very narrow nose bridges and, as the authors have observed, have less nasal discharge than other people in frigid weather.

Modern anthropologists have evidence that an unknown race of people inhabited the Arctic coastline before the arrival of the Eskimos. Some have given a tentative date of several thousands of years before Christ for the time of these people. If one were to accept the theory that human life began independently in North America, then one could combine this with the radiation theory. Eskimos could have been forced north from internal America and, if the unknown Arctic people still lived, have destroyed them and taken over the land.

In any case, the date at which the Eskimos entered the Arctic is not known. We do know that they began a gigantic migration about 1,000 years ago. That migration took them eastward until they at last reached Greenland. It is believed that they arrived there at about the same time as the Vikings. These people are called the "Thule People." Between 400 and 500 years ago, many of them returned across the Arctic to Alaska.

Since there was so little vegetation other than lichens, the Eskimos had to adjust to an all-meat diet. In the short summers, they caught and dried fish. Summer travel was difficult and often impossible along the lowlands because of melting ice and snow. When the freeze set in, the Eskimos could hunt for caribou, musk oxen, and other animals. To a certain extent, they got vegetable matter by eating the stomach contents of these animals. They were sometimes able to get polar bears, and they hunted for seals, walruses, and even whales.

Clothing had to be made from skins and pelts. Summer tents also had to be made from skins. In winter, ice houses or igloos were made. Utensils and hunting weapons had to be made from bones. Heat and light had to come from seal oil or other animal fats, including whale oil.

Men and women were so dependent upon each other that wife sharing was sometimes practiced. Women had to make the clothes, and they had to use their strong teeth and jaws to soften skin boots which had hardened during a day's hunt. Because of their many responsibilities, mothers could only handle one young child at a time and infanticide was sometimes practiced. All the evidence indicates, however, that Eskimos were unusually fond of children. They were, and they still are.

A more or less communistic society existed. The successful hunter and his family often had to share food with less successful hunters, for the successful one had to look ahead to the time when he and his family would be hungry.

Present knowledge indicates that the dog became a domestic animal about 20,000 years ago. It is difficult to imagine that the Eskimos could have survived without the dog. The reindeer was used in Asia but seems not to have been known by even those Eskimos living on the Asiatic side of the Bering Sea. There is some evidence that at least some of the early Eskimos did not own dogs but pulled their sleds and sledges by hand. They lived in low-lying coastal areas.

Those Eskimos living more inland, or in rougher country, must have found it impossible to haul sleds by hand, and certainly not the heavier and larger sledges. The so-called spitz, or Arctic type of dog, is a strongly dominant one, and thus it is possible that the Eskimo dog may represent the oldest of all domestic animals.

Malemut Family with Dog Sled—1881.

Malemut Family from Shaktolik—1881. Drawing is from a photograph.

2

The Malemutes,
the People of Mahle

THE WORD "ALASKA" is a corruption of the Aleut word "A-la-as-ka," meaning "great country" or "vast land." Alaska has also been spelled Alyeska, and Alyeshka. The language of the Eskimos is one with an almost endless number of suffixes, each carrying a subtle grade of meaning. One suffix is "-miut." It has been translated in two ways: "the people" and "inhabitants of."

One group of Eskimos called itself the Mahlemiut. The meaning of "Mahle" is not known, but we can translate the full term as "the people of Mahle." Most Eskimos are rather small in size, a factor permitting greater endurance under Arctic conditions. But E. W. Nelson, who was on the *Corwin* in 1881, wrote as follows:

> The Malemut and the people of the Kaviak Peninsula, including those of the islands in Bering Strait, are tall, active, and remarkably well built. Among them it is common to see men from five feet ten inches to six feet tall, and of proportionate build. I should judge the average to be nearly or quite equal in height to the whites.
>
> As a race, the Eskimos are very hardy and insensible to cold. While the Corwin was at anchor in Hotham Inlet, during the fall of 1881, I found a Malemut woman with two little girls, one about two years and the other about five years of age, lying fast asleep on the deck of the vessel, clothed only in their ordinary garments. A very raw wind was blowing at the time, and it was very difficult for us to keep warm even while moving about in heavy garments.

While I was at the head of Norton Sound during February, when the temperature stood at minus forty degrees Fahrenheit, a boy ten years of age, with a sled and three dogs, was sent back several miles along the previous day's trail to recover a pair of lost snowshoes. He started off alone and returned a few hours later with the snowshoes, his cheeks glowing red from the cold, but without other indication of the effect of the temperature.

In 1877, Nelson was commissioned to make a collection for the U.S. National Museum in Alaska. His report, published in the *Eighteenth Annual Report of the Bureau of American Ethnology,* has much to say about the Malemutes:

> The Shaktolik people told me that in ancient times, before the Russians came (Authors: 1765 and later), the Unalit occupied all the coast of Norton Sound from Pastolik northward to a point a little beyond Shaktolik. At that time, the southern limit of the Malemut was at the head of Norton Bay. They have since advanced and occupied village after village until now the people of Shaktolik and Unalaklit are mainly Malemut, or a mixture of Malemut and Unalit. They added that since the disappearance of the reindeer along the coast, the Malemut have become much less numerous then formerly.

Nelson is not writing here of the domesticated reindeer used in Asia for food, milk, skins, and transportation, but of the American reindeer, called the caribou. The latter move in vast herds on long migrations, and they appear to have changed their migration route for unknown reasons. The Malemute population dropped as its food supply lessened.

"Various Russians," Nelson continued, "and others, who were living in that region in 1872 and 1873, informed me that at that time there were about 200 people living in the village of Kigiktauik, while in 1881 I found only about 12 to 14. At the time first named, the mountains bordering the coast in that neighborhood swarmed with reindeer, and in addition to the Unalit, many Malemut had congregated there to take advantage of the hunting.

"During November, 1880, I found a family of Malemut living in a miserable hut on the upper part of the Anvik River. As stated elsewhere, these people have become spread over a wide region."

Dr. John Simpson, the ship's doctor, who had wintered at Barrow in 1827, was one of the first white men to reach that point. He wrote of four great Eskimo trading centers, one of which was on the shores of the Kotzebue Sound. This was the land of the Mahlemiuts, or as we now spell it, Malemutes.

Two great rivers empty into Kotzebue Sound, the Kobuk and the Noatak. Indians and inland Eskimos could bring their furs down to the trading center and sell them for goods of Asiatic origin, and they could buy dogs.

Lieutenant George M. Stoney, who took part in a naval exploration of Alaska in 1900, reported seeing forty Kobuk Eskimos, fifty dogs, and twelve sleds. They were returning to the mountains after trading with the Malemutes. These Eskimos were probably also Malemutes. For in 1887, Lieutenant John C. Cantwell had reported that the Kobuk River Eskimos spoke the "Malamiut dialect of the coast."

Lieutenant Stoney reported that some sleds were drawn by men, women, and dogs all hitched up together. And he noted one woman with a child in her parka, dragging a sled while her husband pushed and guided from behind. A single dog helped the woman pull. Lieutenant Stoney observed that the inland Eskimos seldom used many dogs. Food was scarce so they used only one or two as helpers.

The Malamute dogs of that time were heavy freighting dogs and they were probably as nearly purebred as an Eskimo society could manage. But in 1896, gold was discovered on Bonanza Creek in the Klondike. The massive rush of the gold miners created a demand for Malamutes which could not be met.

Outside dogs were brought in by both the miners and other fortune hunters. Among others, St. Bernards were used. They were great "pullers," as the miners said. All these dogs were crossed with Malamutes and other Arctic dogs. Good dog teams could bring as much as $1700, and an individual dog might cost as much as $500.

From that time on, people began to boast of wolf crosses and even of harnessing purebred wolves which had been captured as puppies. Probably very little of this was true, but what was true was that the fame of the Malamutes caused all of these dogs to be called Malamutes.

What was also true was that the crossbreds quickly began to return to the so-called spitz type to which all the northern breeds belong. This Arctic type has been dominant for more centuries than man can unearth. So even the first generation of crossbreds tended to look more like the spitz dogs than the other half of their breeding. Within three generations, there would be no sign of outside blood.

There would, of course, be slight variations within the Arctic type, since dogs in isolated communities would be inbred. These differences can partially account for slight variations found in modern Alaskan Malamutes. They do not indicate any impure breeding in present-day dogs, nor any departure from pure type.

A rare photograph taken about 1895 of commodity trains at a Hudson Bay Company far north trading post.

3

Arctic Explorers Tell
of Their Great Dogs

PEOPLE WHO OWN Alaskan Malamutes, or for that matter any of the Arctic breeds, ought to know something of the proud record their dogs have made in the service of the Arctic peoples. All the Arctic breeds share much in common—their ability to work under near-killing conditions, their hardihood in the Arctic cold, and their willingness to work even on near-starvation diets. Many of their great services were rendered to Arctic explorers, and so here we tell something of those explorers.

The search for a Northwest Passage to Asia began in the early 1700s, but the great age of Arctic exploration is roughly dated from 1740 to 1890. Most of the explorers went north from Europe and tried to go west. Others, the Spanish for example, went around Cape Horn and then began to explore the Pacific Coast of America northward. The great George Vancouver did the same for England.

Meanwhile, the Russians moved across Siberia. In 1728, Vitus Bering passed through the strait which bears his name. Three years later, the explorer Girondeff sighted the American coast. In 1741, Bering and Alexei Chirikov also located the American coast. Bering's ship was wrecked on the shore of the island that bears his name, and he died there December 8, 1741. By 1775, the Russians had set up a series of trading stations along the southern coast of Alaska.

In one of history's greatest land trips, Alexander Mackenzie crossed along the Arctic shores to Cape Menzies and returned. The great river bears his name, and one sometimes reads of dogs called Mackenzie River Malamutes. His journey was in 1792–93.

The first explorers to reach the north coast of Alaska, however, were the Englishmen, Sir John Franklin and Captain F. W. Beechey. They had been sent in 1826 to map the coast west of the Mackenzie River. John Simpson, a ship's doctor, wintered at Barrow which was then, as now, the largest Eskimo village in the world. Point Barrow is the northernmost tip of the continent. This John Simpson is not to be confused with George Simpson, a Hudson's Bay Company employee who walked 1,910 miles from Fort Confidence to the Red River settlement from September 26, 1839 to February 2, 1840.

John Simpson describes in his journal four great Eskimo trade centers, and one of these is important to our story. It was near Kotzebue where the inland Eskimos and Indians of the Noatak and Kobuk river areas came to exchange furs for goods of Asiatic origin and dogs.

With this background, let the explorers themselves tell about their dogs. In 1824, *The Private Journal of Captain G. F. Lyon* was published. Captain Lyon had commanded one of the ships of Captain Parry on his 1821–23 trip. The ships were the *Hecla* and the *Fury.* Here are excerpts from his journal:

> They bear young at every season and seldom exceed five at a litter. In December, with the thermometer at 40 degrees below zero, the females were in several instances in heat. [My dogs] at the ship had no shelter, but lay alongside with the thermometer at 42–44 degrees (below zero), and with as little concern as if the weather had been mild.
>
> I found, by several experiments, that three of my dogs could draw me on a sledge weighing 100 pounds, at a rate of one mile in six minutes; and as proof of the strength of a well grown dog, my leader drew 196 pounds singly, and to the same distance in eight minutes.
>
> At another time, seven of my dogs ran a mile in four minutes, 30 seconds, drawing a heavy sledge full of men. . . . Afterwards, in carrying stores to the Fury, one mile distant, nine dogs drew 1611 pounds in the space of nine minutes. My sledge was on wooden runners, neither shod nor iced; had they been the latter, at least 40 pounds might have been added for every dog.

Writing of their marvelous ability to find their way, and their "homing instinct," he wrote: "I have often returned home from the Fury, a distance of near a mile, in pitchy darkness, and admidst clouds of snow drift, entirely under the care of those trusty servants who, with their noses down to the snow, have galloped on board entirely directed by their sense of smelling. Had they erred, or even been at all restive, no human means could have brought us on board until the return of clear weather."

The dogs were, of course, hungry all the time, and Captain Lyon

Harper's Bazar for June 12, 1882, depicts the struggle of men and dogs to save equipment from the sinking cruiser *Jeannette*.

11

remarks that "the dogs ate at least two dead Eskimos." These were bodies exposed on the ice when burial was impossible. Other accounts tell of the curious sense of conscience possessed by some of the dogs.

There is an Eskimo saying that when a marooned Eskimo starts to eat his dogs, he is doomed, for he is destroying his only means of transportation. But it has been noted that some dogs will ravenously devour a dead comrade, sometimes before he is quite dead. Others will not touch the body until it has been frozen for a day or so. Still others will not touch it at all, and prefer to starve to death.

Franz Boas had some interesting comments on the character of the dogs, as reported in "The Central Eskimo" in the *Sixth Annual Report of the Bureau of Ethnology,* Smithsonian Institution, in 1888:

> If any dog is lazy, the driver calls out his name and he is lashed, but it is necessary to hit the dog called, for if another is struck he feels wronged and will turn upon the dog whose name has been called; the leader enters into the quarrel, and soon the whole pack is huddled up in one howling mass, and no amount of lashing and beating will separate the fighting team. The only thing to do is to wait until their wrath has abated and clear the traces.

One of these authors had an experience worth mentioning at this point. It happened at Point Barrow. Heavy polar winds had broken up the ice and had piled huge cakes as large as the sides of houses upon the shore. The weather had calmed and the ocean beyond was again frozen over. The temperature was 35 degrees below zero.

In searching for a passage to the ocean, a comparatively round mound was found, but as the leading dogs went over the mound, they disappeared. Three of them had fallen into the carcass of a whale. They hung by their harness and tried to fight, and those outside set up their own fight.

The driver and the author had to jump into the carcass, take the dogs out of harness, and then haul them out. But not until the other dogs had stopped their own brawl.

One thinks of the Arctic Ocean ice as being as flat and smooth as on a pond, but the winds often break up the ice floes, leave open-water areas, and pile blocks upon blocks. Nor is the going always smooth on land. The gentle naturalist, John Muir, in *The Cruise of the Corwin* gives several excellent descriptions of both the driving and the way in which the Eskimos kept their dogs:

> . . . we found the dogs, nearly a hundred of them, with eleven sleds, making, as they lay at their ease, an imposing picture among the white ice. Three teams were straightened out . . . the Captain and I were taken on behind the other two; and away we sped over the frozen ceiling of the sea, two rows of tails ahead.
>
> The distance to the village . . . was about three miles, the first mile very rough and apparently hopelessly inaccessible to sleds. But the wolfish dogs and drivers seemed to regard it all as a regular turnpike, and jogged merrily

on, up one side of a tilted block or slab and down the other with a sudden pitch and plunge, swishing round sideways on squinted cakes, and through pools of water and sludge in blue, craggy hollows, on and on, this way and that, with never a halt, the dogs keeping up a steady jog trot, and the leader simply looking over his shoulder occasionally for directions in the worst places. My sled was not upset at all, the captain's only twice . . . [the dogs] are as steady as oxen, each keeping its trace line tight, and showing no inclination to shirk.

These Eskimos were Chukchis, living on the Siberian coast, and Muir tells how they lived:

Three or four families live in one [hut], each having a private polog of deerskins of which there are several thicknesses on the floor. We were shown into one—the snuggest storm nest imaginable and perfectly clean.

The common hut is far otherwise; dogs mingle with food, hair is everywhere, and strangely persistent smells that defy even the Arctic frosts. The children seemed in fair ratio to adults. When a child is to be nursed, the mother merely pulls out one of her arms from the roomy sleeve of her parka and pushes it down until the breast is exposed. The breasts are pendulous and cylindrical like those of the Tlingits.

The dishes used in domestic affairs are of wood, and in the smallest of these the puppies, after licking them, were often noticed to lie down. They seemed made specially for them, so well did they fit. Dogs were eagerly licking large kettles, also, in which seal meat had been boiled.

[Again:] . . . while puppies and nursing mother dogs and children may be seen scattered here and there, or curled snugly in the pots and eating troughs, after they have licked them clean, making a squalor that is picturesque and daring beyond description.

In all the huts, however, there are from one to three luxurious bedrooms. The walls, ceilings, and floor are of soft reindeer skins, and (each polog) has a trough filled with oil for heat and light. After hunting all day on the ice, making long, rough, stormy journeys, the Chukchi hunter, muffled and hungry, comes into his burrow, eats his fill of oil and seal or walrus, then strips himself naked and lies down in his closed fur nest, his polog, in glorious ease, to smoke and sleep.

Muir has this description of summer travel:

. . . eight canoe loads of Eskimos, with all their goods, tents, children, etc., passed close along the shore going toward Icy Cape; all except one were drawn by dogs—from three to five to each canoe—attached by a long string of walrus hide, and driven by a woman or half-grown girl, or boy. "Ooch, ooch, ooch," they said while urging them along. They dragged the canoe with perhaps two tons altogether at two and one half miles per hour. When they came to a sheer bluff, the dogs swam and the drivers got into the canoe until the beach again admitted of tracking. The canoe that had no dogs was paddled and rowed by both men and women. One woman, pulling an oar on the starboard bow, was naked from the waist. They came from Point Hope.

John Muir wrote this journal in 1881 as the *Corwin* searched for the remains of the lost explorer De Long and his ship, the *Jeannette.* We have quoted from the Houghton-Mifflin edition of 1917, edited by W. F. Badé.

By far the greatest and most tragic description of the Arctic dogs was written by Lieutenant Commander George Washington De Long. His cruise in the *Jeannette* began at San Francisco July 8, 1879. He kept a daily log, until he died of cold and starvation early in October 1881. The *Jeannette* was trying to reach the North Pole via the western Arctic. On August 25, 1879, George De Long in command wrote that he was at St. Lawrence Bay, Siberia, and that he had forty dogs and nine sleds.

> They are all good sized and strong, and thus far roam around the deck in a happy go lucky kind of way, fighting every five minutes and seemingly well contented. . . . The nature of these dogs is to fight at all times, and unless they are beaten well, they will not keep the peace at all.

When four of the dogs had to be rescued from an ice floe, De Long wrote: "The remaining dogs were very indignant at the absent but returning ones, and had they not been prevented would have given them a fight as a celebration, looking no doubt on the enforced separation as some new dodge for shirking work."

At one point, the dogs had to be fed frozen food, and De Long observed that some had rotting teeth and some none at all. "These, while trying to get the frozen food down, are frequently robbed by the more vigorous dogs who have good jaws, and who can, if necessary, reduce an iron bar to proper size for their stomachs."

The *Jeannette* was locked in ice, and Lieutenant De Long took the time to write an incomparable description of his dogs:

> The weather is gloomy, depressing, and disagreeable. Velocities ranging from 10 to 23 miles drive the snow from the face of the floe in clouds, and other snow falling makes distant objects, say 100 yards, invisible. Here and there alongside the ship a little white lump indicates that there is a dog beneath it, and even the regular and irregular dog fights are discontinued until the weather gets clearer and friend can be distinguished from foe.
>
> . . . Why they fight, how they fight, and whom they fight, seem to be purely abstract questions with them, so long as it is a fight. For instance dogs one and two will see dog three in a good position, perhaps enjoying a meat can that has been empty for months and has, of course, no nutriment. As if by concerted plan one and two will spring on three, roll him over, and seemingly tear him to pieces. Fortunately the wool is so long and thick that an attacking dog gets a mouth full of hair before his front teeth reach the flesh, so no great damage is generally done. The vulnerable places are the ears, and the belly.
>
> I have seen an attacked dog run, and, lying on his stomach, shove his head into a snow bank with impunity, while his foes are choking over the hair they tore from his back. However, this is a long digression. Suddenly dog three will turn on dog two and be promptly aided by dog one, his previous foe. By this

Plug ugly.

Foxie.

Bones.

Kas-mat-ka.

SOME OF THE DOGS.
from sketches

Sketches of dogs on the *Jeannette* by Raymond L. Newcomb, naturalist.

time the whole pack has gathered as if by magic, and a free and indiscriminate fight occurs, until the advent of the quartermaster, and a merciless application of the whip breaks up the row.

They divide up into little gangs of three or four, and in these friendly cliques they also fight. For days everything may go on smoothly, when one of the set does something offensive to his mates, and one of them (or sometimes all of them) administers a thrashing, and the offender is sent to Coventry until their feelings calm down. It is a common occurrence to see a dog on the black list, a quarter of a mile from the ship, all alone and afraid to come in until his time is up.

He then approaches fawningly, wagging his tail deprecatingly to become reconciled, and is either welcomed with wagging tails or snarling teeth, in which latter case he retires to his isolated position for another spell.

Another peculiarity is, that though they make no demonstration at any dog singly, or a team, going away, except the most doleful howling in concert, they seem to consider it a terrible indignity that he, or they, should presume to come back. The remainder of the pack scent the arriving one, several hundred yards off, and gather awaiting him. If the team comes in, a rough-and-tumble fight commences between the harnessed and the free, which requires two or three men to stop. As soon as the harness is off, they are all smooth and quiet again, the cliques reassembling and moving off to their usual haunts.

If a single dog, so much the worse luck for him. As soon as he appears, they are all on him. Let him be never so wary, and slink around the hummocks to reach the ship unobserved, some one dog sees his head, or his tail, gives the signal, and away they go. It is then a question of speed, for if the single dog but reaches his usual sunning or stopping place, he is safe; for, by some rule always observed, the getting to home base restores him to the full rights of citizenship. The cautious approach, and the great speed on the last stretch, are worthy of much higher intelligence than we usually give to dogs.

The care they bestow on each other in distress or trouble, arising from disability, has a marked exhibition in the case of Jack and Snuffy. Snuffy had his nose bitten into in a fight at St. Michael's last summer, and in consequence his head is twice the natural size, by swelling and diseased bone. Jack is seemingly Snuffy's brother, and he is devoted to him beyond much human fraternal affection. He stays by Snuffy, cleans him, sees that he is not molested by other dogs, follows him into enemies' camps, leads him through in safety, and guards his retreat. Let Snuffy get a tid-bit, like an old moccasin or a piece of hide, Jack sees him secure it, stands by him while he chews it, and if he leaves it, chews it for him until he seems to want it again, when it is promptly surrendered. So accustomed have the pack become to this sort of thing that they permit many liberties with their food which they would resent with a well dog.

Their cunning is extraordinary. Going out the other night at 12 for meterological observations, about a dozen of them came around me in great excitement about something or other. Looking around for a cause, I observed a good-sized dog head first in a barrel at an angle, with only his tail and flanks sticking out.

He had gone in for some walrus meat at the bottom, and no dog had driven him out, because his stern view was not recognizable as belonging to a bully or not. Anxious to save the meat, I went to the barrel and drove him out, when half of the gang recognizing him as no great fighter, pitched into him, while the other half fought among themselves for entry into the barrel. For fear of catching a Tartar, they had waited for some one to solve the conundrum "Who is in the barrel?"

In another entry in his log, De Long writes:

Having great difficulty in getting any work out of our "hoodlum gang," Jack, Tom, and Wolf, a method of punishment had to be devised. Ordinarily they lie around on ash-heaps all day in the sun, blinking lazily, and ready to head an attack on some wandering dog in search of a bone, or more particularly sallying out to meet some dog returning with the hunters, who has incurred their grave displeasure by assisting at any work. The sight of a harness, merely, reminds them of a pressing engagement elsewhere; and the moving of a dog sled in their range of vision seems suggestive of the advisability of a change of base.

Accordingly, each morning, when the ice has to be dragged in for melting, these three are occupied surveying the work from a distance until it is completed, and then they unite in an attack on those dogs who did the dragging. They were caught by strategy today, however, and harnessed up; but Tom slipped his harness quietly and bolted, while Wolf chewed his through and escaped. When caught they were securely tied to a rope over the stern, and kept there until 10 P.M. when, in order that their howls might not keep everybody awake, they were anchored with an ice-claw some distance off. This disgusted them. Tom took his punishment solemnly and quietly, but Wolf yelled incessantly, so much so that Tom got provoked and thrashed him twice into silence.

Toward the end of June 1881, the *Jeannette* was crushed by ice and sank. The men left in two boats but got separated in a storm. The De Long boat was wrecked and the men began a long overland trek in search of some habitation, food, and shelter. Their food ran out, and one by one, the dogs had to be killed for food. And one by one the men began to die. On the 113th day, the last dog was killed. And on the 140th day, the last entry was made in Lieutenant De Long's log. It said: "Boyd and Gortz died during the night. Mr. Collins dying." His own death came shortly after.

Emil St. Godard, winner of the 1927 World Dog Race, The Pas, Manitoba.

4

The First International Dog Sled Race

THE GORHAM, New Hampshire, winter carnival of 1920 brought in a dog team which gave exhibitions. The team was that of Arthur T. Walden of Wonalancet. His dogs were crossbreds, and the leader was the famous dog Chinook. Walden and his team created so much interest that an international race was planned for the next season. It did not, however, take place until 1922.

It was this race which truly sparked national interest in the sport of driving teams of dogs. Viewed from this distance, it seems unlikely that either Siberian Huskies or Alaskan Malamutes would have come onto the North American scene as purebred breeds had not this and other races been held. For that reason, we give an account of the race here.

W. A. Brown of Berlin, New Hampshire, organized the race. Brown was the owner of the Brown Paper Company, and he was famous for his stable of Arabian horses. Brown sponsored two teams. Walden was the driver of one, and Henry Skeen drove the other. Jean Lebel of Quebec drove the third, and Jacques Suzzaine, a Canadian then living at Lake Placid, New York, the other.

The race was 120 miles, split into segments of 40 miles each day for the three days. The course went from Berlin to Colebrook, to Lancaster, and back to Berlin. That race actually was held under the title of the Eastern International Dog Derby. Camera crews from both news and motion picture services attended to film the great event. Walden won. Henry Skeen was second; Jacques Suzzaine was third; and Jean Lebel was fourth.

The race was then moved to Quebec. That first race had created such interest that it made North America wake up to the fact that dogsledding could be a great sport. The Quebec races brought Early Brydges from The Pas, Manitoba, in 1924. He had learned the gang hitch from Walter Goyne, who had seen it in Alaska. Brydges was the first to use it in the East.

In 1925, Emil St. Godard, then only nineteen years old, came to race from The Pas, as did "Shorty" Russick, the "little Russian" from Flin Flon. Walden also returned for the 1925 race. These three, plus Leonhard Seppala, became some of the immortals of North American sled dog racing.

Emil St. Godard won the 1925 race. He gained an almost two-hour lead over the heavier, freighting type Walden-Chinook team. His time for the race was 12 hours, 49 minutes, 45 seconds, as compared to Walden's 14 hours, 3 minutes, and 20 seconds. St. Godard finished with seven dogs.

Two things ought to be remembered in this connection. The lighter, faster dogs were coming into vogue for racing. And, although crossbreds did well, and made records, it became evident that the purebred northern dogs had greater stamina and endurance under severe conditions in day-after-day work. Also, men like Emil St. Godard, Shorty Russick, and Roland Lombard trained equally as hard as their dogs. Some of the younger drivers would run all or most of the way, so as to lighten the load drawn by the dogs.

5

Allan Alexander "Scotty" Allan

IT IS A NAME no Alaskan Malamute owner should ever forget, as "Scotty" Allan surely ranks with the greatest in the history of the international ranks of sled dog trainers and drivers. Moreover, his influence upon what was to become the purebred Alaskan Malamute was incalculable. It was Scotty who showed Short Seeley what great freighting dogs of the North looked like, and who gave her the dog she named Rowdy of Nome.

He was born Allan Alexander Allan in a small town in Scotland. His father raised sheep and had a blacksmith shop; he was also noted for his ability to understand animals, and their ability to understand and obey him. Young Allan had this rapport to an even greater degree. Short but athletic, Allan once won a footrace for boys under eight, and after that he won races against older boys.

In his early teens, he took over the training of a Border collie which refused to work for its owner. Scotty Allan won the dog's confidence, and the team went on to win the Grand National Sheep Dog Trials.

His father then sent the boy to a training school for horsemen. There his remarkable ability to gain the confidence of animals again proved itself. At nineteen, he was hired to take a registered purebred Clydesdale stallion to South Dakota. The horse was notably bad-tempered. During a furious North Atlantic storm, Scotty was able to calm all of the horses being shipped. The big horse was put in quarantine, as required. Scotty and his dog waited it out. Then horse, dog, and Scotty made their home in a boxcar during the long trip to South Dakota.

Scotty worked about in the Dakotas and Montana, then met and married a girl from Oregon. But the lure of adventure was still strong, and the Klondike gold strike was even stronger. Scotty went north, promising to come back for his wife, which, eventually, he did. He finally reached Nome. By this time, he had a dog team of his own. It consisted of a leader named Dubby, and four pups from one litter which no one wanted. He had bought Dubby from a Hudson's Bay Company kennel.

Scotty had arrived in America in 1887. Now, in Nome, his exploits and his astonishing ability with dogs had given him a great reputation. He joined Judge Albert Fink in organizing the first official dog sled race. They called it the All Alaska Sweepstakes. It was a nonstop race of some 408 miles from Nome to Candle and back. Fink won the first race, in 1908. The next year, Jacob Berger won, with Scotty driving. Scotty joined with the writer Esther Darling to form the kennel of Darling and Allan.

They were so successful that Scotty had a record of three wins, three seconds, and a third in ten years. Darling wrote several books about racing, and about Scotty's famed lead dog, Baldy of Nome. It used to be said that the driver is the hardest worker on the team. Scotty Allan proved that. He practiced by running long distances with his team, eating a minimum amount of food, staying up twenty-four hours, etc.

Doctors warned Scotty that he had to slow down. But Scotty only shrugged. He wanted to experience life, all of it. When the Lord summoned him, Scotty would go willingly. But meanwhile, life had changed and there was much to experience.

Arthur Treadwell Walden had moved to New Hampshire, where he bred, trained, and raced. Richard E. Byrd was preparing for an exploratory trip to the Antarctic and to the South Pole. Walden was commissioned to collect the dogs and train both dogs and drivers. He called upon Scotty to help, and, of course, Scotty responded. That is how he happened to meet Eva "Short" Seeley.

But Scotty could not go to Antarctica. Walden, who lived to be ninety-one, went on without him. Scotty returned to join his family in California. There, on December 1, 1941, he died peacefully in his sleep.

There are many periodicals and books which have material on Scotty. Putnam published a book by Scotty himself. In addition, Esther Darling wrote a number of books about the Alaskan sled dogs, their races, and their owners. One of these, *Baldy of Nome,* is about Scotty and his famous lead dog.

6

The Early Years—
Sled Dogs in
New England

by Eva B. Seeley

ARTHUR TREADWELL WALDEN, veteran of the
Alaska freighting trials and winner of the first international sled dog race,
had settled in Wonalancet, New Hampshire. He bought the Wonalancet
Inn, and set up his kennel behind it. His wife, Kate "Sleeper" Walden,
operated the inn.

Eva Brunelle, a physical education instructor, and a small package
loaded with energy, would one day be world-renowned as the founder of
the breed we know as the Alaskan Malamute. But now she was coming
north from Florida to help set up a winter carnival in her hometown of
Worcester, Massachusetts. On the way north, she saw a newspaper article
about Walden and his dog team. It occurred to her that the sled dogs (called
wolf dogs in the article) would be a great attraction at the carnival, and the
promoters of the carnival agreed. She called Walden and engaged him. As
it turned out, a second team also appeared.

The trail for the sled dogs was on a golf course. Walden took Eva
Brunelle for her first ride. Along the way, a cat scooted across the trail and
the nine-dog team gave chase. Walden upset the sled, possibly saving Eva
from serious injury, but injuring his own hand. Eva was thrilled by the ride
and became a sled dog enthusiast forever. The year was 1923.

Chinook Kotzebue Gripp; breeder-owner, Eva Seeley.

Eva Brunelle's fiancé, Milton Seeley, worked with chemicals. He had come to Worcester for the carnival, and he too was thrilled by the dogs. When he and Eva married, they decided to honeymoon at Wonalancet. Milton's health was not good and eventually the Seeleys decided that he should retire and they should move to Wonalancet. They bought land, set up their own home and kennel, and laid out a sledding trail. That was in 1927.

That January, Arthur Walden was busy collecting dogs and training dogs and drivers for the first Byrd Antarctic Expedition. There was a need for fifty more dogs than were present, and they arrived by train and truck. Among Walden's aides was A. A. "Scotty" Allan.

Scotty called Eva over to see one of the dogs. This was a big, gentle dog which seemed to love to be petted. Scotty told Eva (by this time known to everyone as "Short") that this dog was the true type of Alaskan freighter dog. Since the dog had no name, she was allowed to name him—Rowdy of Nome. He was assigned to Edward Goodale's team.

Short did not have many dogs of that type in her growing kennel. She had fallen in love with Rowdy, and now she began to try to find dogs of his type. Thus, it can be said that it was Scotty Allan who instilled in her mind the picture of what the Alaskan Malamute should be.

Arthur Walden had started the New England Sled Dog Club in 1924, and there had been racing ever since. However, he was busy training dogs for the Byrd Expedition, and the racing schedule had declined. Walter Channing was president, but wished to resign. He agreed to stay on until a successor could be found, provided Short Seeley would help him. She did, and restored the racing season to its normal schedule, with help from her husband, Milton.

The Seeleys now began their search for dogs of Rowdy's type. Leonhard Seppala had decided to race only Siberians, and had established his kennels at Poland Spring, Maine. He gave the Seeleys a dog. The Seeleys also obtained Yukon Jad and Bessie at that time.

Elizabeth Ricker of Poland Springs Hotels raced Siberians, and she decided to seek recognition of the breed at the American Kennel Club. This gave Short Seeley the idea of registering a truly American breed, which she was developing at Wonalancet.

The second of Admiral Byrd's expeditions—called BAE II—required more dogs. The Seeleys, who had been racing Siberians as well as breeding the dogs to be called Alaskan Malamutes, were able to supply dogs of their own breeding. In 1929, Yukon Jad and Bessie had produced four sons. This was the first litter to be bred of similar stock. They can, therefore, be called the first Alaskan Malamute puppies.

The four were Gripp of Yukon, Tugg of Yukon, Kearsarge of Yukon, and Finn of Yukon. Finn was sometimes heard on radio broadcasts from Little America. Gripp became the first champion in the breed. Kearsarge did not return from the Antarctic. His fate is not known.

Saturday Evening Post cover artist Norman Rockwell (right) spends an afternoon with Hall of Famers Robert and Elizabeth Aninger and their dogs.

7

Recognition and
the Parent Club

FOLLOWING THE DEPARTURE of the first Byrd Antarctic Expedition, BAE I, Eva and Milton Seeley began an intensive study of the Alaskan dogs. They had already produced a uniform litter. Now they wished to continue and expand. Through A. A. "Scotty" Allan, they began extensive correspondence with owners and breeders in the Pacific Northwest, Alaska, and the Yukon Territory. The recognition of the Siberian Husky in 1930 encouraged Malamute owners to try for their own breed.

Frank Gough sent pictures of his dogs and explained his breeding plans. Gough had not previously considered asking for breed recognition by either the American or Canadian Kennel clubs. He was merely trying to produce uniform large freighting dogs.

Among those with whom the Seeleys corresponded, and who helped in their concept of a pure Alaskan Malamute breed, were Bishop Bentley, who traveled by dog sled over much of Alaska; the famed "Glacier Priest," Rev. Father Hubbard; and Frank DuFresne, the Alaskan judicial chief and one of the most noted sportsmen of Alaska. He had owned a team of pure white Siberian Huskies.

The Seeleys had produced a lovely home-bred bitch, and obtained another, Holly, when she returned from BAE I. A Coast Guard captain who cruised the Pacific Arctic seas brought a male which he had obtained on St. Lawrence Island. This dog was named St. Lawrence Mukluk. Mukluk was a great worker, and he was noted for both his strength and his intelligence. Mukluk was bred to a bitch of good type, and the mating produced some uniform pups. In 1932, during BAE II, the Seeleys' stock had been used for breeding, and seven uniform gray dogs were produced. They were called the Admiral Byrd Grays. Correspondents had also told them where they might find other dogs of similar type and character, and after seven years the Seeleys felt the breed was ready for recognition by the American Kennel Club.

Milton and Eva had been showing some of their Siberians at dog shows. George Foley, who had founded the Foley Dog Show Organization and who had helped many clubs and even many breeds made an appointment for them to meet Charles Inglee, president of the American Kennel Club. Foley accompanied them to the meeting.

The American Kennel Club policy is to give a breed only tentative recognition at first. Dogs must be shown in the Miscellaneous class until sufficient numbers have been registered to merit opening up the full facilities of the Stud Book to them.

Mr. Inglee explained that the dogs to be shown had to be uniform, else he could not say how long it might take to grant full recognition. He also warned them against those fringe people who are a curse to every breed since they breed poor dogs to poor dogs, hoping merely to cash in on the increasing popularity of the breed. He suggested that Milton and Eva ought to enter at least six dogs at shows, so that judges could get a chance to study them and to check them for uniformity.

In those days, Geraldine Rockefeller Dodge conducted the fabulous Morris and Essex show. It was the largest and most famous of American shows, and it was held on her great estate, Giralda, in Madison, New Jersey. Mrs. Dodge, and her manager, McClure Halle, invited the Seeleys to exhibit seven Alaskan Malamutes, seven Siberian Huskies, and seven Samoyeds. The exhibit was placed in a special tent, and it created a great deal of interest and enthusiasm. For one thing, people came to realize that these dogs were gentle and had no wolflike characteristics.

The American Kennel Club also sent several well-known judges to visit the Kotzebue kennels and to study both older dogs and puppies. Among those who came were Clarence Gray and William Cary Duncan. Other judges, such as Charles Hopton, also became interested. The original standard was based on their studies and upon their conferences with Milton and Eva. At this time, Volney Hurd, a *Christian Science Monitor* editor, helped the breed immensely. Dr. Hurd had spent a week in the area, much of it in studying the Alaskan Malamutes. Later he wrote a full-page article describing the breed.

Many of the Kotzebue dogs were lost in the Antarctic. Some were lost in accidents. Others were left behind and were destroyed either by time bombs or by starvation. In the meantime, the number of Alaskan Malamute breeders and owners was increasing rapidly.

Rowdy of Nome, born at Nome, 1927—
the dog that began it all.

Dr. Roland Lombard, famous racing driver.

Breed recognition came in 1935. In the years that followed, many dogs were brought from Alaska or the Yukon Territory. And these dogs, along with the Seeleys', formed the foundation stock for final approval of the breed by the American Kennel Club.

On April 17, 1935, the Alaskan Malamute Club was organized. The meeting was held at the Seeley home at Wonalancet. The charter members were Malamute breeders, some who were simply interested in sled dogs and racing, and some who bred Siberian Huskies. Milton Seeley was elected president; Volney Hurd of the *Christian Science Monitor,* Boston, vice president; Grace Bight (later the wife of Samuel Kirkwood, president of the American University at Beirut, Lebanon), treasurer; and Eva Seeley, Secretary.

Here one must explain AKC registration policies which existed at that time. Many dogs were of unknown ancestry. Those which appeared to be purebred would be used for breeding. Sometimes the puppies did not conform, and would be weeded out, or their parents would not be used further.

When final recognition came, there were many dogs of unknown pedigree. At one time, the American Kennel Club would grant such dogs a Stud Book number, that is, registration, provided they could win a certain number of championship points.

Later the rules were tightened. A dog of unknown or defective pedigree had to win a championship. It could still not be registered but if bred to a registered dog, its offspring could be. The American Kennel Club continued this policy as it related to certain foreign breeds, but later canceled it for American breeds. This brought protests from some Alaskan Malamute breeders and for a time, the American Kennel Club excepted certain dogs from the application of the rule. This explains why Alaskan Malamute pedigrees go back to "unknown" ancestors in so few generations.

The first recorded American Kennel Club registrations came in July 1935. The first was Gripp of Yukon, born August 24, 1929. He was sired by Yukon Jad out of Bessie and he was wolf-gray in color. Gripp also became the first champion in any country. Rowdy of Nome also was registered, as was Taku of Kotzebue.

The next year, Finn of Yukon, Kearsarge of Yukon, Patsy of Kotzebue, and Sheila of Kotzebue were registered. In 1938, Kobuk of Kotzebue, sired by Gripp out of Taku, was registered, as were his litter mates Kotlag, Navarre, and Wanda. The Chinook name did not appear until February 1944, with the registrations of Chinook's Karluk of Kotzebue, and Chinook's Sheila of Kotzebue.

In the history of North American sled dog racing, no name is as well known as that of Dr. Roland Lombard. In 1946, he registered Igloo Pak's Gripp, sired by Jiffy of Kotzebue out of Tanana of Igloo Pak. But Dr. Lombard's amazing career had begun in 1930 when he won a race against the best drivers in the world at that time. Since then he won more races than

Ch. Gripp of Yukon, first champion in the breed. Bred by Mr. and Mrs. Milton Seeley.

can be remembered. Among them are eight victories in the world championship Fur Rendezvous race at Anchorage. In half a dozen other famous races he lost by less than a second. Dr. Lombard was a founding member of the Alaskan Malamute Club of America, and for a time was its representative at the American Kennel Club.

In 1950, Earl Norris registered Klutina of Kobuk, a son of the Norris champion, Toro of Bras Coupe. Earl and Natalie Norris have played a continuing part in the progress of the breed. Earl won the Anchorage world championship race in 1947 and 1948, and Natalie won the women's race in 1954. Toro of Bras Coupe was one of history's greatest Alaskan Malamute sires, and he worked in harness for seven years before being shown to his bench championship.

We now come to the names of Paul Voelker, Robert Zoller, and Ralph and Marchetta Schmitt. They were developing and registering a different strain of Alaskan Malamutes. This is a story to be told by Robert Zoller of Husky-Pak.

The Byrd Antarctic Expeditions and World War II had taken a heavy toll of registered Alaskan Malamutes and of others which were not registered but which in the course of time might have been. By 1947, it was estimated that there were only thirty registered "base stock" dogs left. It was therefore determined to reopen the Stud Book in order to accept new foundation blood.

One effect of this was to bring about the development of the M'Loot and Husky-Pak strain. Another was to spread interest in the breed into the Midwest, the Pacific Coast, and even into Canada and Alaska itself.

As new strains developed, the Alaskan Malamute Club of America grew to encompass a truly national membership. In October 1953, the club applied for membership in the American Kennel Club. The contribution and perseverance of those original seventy-six members was so broad in scope that many have been among those selected for permanent recognition as members of the Parent Club Hall of Fame.

HALL OF FAME

The Hall of Fame is dedicated to those individuals who have made significant voluntary contributions to the breed. This recognition encompasses those who have made an impact upon the breed by promoting an improved understanding and appreciation of Alaskan Malamutes as a whole. This recognition of merit is further intended for those individuals who have contributed through an outstanding breeding program, and those who performed to protect the health and welfare of all Alaskan Malamutes.

Andre Anctil
Elizabeth Aninger and Robert Aninger: Kliquot Kennels

Dr. Kenneth Bourns and Jackie Bourns: Boru Kennels Reg. (Canada)
Roger Burggraf and Malle Burggraf: Taaralaste Kennels
Mr. and Mrs. J. W. Dawson
Virginia Devaney: Voyageur Kennels
D. C. Dillingham and Dorothy Dillingham: Tigara Kennels
Linda Dowdy: Fire'n Ice Kennels
Eleanore DuBuis: Sena-Lak Kennels
Jane Fulton: Kingmik Kennels
Robert Gormley and Martha Gormley: Barb-Far Kennels
Minnie Graham: Bearpaw Kennels (Canada)
Beth J. Harris: Beowulf Kennels
Arthur Hodgen and Natalie Hodgen: Sno-Pak Kennels
Dr. Roland Lombard and Louise Lombard
Alice Jean Lucus
Sam Maranto
J. Linton Moustakis and Kay Moustakis: Kee-Too Kennels
Earl Norris and Natalie Norris
Hal Pearson and Dorothy Pearson: Redhorse Kennels
Melvin Pokrefky and JoAnn Pokrefky: Coldfoot Kennels
Edward Rodewald and Kay Rodewald: Sky Fyre Kennels
Richard Ross and Dianne Ross: Tote-Um Kennels
Robert Russell and Nancy Russell: Storm Kloud Kennels
Ralph Schmitt and Marchetta Schmitt: Silver Sled Kennels
Eva B. (Short) Seeley and Milton Seeley: Chinook Kennels
Mr. and Mrs. Robert Spawn
Merry Stockburger
Richard Tobey
Roy Truchon and Elsie Truchon
Paul Voelker: M'Loot (strain)
Robert Zoller and Laura Zoller: Husky-Pak Kennels

AND SPECIAL MENTION

Arthur Walden
A. A. (Scotty) Allan

Eva Seeley with, l. to r., Ch. Gripp of Yukon, Finn of Yukon, and Kearsarge of Yukon. Latter was abandoned in Antarctica.

Men and dogs in an air transport plane headed for France.

34

8

The Admiral Byrd Expeditions and World War II Dogs

O N THAT OCTOBER DAY in 1939, a thousand people gathered at Wonalancet to pay tribute to the dogs who had given their lives during the two Byrd Antarctic Expeditions. A major actor that day was the Seeleys' old Alaskan Malamute, Rowdy of Nome. He was a veteran sledge dog who weighed eighty-five pounds. Rowdy had been born in Alaska, and he had been a member of the team that made a thousand-mile trek at the bottom of the world. Now he wore his Antarctic harness to which was attached the gang line. Rowdy walked slowly toward Eva Seeley, and in doing so pulled away the hemlock branches which unveiled the bronze memorial plaque.

Rowdy had never asked anything in life except to work for his masters and perhaps to lie at their feet. Now he lifted his ears, sighed, and settled down, and at that moment, a loudspeaker spoke the message sent by Sir Wilfred Grenfell to that other guest of honor, Rear Admiral Richard E. Byrd: "For this recognition of our debt to our dogs, we owe the admiral an additional debt for his presence today. 'Love me, love my dog,' is an old adage, and in the case of our Husky dogs, he would be indeed an ingrate who, having lived and traveled with them, and whose life has depended upon them, if he would not rise to the toast of today, 'To Admiral Byrd and his dogs,' coupled with: 'Our dogs, our best of friends.' " The message was signed "Wilfred Grenfell."

It all began when the then Commander Richard Evelyn Byrd was named to head an expedition of exploration on the Antarctic continent. It was necessary to assemble a large number of dogs for the expedition. And, of course, it was necessary to get thoroughly experienced drivers, to get adequate food for the dogs, and sufficient harnesses, sleds, kennels, and other things.

Arthur Treadwell Walden, one of the most famous dog drivers of his time, was selected to assemble the dogs, drivers, and equipment. Walden had won the first international sled dog race. But more important, he was a thoroughly experienced freight driver.

Walden was then living at Wonalancet, where his wife, Kate, ran the inn, and his Chinook Kennels were behind the inn. The Chinook Kennels were named after Walden's lead dog, a mongrel whose name means "warm west winds." Walden brought in another famous Alaskan driver, Scotty Allan of Nome. It was Allan who encouraged Eva to purchase Rowdy of Nome. Rowdy joined the team of Edward (later Colonel) Goodale.

In the group of dogs assembled, there were a dozen or more large freighting dogs resembling Rowdy. These were the Alaskan Malamutes. Neither they, nor the Siberian Huskies, were at that time recognized by any kennel club as being distinctive breeds. In fact, Captain Alan Innes-Taylor, who commanded the contingent of drivers and dogs in the second expedition, wrote that there was only one pure Arctic breed at that time, the Eskimo.

During 1927, many dogs were tested and many were discarded. In addition, clothing, tents, sledges, and rations for both men and dogs were worked out. Roald Amundsen sent his formula for pemmican for people.

One hundred dogs were taken by ship to Dunedin, New Zealand, and were placed in quarantine on Quarantine Island, seven miles off the coast. The dogs had not fared well on the long trip, and it was decided that they had not received the proper food. During the past year, Milton Seeley, a food chemist, had experimented with a food formula.

Expedition leaders cabled for this formula. Dr. John Malcolm, professor of dietetics at Orange University, and others were brought in as consultants. A Mr. Hudson, who operated a chocolate factory, loaned the use of his ovens at night. After two weeks, twenty-five tons of pemmican biscuits had been made. Seal and whale meat were also to be eaten during the long Antarctic winter night.

At Little America itself, dogs were tethered "on top" until tunnels and pathways through the ice could be dug. Their crates were placed in alleyways, and dogs were tied far enough apart so that they could not get into fights. Drivers began testing their dogs again. In this, they were mostly

Duke, a Seeley lead dog sent to Rimini Mountain with an Army unit, and lost with entire team in a training accident.

Byrd fliers, l. to r., Clare Alexander, Ralph Shropshire, Richard Brophy, Harold June. Commander Byrd is kneeling.

Shipboard crates for housing dogs.

Dogs on shipboard returning through the tropics from Antarctica.

cold-blooded. For their lives depended upon the dogs. But a Norwegian, who had been a mate on the *City of New York,* the ship which had brought the expedition to the Antarctic, gathered up the cast-off dogs. He then trained them in his own fashion, and he made them into one of the most efficient teams. That driver's name was Sverre Stromm, and he was technically a member of the ice party rather than of the dog drivers.

In his book *Cold,* the noted geologist Dr. Lawrence Gould, second in command at Base Two, pays tribute to the dogs. He could not, he wrote, have made his geological explorations without the dogs, for all his trips were made by dog sled. For example, he logged 1500 miles in 90 days during severe weather. Admiral Byrd himself, made the exploratory trip by dogsled which led to the final location of the Little America base.

Walden's great lead dog, Chinook, had been badly injured when a number of dogs jumped him at once. Later he escaped from his quarters. He was never seen again, and it has been assumed that he went off alone to die.

Before leaving for the Antarctic, Walden had sold a half-interest in Chinook Kennels to the Seeleys. Upon his return to Wonalancet, he sold his interest to them. Chinook Kennels was moved to a new location. It was there that the Seeleys got the commission to assemble 150 dogs for the second expedition.

Between the two expeditions, both Siberian Huskies and Alaskan Malamutes were being selectively bred. They were pure breeds now ready for recognition by the American Kennel Club. In addition to these dogs, Eskimos were brought from Greenland, and mixed-breed dogs from Canada. Among the dogs were seven Alaskan Malamutes, called the Admiral Byrd Grays. They had been born in Little America. In addition, there were both Alaskan Malamutes and Siberian Huskies which had been born at Chinook Kennels.

It should be noted here that every Antarctic expedition followed a sad and distasteful rule. They put down by shooting the weakest of their dogs at the conclusion of their long treks. This practice was followed by the Byrd Expeditions.

For the most part, the dogs were free of contagious diseases, particularly distemper. Between the first and second expeditions, the Laidlaw-Dunkin immunization vaccine had been placed on the market. This first of the live-virus vaccines was used on all the dogs which had not had distemper, and it gave them complete protection for the second expedition.

The Laidlaw-Dunkin vaccine was tested at the Chinook Kennels before its use on the expedition dogs. A report issued by Lederle Laboratories gives this account of the vaccine's use at Chinook Kennels:

Since the advent of the preventive in June, 1929, four and a half years ago, every dog and all the puppies in these kennels have received the protective

Antarctic Kim, born in Little America.

injections. To date, more than 600 dogs have been vaccinated, and in not a single instance has there been a case of distemper in a dog so treated. With regard to the safety of the vaccination, only three of the 600 dogs showed reactions after the injections. These consisted only of a rise in temperature, which disappeared in 12 to 24 hours and did not require treatment.

This official report of Chinook Kennels' part in the early testing of live-virus distemper vaccines "in the field" also states that before the use of the vaccines, Chinook lost an average of fifteen dogs a year from distemper, and it noted that in severe outbreaks, the kennel had lost from thirty to seventy-five dogs. It had, in fact, lost twenty choicely bred Alaskan Malamute and Siberian Husky puppies who had contracted the disease from one of the Greenland dogs. The puppies were too young to be vaccinated.

Dogs in the Antarctic were lost through injuries and sometimes from disasters. Captain Finn Ronne, son of one of Roald Amundsen's men who first reached the South Pole, lost an entire team. He was attempting passage at a deep ice barrier when his heavily loaded gee-pole-type sledge slipped, overturned, and dragged the dogs to their deaths.

As the expedition prepared to return home, the ship faced severe weather conditions which threatened to break up the ice prematurely. The men were notified to board ship immediately. The dogs were to be left behind. For the men, this was a staggering blow. They had had long months with their dogs and had depended upon them for their very lives. Some of the men had planned to take their favorite dogs into their own homes when they again reached North America. The rest of the dogs were to be returned to Wonalancet.

The orders of the ship's captain were law, and these men had lived under a rigid discipline in which obeying orders often meant survival. In the captain's judgment, their lives were now in peril. They staked the dogs to the ice and planted time bombs about them. Then they sailed away. No one aboard ship heard the explosions. It should be noted that when the United States returned to Antarctica for the great international geophysical years 1955–57, sixty dogs from Wonalancet accompanied the expedition.

Wonalancet was also a staging area for dogs collected and trained for the U.S. Army in World War II. Chinook supplied many Alaskan Malamutes and collected others. These dogs were later sent to an Army mountain training area. Many never returned after the war.

The Armed Forces conceived the idea of using sled dogs for three purposes. Dogs could go where horses, tractors, and airplanes could not. This had been shown in Antarctica when the dogs had had to rescue a seriously ill man during weather too rough for flying. Dogs had been used in the Arctic as pack animals, thus they might be useful in lugging gun parts, ammunition, and other supplies in mountainous country. St. Bernard

This team, trained at Chinook Kennels for U.S. Army service, pulled an Army truck loaded with men six miles. There were fifty-three dogs in the team, and not a single fight took place.

Army pack dogs from Chinook Kennels were trained to carry machine-gun parts over rugged terrain.

By-Line Features

dogs had been used in the Alps, basically to discover and warn of snow-covered crevasses into which men might fall. But they had also been used to locate bodies under snow, and to carry provisions to snow-trapped travelers.

The Armed Forces, therefore, decided to use the sled dogs. They had excellent noses. For example, Canadian Lorna Jackson's Ch. Lorn-Hall Oogorook M'Loot had located a body under many feet of rubble following a hurricane. The sled dogs, therefore, could be avalanche dogs. They were smaller, more agile, and swifter than St. Bernards, and they could stand severe cold.

Many of the sled dogs were brought to Wonalancet for early training. Most were then sent to the rugged mountains of Colorado for further and final training. Pack dogs and search-and-rescue dogs were also trained in the Rockies.

Some of the Alaskan Malamutes were among dogs killed in training accidents. Search-and-rescue dogs were not returned after the war. Instead, they were sent to Greenland and Baffin Island to serve at U.S. Weather Bureau stations.

These losses, plus those in the Antarctic expeditions, account for the perilously low base of registered stock which faced the Alaskan Malamute breed in 1947. It was at that time that the Stud Book was reopened to admit new blood from other sources.

Artist's head study of the immortal champion and sire Ch. Toro of Bras Coupe, owned by Earl and Natalie Norris.

9

Our Alaskan Malamute

An article by Natalie Norris

THE THIRST *for knowledge of the origins of the Alaskan Malamute does not cease with the passing of the years. As recorded elsewhere, Natalie Jubin of Lake Placid drove a dog team and gave passenger rides in order to earn money for her college education. She then went to Alaska, where she met and married Earl Norris. Both won the great Alaskan races.*

Later, as a member of the Alaskan Sled Dog Racing Association, Natalie Norris wrote an article on the Alaskan Malamute. She researched well, both among the Eskimos and among the white men who had followed the gold rush to Alaska.

One of the authors of this book would like to point out two important facts in the article. Mrs. Norris quotes one of the early Alaskan authorities as saying that he asked again and again whether wolf crosses were made. All said no. Also quoted is Bill Burke, one of the great mail-team drivers, on the size of the dogs used.

One of your authors also asked the wolf-dog cross question of a dozen Eskimo drivers and got the same answer. He also spent some hours with Bill Burke, and thus can verify the report quoted by Natalie Norris.

In this article, an attempt will be made to clarify data on the Alaskan Malamute, the only dog originating in Alaska recognized by the American Kennel Club.

There were some men of the many that came to the Territory before and around 1900 that were not only observant but recorded their observations. These narratives were written by authors of many vocations: government employees, journalists, gold seekers, fur traders, churchmen, and so forth. Although many an account describes the sled dogs of that era, each description varies in detail to some degree. It is important, however, and noteworthy to mention, that a canvassing of available works reveals many points on which all agree. It is these points that I should like to emphasize and show how they fit into the pattern from which the present standard on conformation was taken.

I quote from three books to illustrate the differences and the likenesses of sled dog descriptions of authors from around 1900.

The Klondike Stampede of 1897–1898, by Tappan Adney, published by Harper and Brothers, copyright 1899. This book has a complete chapter on dogs and equipment; it is well illustrated with drawings and pictures and is in excellent detail. The data is authentic and compares favorably with that of other authors of the time. Tappan Adney was a journalist writing for *Harper's Weekly.* Here are some excerpts:

> The best type of the Yukon dog is the true Eskimo, known by the miners as "Malamut," from a tribe of Eskimo of that name at the mouth of the Yukon. It stands about as high as the Scotch collie, which it resembles a little; but with its thick, short neck, sharp muzzle, oblique eyes, short, pointed ears, dense coarse hair, which protects it from the severest cold, it is more wolf-like than any other variety of dog. With its bushy tail carried tightly curled over its back, with head and ears erect, and with its broad chest, it is the expression of energy, vitality, and self-reliance. In color it varies from a dirty white through black and white to jet black; but there is also another sort, a grizzled gray, which suggests an admixture of gray wolf, with which it is known to mate. **Indeed, these wolf-colored dogs so closely resemble a wolf that if the two were placed side by side a little distance off it would be difficult to distinguish them, but at a nearer view the dog lacks somewhat the hard, sinister expression of his wild relative.** The best type of dog is still to be found among the Eskimos, as well as among the Indian tribes of the interior, but these latter, known as "Siwash" dogs, are frequently inferior in size, though very tough. The purple type has undergone further change by an admixture of "outside" dog, such as St. Bernard, Newfoundland, and mongrel, that the miners have brought in. The "inside" dog, as the native dog is called by the miners, endures hunger and cold better than the "outside," and is therefore preferred for long journeys over the snow, where speed is desired and food is scarce or hard to carry or procure. For short-distance, heavy freighting, the large St. Bernard or mastiff is unsurpassed, but it eats more. . . .
>
> . . . It has been said that the native dog does not manifest affection for its master; but that is not always the case. It depends upon what has been his early training—like master, like dog. As a rule, he is stolid and indifferent, deigning to notice a human only in sharp barks and howls, the most dismal sound in nature, but he hardly ever snaps, and after the first surprise

at an act of kindness has worn off he shows himself capable of marked affection. . . .

Ten Thousand Miles with a Dog Sled by Hudson Stuck, published by Charles Scribner's Sons, 1914. Hudson Stuck was an Episcopal bishop whose headquarters were at Nenana, Alaska. Stuck's books, of which there are four, are fertile material for persons interested in sled dogs. I quote:

There are two breeds of native dogs in Alaska, and a third that is usually spoken of as such. The Malamute is the Esquimau dog; and what for want of a better name is called the Siwash is the Indian dog. Many years ago the Hudson Bay voyageurs bred some selected strains of imported dog with the Indian dogs of those parts, or else did no more than carefully select the best individuals of the native species and bred from them exclusively—it is variously stated—and that is the accepted origin of the "husky." The malamute and the husky are the two chief sources of the white man's dog teams, though cross-breeding with setters and pointers, hounds of various sorts, mastiffs, Saint Bernards, and Newfoundlands has resulted in a general admixture of breeds, so that the work dogs of Alaska are an heterogeneous lot today. It should also be stated that the terms "malamute" and "husky" are very generally confused and often used interchangeably.

The malamute, the Alaskan Esquimau dog, is precisely the same dog as that found amongst the natives of Baffin's Bay and Greenland. Knud Rasmunsen and Amundsen together have established the oneness of the Esquimaux from the east coast of Greenland all round to Saint Michael; they are one people, speaking virtually one language. And the malamute dog is one dog. . . .

. . . There was never animal better adapted to environment than the malamute dog. His coat, while it is not fluffy, nor the hair long, is yet so dense and heavy that it affords him a perfect protection against the utmost severity of cold. His feet are tough and clean, and do not readily accumulate snow between the toes and therefore do not easily get sore—which is the great drawback of nearly all "outside" dogs and their mixed progeny. He is hardy and thrifty and does well on less food than the mixed breeds; and, despite Peary to the contrary, he will eat anything. . . . The malamute is affectionate and faithful and likes to be made a pet of, but he is very jealous and an incorrigible fighter. He has little of the fawning submissiveness of pet dogs "outside," but is independent and self-willed and apt to make a troublesome pet. However, pets that give little trouble seldom give much pleasure.

His comparative shortness of leg makes him somewhat better adapted to the hard, crusted snow of the coast than to the soft snow of the interior, but he is a ceaseless and tireless worker who loves to pull. His prick ears, always erect, his bushy tail, carried high unless it curls upon the back as is the case with some, his quick narrow eyes give him an air of keenness and alertness that marks him out amongst dogs. When he is in good condition and his coat is taken care of he is a handsome fellow, and he will weigh from seventy-five to eighty-five or ninety pounds.

The husky is a long, rangy dog, with more body and longer legs than the

Spot, a Malamute in Ely Whitney's team. Reprinted from *Wolf The Storm Leader. Dodd, Mead & Co.*

"Finest Dog Team on the Klondike" was Tappan Adney's boast about this team photographed in 1897. From the book *The Klondike Stampede* (Harper & Brothers).

malamute and with a shorter coat. The coat is very thick and dense, however, and furnishes a sufficient protection. A good, spirited husky will carry his tail erect like a malamute, but the ears are not permanently pricked up; they are mobile. He is perhaps, the general preference amongst dog drivers in the interior, but he has not the graceful distinction of appearance of the malamute.

The "Siwash" dog is the common Indian dog; generally under-sized, uncared for, half starved most of the time, and snappish because not handled save with roughness. In general appearance he resembles somewhat a small malamute, though, indeed, nowadays so mixed have breeds become that he may be any cur or mongrel. . . .

Here it may be worth while to say a few words about the general belief that dogs in Alaska are interbred with wolves. That the dog and the wolf have a common origin there can be no doubt, and that they will inter-breed is equally sure, but diligent inquiry on the part of the writer for a number of years, throughout all interior Alaska, amongst whites and natives, has failed to deduce one authentic instance of intentional interbreeding, has failed to discover one man who knows of his own knowledge that any living dog is the off-spring of such union.

While, therefore, it is not here stated that such crossbreeding has not taken place, or even that it does not take place, yet the author is satisfied that it is a very rare thing, indeed, and the common stories of dogs that are "half wolf" are fabulous.

Wolf the Storm Leader by Frank Caldwell, first published by Dodd, Mead and Company in 1910, copyright 1937, illustrates the Alaskan life of Ely Whitney as well as his trek across the States by dog team; he had been sent from Nome to Washington, D.C. by dog team to attract government officials' attention to problems in Alaska. Ely, in the book, describes each of his team dogs to a Washington audience. The following reprinted with permission of the publishers:

Spot is a gray malamoot. Don't ye think he's a good-lookin' feller? Well, he's jist as good as he looks, always in a good humor an' ready to play or fight, an' never was known to shirk in harness. . . . A malamoot is a Bering Sea Eskimo dog . . . he's not a extra big dog, but for work on the mail-trails where ye want a animal what's tough an' has good wind an' speed, ye can't find none what kin quite take the place of the malamoot. . . . An' what's more, they're the friendliest an' most affectionate dog I ever see. Now take this here Spot; he likes to be petted, an' if I so much as raise my hand as if I was a-goin' to strike him, er if I jist hits him a little tap with my mitten, he'll up an' whine an' cry like a baby an' like he was a-bein' killed. It's his feelin's what's hurt an' not his hide. . . . A husky is different. He's a Hudson Bay dog, an' is part English er Scotch hound an' part northern wolf. There's two kinds of huskies, too; the lop-eared, whose ears hang down like a hound's, an' the straight eared, whose ears stand up like a wolf's. Now I'm not a-runnin' down the huskies, fer I've owned an' worked, not one, but many of 'em, an' liked 'em too. They're good workers, but some way I can't like 'em quite as well as I do the malamoots. . . .

A cross-section of works such as the ones I have quoted, as I said, reveal many points on which there is agreement. A clear picture of what the true Malamute was like can be ascertained after digesting the likenesses from a variety of descriptions.

Descriptions by those personally acquainted with the Alaskan dogs at the time early Malamute Breed Club members were gathering all information available in order to draw up a written standard for the Malamute contributed greatly towards perfecting the Standard (conformation points).

The following description of an Alaskan Malamute by Lester Corliss, currently of Anchorage, gives us an idea as to what type of information the first members of the Breed Club obtained from contemporaries. Mr. Corliss bred Malamutes during the twenties in Nenana, Alaska, and some of his dogs are behind the foundation stock bred in New Hampshire. In a recent interview Mr. Corliss said:

> A Malamute should be active as a terrier; even a big Malamute should be jaunty, not sluggish or slow-moving. I liked them tapering from front to back, the withers higher than the rump, chest broader than the hips. The tail should be carried high or curled, with the coat standing off, not long or flat. My Malamutes averaged 70 to 75 pounds for males, 55 to 60 pounds for the females. I preferred my dogs to be longer, rather than too shortly coupled; and, I preferred the black and white, masked face Malamutes with silver shading above the white under-quarters, comparable to the shading in a silver fox. These, in my estimation, were the most beautiful.
>
> The mail teams preferred dogs around 80 to 90 pounds, but seldom did they use a dog over 90 pounds because the over-sized dog could not stand the work. Bill Burke, who had the mail run between Nenana and McGrath on the Kuskokwim used dogs of Malamute type and these averaged 85. He had two teams constantly on the move of some 15 to 20 dogs in a team and around 10 dogs constantly in reserve.

There is conflicting information in the accounts used, but again I point out there is much agreement also. The "husky" used throughout this article should not be confused with the Siberian Husky, which has not been included in this discussion and was an importation in Alaska.

In my opinion, the references to the oneness of the Malamute and the Eskimo dog can be explained somewhat as follows: To one not actually picking the animals apart limb by limb, comparisons were not noteworthy. The differences as set up in the standards are minute, but very important. The set of the ear, shape of the ear, shape of the foot, length of the coat, shape and size of the muzzle in comparison to skull are all points of difference an observer looking for these differences can readily note. There is more data to be had on the Eskimo dog in the Canadian Arctic and Greenland than any of the other northern breeds, which a visit to a well-stocked library would reveal. In the early part of this century, most observers had not trained themselves to differentiate between these characteristics

Earl Norris, a pioneer Alaskan Malamute breeder, is shown hauling supplies up Muldrow Glacier on the slopes of Mt. McKinley in 1947. *Bradford Washburn*

so important to the breeders of today. Hence, their data does not read like a breed standard. I think it can be said, however, that the Malamute, thanks to those who fancied these dogs thirty and forty years ago, has changed relatively little in the past decades.

The Malamute is too fine and distinguished a breed to be changed into anything but what centuries of adaptability to its environment has produced. Our efforts should be to breed not only beautiful Malamutes, but as good specimens physically as were originally found in Alaska. It isn't a question of breeding a better Malamute but as good a Malamute. If this article has sparked Malamute breeders into digging for more firsthand information, I shall feel well rewarded for my effort.

10

Two Foundations

THE ALASKAN MALAMUTE is a breed with an evolutionary history like no other. The destiny of this native American breed has long been intertwined with the history of the United States. The people who are the architects of the breed have been extraordinary for their depth of research and their dedication. Several such individuals are introduced in other sections of this book. In this chapter, we present two whose breeding research has served as a foundation for many successful fanciers today.

THE BEGINNING OF HUSKY-PAK

While serving as a junior officer in the Navy during World War II, Robert J. Zoller saw his first Alaskan Malamute. He immediately fell in love with the dog. Zoller saw service in both the Atlantic and the Pacific, and ended up a commander. At the war's end, he remained in the reserves. However, he never forgot the Alaskan Malamute he had known during the war.

Robert Zoller was one of the founders of the Alaskan Malamute Club of America. He served as its president, and for some years edited and produced the newsletter which has done so much to promote the breed and to acquaint Alaskan Malamute breeders and fanciers with each other across the "lower 48," Alaska, and Canada. He has kindly provided us with the Husky-Pak story.

Almost everyone agrees that the Alaskan Malamute is a product of canine development in a particular region of the Arctic. But there are many differing opinions as to where the registered Malamutes of today began. You can go back to a certain point in the 1930s and 1940s to fifty or fewer individual dogs and suddenly you get to "unknown."

I am sure that here and there people had been bringing a few dogs out of Alaska for generations, but it all began to add up to a breed perhaps in the 1930s, but mainly in the 1940s, when several people began to breed and sell these dogs. And they began to give the people who bought them a pedigree with "Alaskan Malamute" written across the top.

At the starting point, who really knew what a Malamute was, or whether this dog or that one was purebred? Obviously, nobody knew. There was no Eskimo Kennel Club keeping track. So the selections and the labeling were all based on opinion, and opinions varied. That is why there were so many "Alaskan Malamutes" of widely varying type.

I'm convinced a lot of mistakes were made. I've seen a number of dogs claimed to be Malamutes that weren't even close, including a 150-pound part timber wolf in Iowa and a huge blue-eyed crossbred that was apparently half St. Bernard. The latter was actually shown in Baltimore in 1947. I know that neither of these dogs appears in the pedigree of any present-day Malamute. But it seems logical that some questionable early dogs do. It is important, however, to understand that we owe no apologies to any other breed. In Malamutes, you finally get back to the unknown; in most other breeds you can get back to known dogs of other breeds.

What of the Malamutes of today, and where did they come from? The early major contributors were Arthur Walden, who assembled a number of sled dogs in New England, some of which were ancestors of many registered Malamutes today; Milton and Eva Seeley, who developed the Kotzebue line and who got them recognized and registered by the American Kennel Club; and Paul Voelker, who developed the M'Loot line. Voelker never registered his dogs but sold them to people who eventually did.

The logical next question is, where did Walden and Voelker get their dogs. Some they brought from the Arctic, and others they bought from people who did. A lot of the early fanciers of sled dogs knew each other, and the dogs were bought and sold among them. A number of men were part of a U.S. Army sled dog program during World War II. The Army assembled hundreds of sled dogs. Some were Malamutes, and some of these were bought by their drivers at liquidation sales when the war ended. At least two of these dogs ended up with Paul Voelker and became a part of the M'Loot line. A few others also ended up as ancestors of various Malamutes of today.

The important points to be made are that in the mid-1940s, all Malamutes went back only a couple of generations to "unknown"; that most people who brought dogs out of Alaska, or bought them from people who did, really didn't have much to go on but opinion, and opinions varied widely; that most were more interested in good sled dogs than in scientifically isolating pure Malamute type and in starting a registered Malamute breeding program.

While dozens had been involved in some way, only the Seeleys and Paul Voelker were sticking it out in the late 1940s. At that point, newcomers suddenly became involved. They brought a new level of interest to the Alaskan Malamute breed. My wife Laura and I were two of these people. I became interested when I saw my first Malamute at a U.S. Navy officers' club in Newfoundland in 1941. I began an intensive study of the breed, and we acquired our first Malamutes in 1947 and 1948.

Along with other newcomers to the breed, we added a new dimension. We felt the breed had proved its ability as a working sled dog but deserved more than that. I became dedicated to positioning the Malamute in a new role as a pet and companion to people who wanted a rare and beautiful dog. Type and quality thus became of overriding importance to us.

We immediately encountered the Kotzebue and M'Loot strains and researched them intensively. We also discovered that certain other dogs that were neither M'Loot nor Kotzebue had contributed to the Malamute breed, and their influence cannot be ignored. For want of a better term these dogs are sometimes referred to as the "third strain." This is not an accurate description because these were just individual dogs, not a strain, owned by different people.

Only a handful of these dogs were involved, but some were good enough to be included in early breeding programs that eventually led to AKC-registered progeny. At least a couple, in my opinion, materially affected the quality of our breed perhaps for all years to come.

In the mid-1940s, we read everything we could find, journeyed frequently to see dogs all over the country, and corresponded with everyone we could locate whose name had ever been linked with the breed. My wife and I believe that our own major contributions were an all-consuming interest in the Malamute as a purebred dog, intensive effort, and most important, a degree of objectivity.

We may have been the first to see both the strengths and the weaknesses of the two existing strains. This immediately got us into serious difficulties with both camps. In the course of our studies, we developed some firm opinions. The Kotzebues were good type, mainly because of good heads and general proportions, but they were smaller than we believed Malamutes should be. The M'Loots had better size, but some were rangy, some considerably lacking in substance. Their fronts were generally better than the Kotzebues, who tended to be somewhat wide in chest and sometimes out at the elbows. The rears of the M'Loots were lacking in angulation, and this led to stilted gait. The M'Loots also tended to long ears and long muzzles.

The Kotzebues were gray dogs with white trim. The M'Loots had a

Ch. Arctic Storm of Husky-Pak, owned by
Robert J. and Laura Zoller.

Ch. Cliquot of Husky-Pak, C.D.X., had his picture taken with his
trophies when he was twelve years old. Owned and bred by the
Zollers, he died at fourteen.

Ch. Husky-Pak Jingo is the last
known survivor of Robert Zoller's
Husky-Pak dogs. She is the dam
of Ch. Jingo's Silver Trumpet.
Owner is Virginia Devaney of
Cedar Crest, New Mexico.

56

wider range from light gray to black and white. Dispositions differed somewhat. The Kotzebues were less aggressive and easier to control. The M'Loots were often aggressive with other dogs, prone to fighting, and sometimes difficult to handle.

We liked much of what we saw in both strains, but we felt there was more to be done. We got lucky almost right from the start. At Great Barrington, Massachusetts, we found a pair of pups sired by a dog named Alaska (he later became Ch. Spawn's Alaska) that we bought and raised, and took to national championships. This brother and sister pair were Ch. Apache Chief of Husky-Pak and Ch. Arctic Storm of Husky-Pak.

Both became milestones of breed progress. They were three-quarters M'Loot and one-quarter "other." I never saw Alaska's parents, but his dam, Kiska, was by Gemo out of Sitka. I did see Gemo in the flesh and a number of photographs of Sitka. I am now convinced that, by the standards of the time, these two were outstanding, and from what appeared later on, they deserve much credit for adding good things to our breed.

Gemo was produced by Dave Irwin, the Arctic explorer, from two Malamutes he brought out of the Arctic. Gemo was sold to Lowell Thomas, the famed explorer-newsman, who showed him at least once as a listed dog at the Westminster show at Madison Square Garden. He was probably the breed's first Best of Breed winner at Westminster.

Lowell Thomas sold or gave Gemo to Dick Hinman of Newbury, Vermont. In early pedigrees, this dog is shown as Erwin's Gemo, Irwin's Gemo, or sometimes, Gimo, or even Chimo. Early pedigrees were often made out in handwriting. Misspellings were frequent, and to add to the confusion, there were dozens of Alaskas, Sitkas, Wolfs, etc.

Based on Spawn's Alaska and two of his litter brothers which I saw and studied, Chisholm's Viking and Duke, Gemo and Sitka through Kiska produced progeny which influenced the quality of our breed. Sitka appears in some pedigrees as Hinman's Sitka. She could well have been a better bitch than Gemo was a dog. At any rate, I liked what I saw in her pictures.

Spawn's Alaska was one of the top winners in our breed from his start until Apache Chief and Arctic Storm took over. Included were two Best of Breed victories at Westminster, in 1951 and 1953. He won consistently over Ch. Mulphus Brooks Master Otter and Ch. Toro of Bras Coupe, two other top dogs of their time.

Ch. Spawn's Alaska and his offspring Ch. Apache Chief of Husky-Pak and Ch. Arctic Storm of Husky-Pak had that ingredient for which we had been searching. So did their offspring. In the five years from 1953 to 1957, in national specialty competition, Zoller dogs won four Bests of Breed, five Bests of Opposite Sex, five Bests of Winners, and every Winners Dog and Winners Bitch when Husky-Pak dogs were there to compete.

We found that our strain, compared with the pure M'Loot strain, resulted in dogs of equal size but of heavier bone and more powerful build.

Ch. Tigara's Artica Eve shown with owner, Dorothy Dillingham.   *Ludwig*

In body structure they were not unlike king-size Kotzebues. While their heads, overall, were not as good as the Kotzebues, they had broad skulls and wide-set ears. They had good fronts like the M'Loots, good rears like the Kotzebues, and good overall coats, colors, and balance.

To set the type and heavy up the muzzles, we searched for a good-quality, not too small Kotzebue and came up with the name of Ch. Toro of Bras Coupe, then owned by Earl and Natalie Norris of Anchorage, Alaska. Toro was a good one. He had been produced at Chinook Kennels, with Eva Seeley listed as his breeder. Toro and all his litter mates, and an entire second litter of the same breeding, were sold en masse to the Bras Coupe winter sports club in Alaska.

Toro was by Ch. Kim of Kotzebue out of Kotzebue Cleopatra. Later, when he was offered for sale, I had first chance at Toro, the best of the two litters. To my eternal unhappiness, I passed him up. At the time, I just couldn't add another dog to my kennel. When we bred Ch. Arctic Storm of Husky-Pak to Toro, she produced a litter of six. Five became champions. The owner of the sixth did not show it.

These dogs made important contributions. Ch. Cliquot of Husky-Pak became the official symbol of the Alaskan Malamute Club of America. Ch. Cherokee of Husky-Pak won the national specialty show three years in a row and was AMCA "Dog-of-the-Year" for three consecutive years.

To sum it up, our breed, as it exists today, is the result of a lot of work by a lot of people. It began with the development, distribution, publicizing, and registering of the Kotzebues in New England, and later in Alaska and California. The same goes for the M'Loots, developed in Michigan, and shown, publicized, and registered in various parts of the country. Our own part came in the development of what we term "the three-way cross" as we have told it here.

THE TIGARA FORMULA

No history or understanding of the breed may be considered complete without at the very least, some knowledge of D. C. and Dorothy Dillingham's Tigara Kennels. When D. C. married Dorothy in 1953, he "married" into a "family" of Malamutes. At that time D. C. was also a successful breeder and exhibitor of Chow Chows, including the famous Ch. Sing Fu Brilliantine.

Through their understanding of the Alaskan Malamute Standard and genetics, over the years the Dillinghams set a breed "type." The consistency established in their breeding program has never been duplicated.

Alaskan Malamutes were not known for having a "correct" type of movement prior to the Dillinghams' involvement. According to the Dillinghams' "formula of balance" for the breed, the dogs must be able to move easily with a ground-covering stride. They must have excellent reach in the forequarters and powerful follow-through with the rear. A proper layback of the shoulders allows dogs to have correct reach in the forequarters. Without the proper layback, the dogs will likely "toe in". The rear may move in a cow-hocked manner as compensation for being either out at the shoulder or straight-shouldered.

"A dog's layback of the shoulder must match the angulation of the hind-quarters (the stifles' angulation). As the dog stands, the dog's hock-to-the-ground must not be perfectly perpendicular. It must have a moderate bend. This translates visually to the fact that the foot of the dog, as it is standing, should be somewhat slightly ahead of the hock."

The Dillinghams' success formula for breeding was based upon a very simple premise for establishing and maintaining type. The sire's sire must be the same dog as the grandsire of the dam, through her sire. This may be reversed to effect a linebreeding on the dam's sire as well. This formula is known as close linebreeding. This is what makes it possible to set "type."

11

The Breed Standards
—Then and Now

LET US RETURN TO 1935. During that year, the first breed Standard was approved by the American Kennel Club. We give it here in full. It remained the Standard of the breed until April 12, 1960, when, during the presidency of Robert Zoller, the Standard was revised. The present Standard was adopted in 1982.

DESCRIPTION AND STANDARD OF POINTS

(As Adopted by the Alaskan Malamute Club, April 17, 1935, and Approved by the American Kennel Club)

Origin—The Alaskan Malamute is a native sled-dog of Alaska and is the oldest native dog known to that country. It was originally named "Mahlemut" after a native Innuit (Mahlemut) Tribe.

General Appearance and Characteristics—A large size dog with a strong, compact body, not too short coupled; thick dense, coarse coat and not too long; stands well over pads and has appearance of much activity; broad head, ears erect and wedge-shaped; muzzle not too pointed and long, but not too stubby (other extreme); deep chest, proud carriage, head erect and eyes alert.—Face markings are a distinguishing feature and the eyes are well set off by these markings which consist of either cap over head and rest of face solid color, (usually greyish white) or face marked with appearance of a mask, thus setting off eyes; tail is plumed and carried over back when not working, but not too tightly curled, more like a plume waving. Malamutes are of various colors, but usually wolfish grey or black and white. Their feet are of the "snowshoe" type with well cushioned pads giving firm and compact appearance; front legs straight and with big bone; hind legs well bent at stifles and without cowhocks; straight back gently sloping from shoulders to hips; endurance and intelligence are shown in body and eyes; the eyes have a "wolf-like" appearance by position of eyes, but expression is soft; quick in action, but no loss of energy in moving; affectionate dispositions.

Head—The head should indicate a high degree of intelligence—it should be in proportion to the size of the dog so as to not make the dog appear clumsy or coarse. **Skull**—Broad between ears, gradually narrowing to eyes; moderately rounded between ears, flattening on top as it approaches eyes, rounding off to cheeks, which should be moderately flat; there should be a slight furrow between the eyes; the top line of skull and top line of muzzle showing but little break downward from a straight line as they join.

Muzzle—Large and bulky in proportion to size of skull—diminishing but little in width or depth from junction with skull to nose—lips close fitting—nose black—upper and lower jaws broad with large teeth—the front teeth meeting with a scissors grip, but never "overshot."

Eyes—Almond shaped—dark in color—moderately large for this shape of eye—set obliquely in skull.

Ears—Medium—upper half of ear triangular in shape—slightly rounded at tips—set wide apart on outside back edges of top of skull with lower part of ear joining the skull on a line with the upper corner of eye; giving the tips of the ears the appearance when erect of standing off from the skull; when erect, ears are pointed slightly forward, but when at work the ears are usually folded back on the skull.

Body—Chest should be strong and deep; body should be strong and compactly built, but not too short coupled; the back should be straight and gently sloping from shoulders to hips. Loins well muscled, but no surplus weight.

Shoulders, Legs and Feet—Shoulders moderately sloping; forelegs heavily boned and muscled—straight to pasterns, which should be short and strong and almost vertical as viewed from the side; feet large and compact, toes well arched, pads thick and tough; toenails short and strong; protective growth of hair between toes. Hindlegs must be broad and powerfully muscled through thighs; stifles moderately bent; hock joints broad and

62

strong and moderately bent and well let down—as viewed from behind the hindlegs should not appear bowed in bone, but stand and move true and not too close or too wide. The legs of the Malamute must indicate unusual strength and powerful propelling power—any definite indication of unsoundness in legs and feet, standing or moving, constitutes practically disqualification in the show ring.

Coat—Thick, dense, coarse coat, but not long; undercoat is thick, oily and woolly, while outer coat is rather coarse and stands out. Thick fur around neck. (This allows for protection against weather.)

Color and Markings—The usual colors are wolfish grey or black and white. Markings should be either cap-like or mask-like on face. A variation of color and markings is occasionally found.

Tail—Well furred and carried over back when not working, but not too tightly curled to rest on back, a "waving plume" appearance instead.

Height—Of male dog averaging from 22 to 25 inches; of bitch averaging from 20 to 23 inches.

Weight—Of male dog averaging from 65 to 85 pounds; of bitch averaging from 50 to 70 pounds.

SCALE OF POINTS

	Points
General appearance	20
Head	20
Body	20
Legs and feet	20
Coat and color	10
Tail	10
Total	100

OFFICIAL STANDARD FOR THE ALASKAN MALAMUTE

General Appearance and Characteristics—The Alaskan Malamute is a powerful and substantially built dog with a deep chest and strong, compact body, not too short coupled, with a thick, coarse guard coat of sufficient length to protect a dense, woolly undercoat, from 1 to 2 inches in depth when dog is in full coat. Stands well over pads, and this stance gives the appearance of much activity, showing interest and curiosity. The head is broad, ears wedge-shaped and erect when alerted. The muzzle is bulky with only slight diminishing in width and depth from root to nose, not pointed or long, but not stubby. The Malamute moves with a proud carriage, head erect and eyes alert. Face markings are a distinguishing feature.

These consist of either cap over head and rest of face solid color, usually grayish white, or face marked with the appearance of a mask. Combinations of cap and mask are not unusual. The tail is plumed and carried over the back, not like a fox brush, or tightly curled, more like a plume waving.

Malamutes are of various colors, but are usually wolfish gray or black and white. Their feet are of the "snowshoe" type, tight and deep, with well-cushioned pads, giving a firm and compact appearance. Front legs are straight with big bone. Hind legs are broad and powerful, moderately bent at stifles, and without cowhocks. The back is straight, gently sloping from shoulders to hips. The loin should not be so short or tight as to interfere with easy, tireless movement. Endurance and intelligence are shown in body and expression. The eyes have a "wolf-like" appearance by their position, but the expression is soft and indicates an affectionate disposition.

Temperament—The Alaskan Malamute is an affectionate, friendly dog, not a "one-man" dog. He is a loyal, devoted companion, playful on invitation, but generally impressive by his dignity after maturity.

Head—The head should indicate a high degree of intelligence, and is broad and powerful as compared with other "natural" breeds, but should be in proportion to the size of the dog so as not to make the dog appear clumsy or coarse. **Skull**—The skull should be broad between the ears, gradually narrowing to eyes, moderately rounded between ears, flattening on top as it approaches the eyes, rounding off to cheeks, which should be moderately flat. There should be a slight furrow between the eyes, the topline of skull and topline of the muzzle showing but little break downward from a straight line as they join. **Muzzle**—The muzzle should be large and bulky in proportion to size of skull, diminishing but little in width and depth from junction with skull to nose; lips close fitting; nose black; upper and lower jaws broad with large teeth, front teeth meeting with a scissors grip but never overshot or undershot.

Eyes—Brown, almond shaped, moderately large for this shape of eye, set obliquely in skull. Dark eyes preferred. Blue eyes are a disqualifying fault.

Ears—The ears should be of medium size, but small in proportion to head. The upper halves of the ears are triangular in shape, slightly rounded at tips, set wide apart on outside back edges of the skull with the lower part of the ear joining the skull on a line with the upper corner of the eye, giving the tips of the ears the appearance, when erect, of standing off from the skull. When erect, the ears point slightly forward, but when the dog is at work the ears are sometimes folded against the skull. High-set ears are a fault.

Neck—The neck should be strong and moderately arched.

Body—The chest should be strong and deep; body should be strong and compactly built but not short coupled. The back should be straight and gently sloping to the hips. The loins should be well muscled and not so short as to interfere with easy, rhythmic movement with powerful drive from the hindquarters. A long loin which weakens the back is also a fault. No excess weight.

Shoulders, Legs and Feet—Shoulders should be moderately sloping; forelegs heavily boned and muscled, straight to pasterns, which should be short and strong and almost vertical as viewed from the side. The feet should be large and compact, toes, tight-fitting and well-arched, pads thick and tough, toenails short and strong. There should be a protective growth of hair between toes. Hind legs must be broad and powerfully muscled through thighs; stifles moderately bent, hock joints broad and strong, moderately bent and well let down. As viewed from behind, the hind legs should not appear bowed in bone, but stand and move true in line with movement of the front legs, and not too close or too wide. The legs of the Malamute must indicate unusual strength and tremendous propelling power. Any indication of unsoundness in legs or feet, standing or moving, is to be considered a serious fault. Dewclaws on the hind legs are undesirable and should be removed shortly after pups are whelped.

Tail—Moderately set and following the line of the spine at the start, well furred and carried over the back when not working—not tightly curled to rest on back—or short furred and carried like a fox brush, a waving plume appearance instead.

Coat—The Malamute should have a thick, coarse guard coat, not long and soft. The undercoat is dense, from 1 to 2 inches in depth, oily and woolly. The coarse guard coat stands out, and there is thick fur around the neck. The guard coat varies in length, as does the undercoat; however, in general, the coat is moderately short to medium along the sides of the body with the length of the coat increasing somewhat around the shoulders and neck, down the back and over the rump, as well as in the breeching and plume. Malamutes usually have shorter and less dense coats when shed out during the summer months.

Color and Markings—The usual colors range from light gray through the intermediate shadings to black, always with white on underbodies, parts of legs, feet, and part of mask markings. Markings should be either caplike and/or mask-like on face. A white blaze on forehead and/or collar or spot on nape is attractive and acceptable, but broken color extending over the body in spots or uneven splashings is undesirable. One should distinguish between mantled dogs and splash-coated dogs. The only solid color allowable is the all-white.

Size—There is a natural range in size in the breed. The desirable freighting sizes are:

Males—25 inches at the shoulders—85 pounds.

Females—23 inches at the shoulders—75 pounds.

However, size consideration should not outweigh that of type, proportion, and functional attributes, such as shoulders, chest, legs, feet, and movement. When dogs are judged equal in type, proportion, and functional attributes, the dog nearest the desirable freighting size is to be preferred.

IMPORTANT—*In judging Malamutes their function as a sledge dog for heavy freighting must be given consideration above all else.* The judge must bear in mind that this breed is designed primarily as the working sledge dog of the North for hauling heavy freight, and therefore he should be a heavy-boned, powerfully built, compact dog with sound legs, good feet, deep chest, powerful shoulders, steady, balanced, tireless gait, and the other physical equipment necessary for the efficient performance of his job. He isn't intended as a racing sled dog designed to compete in speed trials with the smaller Northern breeds.

The Malamute as a sledge dog for heavy freighting is designed for strength and endurance and any characteristic of the individual specimen, including temperament, which interferes with the accomplishment of this purpose is to be considered the most serious of faults. Faults under this provision would be splayfootedness, any indication of unsoundness or weakness in legs, cowhocks, bad pasterns, straight shoulders, lack of angulation, stilted gait, or any gait which isn't balanced, strong, and steady, ranginess, shallowness, ponderousness, lightness of bone, poor over-all proportion, and similar characteristics.

SCALE OF POINTS

General Appearance	20	Feet	10
Head	15	Coat and Color	10
Body	20	Tail	5
Legs and Movement	20	TOTAL	100

DISQUALIFICATIONS

Blue eyes.

Approved August 10, 1982

12

Interpretation of
the Standard

by Virginia Devaney and Beth J. Harris

THE ALASKAN MALAMUTE STANDARD could be said to have been "written" by historical events rather than by man. This type of dog has long been known to benefit mankind in myriad ways: as a draft animal, hunter, camp guard, and in those times of man's most dire need, as food and portions of his clothing. Evidence uncovered at some archeological digs indicate this type of dog was utilized as long ago as 5800 B.C. by early men in the Pacific Northwest.

During the periods of easterly migration by early settlers (and camp-following dogs) prior to the glacial epoch, the Bering Land Mass (now the Bering Sea) is believed to have been a huge rich, grassy veldtlike area. Stretching over one thousand miles from north to south, it encompassed an area three times that of the United States and Canada.

The climate changed drastically many times over thousands of years. The earlier melting glaciers created the Bering Sea. People and dogs evolved slowly in their adaptation to the new and progressively harsher climatic conditions. The true standard of the Alaskan Malamute was "written" therefore, by subzero temperatures, scarcity of game, and long hours of darkness during the prolonged winter months. Long hours of daylight, abundance of game, and swarming insects during the brief summer months also had their impact on the dogs we know today.

Due to the climatic conditions, the most important influences on the

Alaskan Malamute's evolutionary development were climate and abundance of game. These climatic conditions dictated that the dogs develop a double coat, one which protects both against extreme temperatures of cold and swarms of insects. The scarcity of readily available game (game being food, converting to calories, and calories to heat) was critical to the evolution of a dog type which has a totally efficient metabolism. This translates to mean the dogs are well able to utilize that food ingested. The efficiency of the metabolism allowed the animals to have sufficient energy to work long hard hours under conditions of extreme deprivation, day after day, subsisting on proportionately small amounts of food. These were the progenitors of today's dogs. As a result, today we are able to enjoy dogs which require comparatively little food when given a nutritionally balanced diet.

Thus are we able to enjoy as companions a breed of dog which evolved totally through survival of the fittest. Through the interpretation of the Standard it will be shown that there are reasons for every aspect of the breed's physiology, from the tip of the nose through the tip of the tail.

ANALYSIS OF THE STANDARD

General Appearance and Characteristics—The Alaskan Malamute is a powerful and substantially built dog with a deep chest and strong, compact body, not too short coupled, with a thick, coarse guard coat of sufficient length to protect a dense, woolly undercoat, from 1 to 2 inches in depth when dog is in full coat. Stands well over pads, and this stance gives the appearance of much activity, showing interest and curiosity. The head is broad, ears wedge-shaped and erect when alerted. The muzzle is bulky with only slight diminishing in width and depth from root to nose, not pointed or long, but not stubby. The Malamute moves with a proud carriage, head erect and eyes alert. Face markings are a distinguishing feature. These consist of either cap over head and rest of face solid color, usually grayish white, or face marked with the appearance of a mask. Combinations of cap and mask are not unusual. The tail is plumed and carried over the back, not like a fox brush, or tightly curled, more like a plume waving.

Malamutes are of various colors, but are usually wolfish gray or black and white. Their feet are of the "snowshoe" type, tight and deep, with well-cushioned pads, giving a firm and compact appearance. Front legs are straight with big bone. Hind legs are broad and powerful, moderately bent at stifles and without cowhocks. The back is straight, gently sloping from shoulders to hips. The loin should not be so short or tight as to interfere with easy, tireless movement. Endurance and intelligence are shown in body and expression. The eyes have a "wolf-like" appearance by their position, but the expression is soft and indicates an affectionate disposition.

Temperament—The Alaskan Malamute is an affectionate, friendly dog, not a "one-man" dog. He is a loyal, devoted companion, playful on invitation, but generally impressive by his dignity after maturity.

68

The breed did not develop a strong territorial instinct (except for what they deemed their food and space), as the Eskimo's culture, his nomadic way of life, helped to shape the dogs' temperaments. "Home" was wherever the village or campsite happened to be—sometimes for but a night, and at other times for months at a time, depending upon the availability of game.

Because the Eskimo way of life was socialistic in the most ideal sense (everything was shared), the dogs were not used for protection. They were, however, "alert" animals, warning the village of any impending danger, such as an errant polar bear or the approach of a stranger.

While not known for its guard dog tendencies, the Malamute has a highly developed pack instinct. The innate urge to establish a place in the social hierarchy of the pack has determined that many Alaskan Malamutes frequently show aggression toward other animals. If a dog is not properly disciplined for social infractions by its owner, the family (which the dogs perceive also as pack members) will be included in the dog push for dominance. It is the inability of many owners to understand and cope with this strong pack instinct that causes most of the temperament problems in the breed.

Some few Alaskan Malamutes have by their aggressive behavior earned an unwarranted negative reputation for the breed. Many of today's dogs are separated too early from their dams, siblings, and other adult dogs with whom they would have "normally" had a social interaction in a "pack" environment. Placed in isolation in a backyard or kennel run, these youngsters have little or no opportunity to learn proper social behavior and, as a result, have a tendency to become in some cases overassertive in their territorialness when being approached, or when approaching other dogs.

During the development of the breed, the youngsters were allowed to be "dogs" during their critical period of socialization. They intermingled freely with the adult population, had older siblings or unrelated "aunties" to watch over them, and were able to establish freely their position of dominance (or subservience) in a safe manner in the pack's social hierarchy (environment).

The temperament of the Alaskan Malamute has, through selective-breeding practices over the past several decades, undergone some major adjustments. These adjustments have rendered the breed more compatible with the living requirements of today's social environment. The result of these selective-breeding practices has been a considerable compromise between what is acceptable in an urban society and those characteristics which allowed the breed's survival in the Arctic.

The correct Alaskan Malamute is an animal which retains its independence, an animal willing to acknowledge and accept responsibility in an eager manner. This trait of independence was a necessary measure of protection for both team and driver. The characteristic of independent thinking is often misconstrued by lay owners and "professional trainers." The breed as a whole, by those without valid experience, is thought to be stubborn and difficult to train. As an example, those dogs which consistently avoid unsteady or questionable footing are faulted by many as being "mentally unsound," whereas in reality this innate characteristic was essential to the survival of working animals and their drivers: those working over soft ice and glacial surfaces.

A large number of breeders are quite diligent about breeding only those dogs which display no aggression toward other animals. This reputation of the breed toward overassertiveness has been quite burdensome. While it is necessary to control this inherent trait of extreme pack drive, it must be remembered at the same time that if today's dogs had to survive under the Arctic conditions of their forebears, they would have to be stubbornly hard and highly competitive, as were their ancestors, who were pushed almost daily to the point of survival.

The Alaskan Malamute is not known as a property type of guard dog. It can, however, be an instinctive "alert" dog, whereby it can alert its owner that something is wrong through a barking-howling combination in a specialized manner. Essentially, however, the breed is friendly to all people. This particular characteristic has been left basically unchanged even though some people have tried to train the dogs to overcome this instinct of open friendly curiosity.

Alaskan Malamutes are diligent guardians of children. They are not, however, a one-man type of dog (being highly sociable), because of their pack orientation. They are also highly intuitive animals. This trait needs to be strongly considered by those who associate with the breed. If a person is either afraid or suspicious of the breed, the dogs are apt to sense this fear and respond accordingly, by questioning the fear or taking advantage of it.

With proper socialization and training, the Malamute can be a perfect pet for the right family. The original function of the breed as a sledge dog for heavy freighting in a harsh environment must not, however, be forgotten.

> *Head*—The head should indicate a high degree of intelligence, and is broad and powerful as compared with other "natural" breeds, but should be in proportion to the size of the dog so as not to make the dog appear clumsy or coarse.

The dogs' skulls appear to be considerably more massive during the winter months. A portion of this appearance is due to the dogs' heavier coats. It is also the result of the increased fatty layers over the skull at this time of the year. These are most readily noticed over the inner corners of the eyes. During the summer, these fatty layers are reduced as they are no longer needed as an eye protection.

> *Skull*—The skull should be broad between the ears, gradually narrowing to eyes, moderately rounded between ears, flattening on top as it approaches the

Head study of Ch. Kotzebue Kanuck of Chinook, owned by Marilyn P. Prouty. Eva Seeley considered this a superb type.

eyes, rounding off to cheeks, which should be moderately flat. There should be a slight furrow between the eyes, the topline of skull and topline of the muzzle showing but little break downward from a straight line as they join.

All arctic animals share a certain basic commonality of a wedge-shaped skull. There is almost no stop whatsoever on any of them: no sharp angles or pockets, places where snow or other moisture would have the possibility of collecting and freezing. The shape of the skull is therefore "weather-repellent."

What appears to be a stop is in actuality the fatty pads above the eye orbits. This also forms the "slight furrow between the eyes."

Muzzle—The muzzle should be large and bulky in proportion to size of skull, diminishing but little in width and depth from junction with skull to nose; lips close fitting; nose black; upper and lower jaws broad with large teeth, front teeth meeting with a scissors grip but never overshot or undershot.

The muzzles of other Arctic canids are proportionately longer than that of the dog because they must, as predators, seize and hold prey which is often larger than they are. The jaws are designed for tearing meat from bone. The muzzle of a wolf for example, including the orbits (bony area around the eyes), comprises nearly one-half the total skull area. Domestication without careful selective breeding tends to reduce the size and length of the carnassial teeth and shortens the muzzle's length.

The Malamute has a relatively short bulky muzzle. It is essential that these dogs have a full complement of strong, properly occluded teeth in order to crush bones and break frozen food. The incisors are used to clean and groom the feet, freeing them of ice and splinters; they are also used to clean bones. The canine teeth seize and draw food into the mouth.

The dogs had to hunt for their food during certain times of the year. Their premolars were critical as crushing tools to break bones for the nutrient-rich marrow, and to cut frozen food. They should be proportionate to the molars in size, meshing perfectly when the jaw is closed. The fourth upper molar and the first lower molar are specialized teeth for cutting tough tendon and flesh. The molars themselves should be massive, meshing in a shearing action to crush heavy bone and large pieces of frozen meat. Proper dentition of these dogs was critical to their survival. The size and existence of these important teeth are threatened today in some stock which is being bred.

Neither level bites nor "open" bites are mentioned in the Standard. A dog with a level bite would soon wear its teeth down with this type of diet. An "open bite" is where the teeth and/or the jaws are misaligned so that the teeth are incapable of meeting properly. This type of dog cannot close its mouth, rendering the animal ineffective in tearing and chewing frozen food. Nor can a bitch with an open bite effectively sever the umbilical cord on her whelps.

The Standard states that the "lips are close fitting." The exposed skin of a drooping lip allows for a greater heat loss and the chance of this delicate moist tissue being frozen.

Pendulous lips, those which are not close-fitting, would expose a large area of moist tissue to the elements, the result of which could be freezing of the lips, gums, and teeth if exposed to the elements. This should not be confused, however, with the looseness of the anterior lip portion displayed when the dogs pant during warm or hot weather.

The Standard does not discuss the tongue of these dogs. Indeed, it would be hard to judge a dog by its tongue! Nevertheless, many veteran drivers, beyond other considerations, do just that. The tongue of these dogs should be of a sufficient length and breadth for the dog to be able when lowering its head on the move to scoop snow without breaking stride. Dogs are not normally watered at intervals during work periods. Yet it is critical to their physiological balance that the necessary body fluids are maintained during work. It therefore becomes critical to the dogs' well-being that they have the ability to take in fluid such as snow while on the move.

The nasal passages in the Malamute's muzzle are rich in blood supply, which warms the air entering the lungs and respiratory system. The warming process is enhanced by the presence of large frontal sinus cavities which are always filled with warm air. These cavities are situated in the "stop" area. This feature is peculiar to Arctic canids.

The cranium is located behind the muzzle and eye orbital areas. It is constructed of a number of bones which, as the puppy grows into adulthood, fuse together to form the brain case. This structure is very strong and is covered by the massively powerful muscles of mastication (chewing). These muscles protect the head from injury and are overlaid, especially during the winter, with a fatty layer also. This fatty layer is an added protection against cold and a buildup of ice which would restrict the movement of the ears. The occiput, therefore, is not readily noticeable in the Alaskan Malamute due to this covering.

The Standard specifically calls for a black nose. This is indicative of all pigmentation. In other words, if the nose is black, then so should the lips and eye rims be black as well. This black pigmentation is common to all Arctic animals and is a protective measure against the very strong ultraviolet rays of the sun at that latitude. Black pigmentation prevents burning and blistering from the sun and also from glare off a frozen surface. This color of pigmentation is also resistant to attack by the heavy swarms of insects which abound in the Arctic during the brief summer months.

A condition commonly called "snow nose" occurs in most Arctic dogs of a spitz background, from the tiny Pomeranian to the massive Mackenzie River Husky (aka Porcupine River dog). There are several theories which explain this unique phenomenon of the lightening of a portion, or all, of the nose during the cold months of the year.

One theory is that cold air causes an increase of mucoid secretion in the nose of dogs (just as it does in humans). Some dogs lick their nose repeatedly to remove the excess moisture. The nose is lightened then by the repeated action of the rough tongue. Those dogs which allow their noses to "run" without repeated licking do not appear to exhibit a "snow nose" during this time of year.

Some few people believe the theory that sunlight, being a rich source of vitamin D, is more readily absorbed through pink skin than black. Accordingly, a "snow nose" should therefore not be faulted when judging dogs during the winter months.

> *Eyes*—Brown, almond shaped, moderately large for this shape of eye, set obliquely in skull. Dark eyes preferred. Blue eyes are a disqualifying fault.

The almond shape and oblique set of the eyes are determined by the skull's configuration. The more stop an animal has, the rounder the eyes will be. Round or protruding eyes are more susceptible to injury and snow blindness.

The formation of the orbital area is enhanced and protected by a layer of fatty tissue which is most noticeable over the inner eye. Here, where the sinus cavities are filled with warm air, the fatty tissue is thickest. The amount of fatty pads about the orbital area also alters the eyes' appearance.

By absorbing body heat, the temperature of this eye covering remains stable, thereby protecting the delicate moist eye tissues. (This protective covering also exists in other Arctic canids.) This particular fatty area, while always present, builds up during the winter months and shrinks during the summer.

The orbital fatty padding provides a jellylike movement as the dog shakes its head to rid itself of snow or other moisture. When working, moving, or shaking the head, ice, snow, and frost breaks away with the movement of this fatty layer.

Additionally, this covering serves to protect the eyes by recessing them from the outer surface. Acting as a "sun shade," the fat deposit droops over the eyes when the lids are slightly lowered, thus protecting the eyes from glare. (Malamutes also have noticeable eyelashes which help to protect the eyes from glare, flying snow, and ice particles.)

Some dog drivers have found that when this fatty deposit is absent, they must resort to oiling some dogs' orbital areas in order to remove ice buildup. The fat layer found over the orbital area is becoming rare and, as such, this important characteristic to the breed must not be lost.

> *Ears*—The ears should be of medium size, but small in proportion to head. The upper halves of the ears are triangular in shape, slightly rounded at tips, set wide apart on outside back edges of the skull with the lower part of the ear joining the skull on a line with the upper corner of the eye, giving the tips

of the ears the appearance, when erect, of standing off from the skull. When erect, the ears point slightly forward, but when the dog is at work the ears are sometimes folded against the skull. High-set ears are a fault.

Not only must the ears be small in proportion to the skull, they must also have very thick leather and be well furred. The size and structure of the Alaskan Malamute's ear is essential to maximize reduction of heat loss from the body, especially when in repose. The mobility of the ear is needed for hearing, snow removal, and also for communication of temper and attitude. Any tendency of an ear either to flop or crease when not in active use (and should not be confused with being folded when actively used) would cut down blood circulation, resulting in an increased opportunity for freezing to occur in this vital area.

The set of the ears allows the cranium and occiput to be covered. The occiput should be nearly "invisible" due to the skull covering. A proper ear set allows a dog to fold his ears together and lay them back against the skull, keeping out snow and cold, and protecting the organs of the inner ear. The ear set also allows the dog to rotate the ear 180 degrees so that it is able to catch the slightest sound of cracking ice, a driver's command, or game on the move.

Neck—The neck should be strong and moderately arched.

The length of the Alaskan Malamute's neck is of vital importance. Not only is a certain length of neck necessary for maximum efficiency as a draft animal, giving the dog balance and stability during work, it is also a feature which is critical to its survival. The dog's neck length must allow the animal to lower its head to or near the ground as necessary for scooping snow, thereby alleviating thirst, tracking, or finding the trail, either when working or hunting and while moving at a brisk pace.

The neck is furnished with a prominant dewlap which is more noticeable in males. This fatty dewlap warms the air descending to the lungs. When a dog pants, air descends directly to the lungs. The dewlap prevents the shock of cold air from being taken directly into the body. The shock of cold air would injure the delicate lung tissues.

When in repose, the dewlap is laid across the thorax, protecting the vital heart and lung area from cold. Many dogs also fold their forelegs under the dewlap when in repose, thereby keeping the forelimbs warm and preventing muscle damage that would occur should they become cold and the animal required to work immediately.

Body—The chest should be strong and deep; body should be strong and compactly built but not short coupled. The back should be straight and gently sloping to the hips. The loins should be well muscled and not so short as to interfere with easy, rhythmic movement with powerful drive from the hindquarters. A long loin which weakens the back is also a fault. No excess weight.

The body of the Alaskan Malamute must have enough depth and breadth to sustain substantial room for the massive heart and the lungs' expansion. A shallow, or too narrow, body could not possibly endure the long hours of hard work, or keep the lungs warm in the subzero temperatures and wind-chill factors of Arctic conditions. Any dog with too much spring of rib that does not narrow somewhat at a point by the elbows is incapable of proper movement. While the Standard calls for no excess weight, the heavy muscle must be serviced by a moderate complementary layer of hard fat.

The Standard does not discuss the croup. A dog with too short a croup, and/or a croup which is level, is readily indicated by an improperly set tail. The tail will be high-set and curled too closely to the body. This is commonly known as a "snap tail." Such short, flat-crouped dogs are incapable of work over any great distances. Few dogs have a croup which is overly long or steep. While such a croup is not pleasing esthetically, it does not impair the animal's performance as a sled dog.

Shoulders, Legs and Feet—Shoulders should be moderately sloping; forelegs heavily boned and muscled, straight to pasterns, which should be short and strong and almost vertical as viewed from the side. The feet should be large and compact, toes, tight-fitting and well arched, pads thick and tough, toenails short and strong. There should be a protective growth of hair between toes. Hind legs must be broad and powerfully muscled through thighs; stifles moderately bent, hock joints broad and strong, moderately bent and well let down. As viewed from behind, the hind legs should not appear bowed in bone, but stand and move true in line with movement of the front legs, and not too close or too wide. The legs of the Malamute must indicate unusual strength and tremendous propelling power. Any indication of unsoundness in legs or feet, standing or moving, is to be considered a serious fault. Dewclaws on the hind legs are undesirable and should be removed shortly after pups are whelped.

The feet of any sledge dog are vital to its survival. As a result of this, the paws' structure must be proper. The furnishings and conditioning of the feet are also of great importance. The paws must be well covered with short bristlelike hair between the toes. Hair that is too profuse or too long should be faulted as an unsoundness, a lack of conditioning in the animal. Such hair will also be prone to collecting moisture between the pads which will then freeze as a result.

Long or profuse hair between the pads causes collection of ice- or snowballs and, more than being uncomfortable for a working dog, can actually cripple it. When such an animal is in repose, it will chew or bite at any collection of snow or ice between the pads. Such chewing and licking causes additional moisture to collect, thereby causing a vicious circle, thus rendering the animal incapable of working.

The Malamute must have strong, tight, compact feet to be an efficient draft animal with great endurance. The pads must be hard and tough, not unlike the sole of a shoe. While the nails of a show-ring specimen are often trimmed very short, survival as a working animal calls for the nails to just barely clear the ground. This allows the dog to bring the nails into service on slippery and other unsound surfaces.

Removal of the front dewclaws is not advocated by many drivers and breeders as it is felt that this appendage is often utilized to hold large bones and food. Other drivers (and breeders), however, feel strongly that the removal of this appendage is in the animal's best interest as the dewclaws have been known to be ripped from a working dog's legs while working in difficult terrain.

Tail—Moderately set and following the line of the spine at the start, well furred and carried over the back when not working—not tightly curled to rest on back—or short furred and carried like a fox brush, a waving plume appearance instead.

The tail of the Malamute developed as a feature critical to the dog's survival ability. It is used as a major insulator; it indicates the temper of the dog; it is a means by which the dogs communicate much of their "language." As an insulator of the extremities during sleep, the tail must be mobile and well furred. It is very important that the tail be of a sufficient length to cover the nose of the dog when in repose. This means that the tail should be at the very least of a length sufficient to reach the hock or an inch below, in order to be able to perform efficiently. The tail is also used as a "rudder" in balancing the dog when making sharp turns during occasional high speeds (such as during a hunt). Too long a tail is inefficient in this performance. Many dogs today also exhibit tails which are short, which snap, or which are lightly or too heavily furred.

On a warm day, dogs stretch out, exposing all their lightly furred portions, thereby maximizing the cooling of their bodies. When the weather becomes colder, the dogs curl up tightly in an oblong which resembles their fetal position. The front feet are curled beneath the dewlap, pads up; the rear feet are turned to the side. In this position the moist pads are not exposed to the ground. The nose is buried in the tail, which can be in any one of several positions, depending upon the severity of the weather.

During cool nights, the tail is draped over the rear legs. In more severe weather, it may be tucked between the rear legs, capturing the warm air exhaled from the lungs; or it may be tucked under the legs if the ground is very cold and damp. In the last position, the rear legs are drawn forward toward the head and dewlap. The head and eyes are tucked under the haunch. In this tightly curled position, the dog has completely protected its vital organs and all the moist areas of the body which could lose body heat and freeze. Only the ears of the dog remain exposed. It is theorized that this developed as a protective measure against danger. This singular exposed area further demonstrates the necessity for a small, thick, and well-furred ear.

The tail is also used to communicate. A tail aloft and wagging denotes a happy and expectant animal while a tail which is tucked between the rear legs denotes an animal in fear. The tail may also be dropped with only the tip wagging nervously when greeting a dominant animal or person. A tail which is carried high over the body or stiffly at a 45-degree angle to the horizontal with the fur "puffed out" indicates an aggressive stance of one dog preparing to challenge another.

> *Coat*—The Malamute should have a thick, coarse guard coat, not long and soft. The undercoat is dense, from 1 to 2 inches in depth, oily and woolly. The coarse guard coat stands out, and there is thick fur around the neck. The guard coat varies in length, as does the undercoat; however, in general, the coat is moderately short to medium along the sides of the body with the length of the coat increasing somewhat around the shoulders and neck, down the back and over the rump, as well as in the breeching and plume. Malamutes usually have shorter and less dense coats when shed out during the summer months.

The double coat of the Alaskan Malamute is a critically important characteristic for the dog's survival. The coarse guard hairs have an oily or waxy-feeling coating which is water repellent. This guard coat protects the thick woollike undercoat which is the insulating factor for the body. Flat-, open-, short-, or soft-coated dogs are not protected well enough to survive the rigors of Arctic conditions. Any dog which has an overly long and/or soft coat cannot survive well in Arctic conditions and should be considered a grave fault to the breed.

A long or soft coat collects moisture from the dog's breathing (panting) when working during cold weather. Such a coat is also prone to collect snow or other moisture which the dog is unable to shake off or jostle loose while working.

During rest periods, these dogs attempt removal of this blanket of snow or frost from their coats by biting at it. This leaves the dog cold and damp at best, as the dog gets its fur wet in its mouth. Then, when the dog moves again, additional frost, snow, or ice collects on the coat, further encasing the dog in cold layers; reducing the dog's body temperature and its effectiveness in work; and making it prone to hypothermia.

As the dog continues to try to work while laden down, the moisture begins to twirl the coat, forming icicles. The icicles grow over time, gaining weight, and twirling ever more tightly, until the dog is in considerable pain. In attempts to alleviate the pain thus caused by the icicles, the dogs bite at them, thereby ripping out their coats. This leaves painfully sore flesh exposed to the freezing temperatures. After a period of time under such conditions, these dogs develop hypothermia and, unless treated immediately, die.

Dogs with too short a guard coat cannot tolerate the wind and severe cold well. They require more food to maintain their body weight. When severe temperatures continue for several weeks, the dogs' fur wears off and sores develop from constantly curling up in their dog houses.

Dogs with a proper thick, coarse guard coat and dense oily undercoat seem oblivious to cold, wind, snow, sleet, or rain. These dogs are ready to work, play, or sleep in any type of weather conditions.

Color and Markings—The usual colors range from light gray through the intermediate shadings to black, always with white on underbodies, parts of legs, feet, and part of mask markings. Markings should be either caplike and/or mask-like on face. A white blaze on forehead and/or collar or spot on nape is attractive and acceptable, but broken color extending over the body in spots or uneven splashings is undesirable. One should distinguish between mantled dogs and splash-coated dogs. The only solid color allowable is the all-white.

Some color combinations primarily found in the Malamutes today are the gray and white dogs, wolf-gray and white, sable and white, wolf-sable and white, seal and white, black and white, silver and white, white, red and white, and biscuit and white. Markings vary greatly from individual to individual: open faces, caplike markings, goggles, bandit masks (color extending down over the eyes and a bar down the top of the muzzle, which may or may not include white spots over each eye); half-masks (which extend down to and over the eyes, but do not include a bar extending over the top of the muzzle, and which may or may not have the white spots over the eyes). Many red or biscuit-colored dogs will have reddish pigmentation rather than black around the eye rims, nose, and lips.

Size—There is a natural range in size in the breed. The desirable freighting sizes are:

Males—25 inches at the shoulders—85 pounds.

Females—23 inches at the shoulders—75 pounds.
However, size consideration should not outweigh that of type, proportion, and functional attributes, such as shoulders, chest, legs, feet, and movement. When dogs are judged equal in type, proportion, and functional attributes, the dog nearest the desirable freighting size is to be preferred.

Many people are concerned and confused over the size of many Alaskan Malamutes bred and exhibited today. Bigger is not better, as is commonly thought by quite a few people. With historical perspective, what must be taken under consideration is that formerly the availability of superior balanced diets for these animals was not that which it is today. With today's nutritional standards, the dogs are able to grow to their fullest genetic potential. This can account for some of the apparent small general increase in the size of today's dogs.

Many people have the tendency to overestimate both the size and

Ch. Fate's Little Miss Priss, one of the top bitches in America from 1982 through 1986, demonstrates a good lateral gait. She was shown by her owner Lynda Birmantas of Chicago.

Ch. Tenakee Chief, owned by Dr. Richard Woods and Dawn Woods, Gardena, California, demonstrates gait. Note great reach. *Callea*

weight of their animals when in a lean, hard condition. Upon putting their dogs under the wicket (the AKC's official measuring standard), or on a walk-on freighting scale, many are astonished to find that their animals remain in a close approximation to the breed Standard as it was written.

It is up to Alaskan Malamute breeders, exhibitors, and judges alike, to maintain the quality of these dogs in accordance with the Standard as it was written. This is a breed of dog which evolved naturally and can only be maintained, not improved upon.

> *IMPORTANT—In judging Malamutes their function as a sledge dog for heavy freighting must be given consideration above all else.* The judge must bear in mind that this breed is designed primarily as the working sledge dog of the North for hauling heavy freight, and therefore he should be a heavy-boned, powerfully built, compact dog with sound legs, good feet, deep chest, powerful shoulders, steady, balanced, tireless gait, and the other physical equipment necessary for the efficient performance of his job. He isn't intended as a racing sled dog designed to compete in speed trials with the smaller Northern breeds.
>
> The Malamute as a sledge dog for heavy freighting is designed for strength and endurance and any characteristic of the individual specimen, including temperament, which interferes with the accomplishment of this purpose is to be considered the most serious of faults. Faults under this provision would be splayfootedness, any indication of unsoundness or weakness in legs, cowhocks, bad pasterns, straight shoulders, lack of angulation, stilted gait, or any gait which isn't balanced, strong, and steady, ranginess, shallowness, ponderousness, lightness of bone, poor over-all proportion, and similar characteristics.

SCALE OF POINTS

General Appearance	20	Feet	10
Head	15	Coat and Color	10
Body	20	Tail	5
Legs and Movement	20	TOTAL	100

DISQUALIFICATIONS

Blue eyes.

Approved August 10, 1982

Some characteristics requisite to the Alaskan Malamute's former survival are no longer readily found among the breed's general populace. Due to the absence in our environment of the survival of the fittest, nature no longer eliminates those less suited for survival under the world's most rigorous conditions. As a result, many of these characteristics have been fading in varying degrees from the breed. If, therefore, the survival of the fittest maintains and/or improves a species of animal, then it logically follows that any relaxation of breeding standards automatically increases the degeneration of fitness. This is due to the fact that some unsuitable individual animals participate in the genetic reproduction pool.

The breed's Standard was established through careful study and consideration. Breeders' interpretations of this Standard (proven in the show rings), have basically been of service in maintaining the breed as a whole. Specialized traits, proven through time to be essential to the breed's survival, may disappear altogether without diligence on the part of all fanciers and judges, protecting these innate characteristics which are unique to the magnificent Malamute.

As owners, breeders, and exhibitors, it is our duty to maintain every one of these survival characteristics, even when that proves difficult in our environment.

13

Gait of the Alaskan Malamute

S<small>INCE THE ALASKAN MALAMUTE</small> is a freighting dog, it follows that its gait is of great importance. The official breed Standard does not have a section on gait. Nor does it mention gait as such. But it does give clues as to what is desired. In its first reference, the Standard says: "The Malamute moves with a proud carriage, head erect and eyes alert."

It goes on to say that the feet are of "snowshoe" type, tight and deep, with well-cushioned pads; the front legs are straight, with big bone; the hind legs are broad and powerful, moderately bent at stifles, and without cowhocks. The back is straight, gently sloping from shoulders to hips.

"The loin," it says, "should not be so short or tight as to interfere with easy, tireless movement." And in another section, it adds: "The loins should be well muscled and not so short as to interfere with easy, rhythmic movement *with powerful drive from the hindquarters. A long loin which weakens the back is also a fault.*"

In another section, it adds: "Hind legs must be broad and powerfully muscled through thighs; stifles moderately bent, hock joints broad and strong, moderately bent and well let down. As viewed from behind, the hind legs should not appear bowed in bone, but stand and move true in line with movement of the front legs, and not too close or too wide."

Let us try to interpret all this, as well as to add what the Standard

Noted dam, Ch. Jingo's Silver Trumpet, here demonstrates the single track, in which the legs move into line under the body but do not cross over beyond that line. Howard and Virginia Devaney are the owners.

A dog team, being trained to pull, shows perfect rear-action drive.
Jack Coolidre

Army dogs in training at Wonalancet show excellent front leg action as they pull a four-wheel gig.
International News Photo

does not say. Viewed from the front, the legs should swing forward perpendicular to the ground, and parallel to each other. Or, one should add, nearly so. There is a tendency to move the feet under the centerline of the body if the dog is trotting under pressure, but this is less true with Alaskan Malamutes than with many other breeds.

If the front legs are viewed from the side, the proper angulation of the shoulder and front leg assembly makes it possible for the dog to reach far forward with its front legs. Dogs which do not reach far forward are said to be "stilted." This can come sometimes from lack of exercise and from confinement in too small quarters. It can also come from faulty shoulder angulation.

If we continue to view the dog from the side, there is neither sway nor roach in the back line. If there is sway (a sinking in the middle of the back) the dog will tire easily because there is no straight line of power. Power is therefore lost. A roach often indicates that the hind leg assembly is not correct. And again, power is lost through the roach.

Note that "straight line" of the back applies laterally as well as vertically. If the dog is viewed while moving away, the body should move in a straight line with the direction of movement. One movement fault is called "crabbing" or "side-winding." This means that while the front legs follow the direction of the head, the body moves slightly to the right or left. The hind legs do not move "true in line with movement of the front legs" as required by the Standard.

Dogs with long loins may also fail in lateral back movement. When viewed going away, and at a slow gait, there will be a sort of caterpillar action. This may be all right for caterpillars, which aren't going anywhere in particular, but it always means lost motion for a Malamute.

Now the true test of movement comes when dogs are actually pulling, either when pulling a sled, or in weight-pulling contests. We are including a number of pictures of teams moving both at a gallop and while trotting. These pictures show that the best dogs do move as the Standard says they should. One can notice the great reach of the front legs; that the dogs' front and hind legs do move parallel and in line; and that there is fair width between both the front legs and the hind ones.

In particular, one should notice the truly sound and beautiful movement of the hind legs of these teams. One of the authors, Maxwell Riddle, once traveled fifty-four miles in a single session, in early December, along the northerly coast of the continent. At the end of that time, the Malamutes were still moving perfectly behind. No finer test of the soundness of movement of the Malamute could be made.

14

Training the Show Dog

by Nancy C. Russell

NANCY C. RUSSELL *is one of the most successful breeders of Alaskan Malamutes of the present day. She is a distinguished officer in the Alaskan Malamute Club of America and has become one of the nation's finest professional handlers of show dogs. She has combined her knowledge of the breed with a natural rapport with all dogs.*

Whereas the average professional handler will take dogs which are mature and train them for shows, Mrs. Russell understands the process from puppyhood on. There is no one more competent to tell the owner of an Alaskan Malamute puppy how to train the dog. We are proud to present her instructions just as she wrote them for this book.

You have just purchased your new puppy and prospective champion. Assuming he has the proper conformation, whether he becomes a champion or a "show-ring dropout" is entirely up to you. So much of a show dog's success depends on his attitude as well as his training. The true "show dog" is the one that walks in the ring with the presence that says, "Here I am; aren't I beautiful?" He ignores the other dogs; gaits on a loose lead with head up and maneuvers corners and turns without breaking his stride; poses alertly for the bait; allows himself to be stacked; and appears to enjoy the judge's examination and almost asks for his attention.

Invariably, you find that the show dog loves to travel. He thinks his crate is home and is content in it wherever it is parked. He thoroughly

Am./Can. Ch. Storm Kloud's Better Than Ever, W.T.D., W.W.P.D., won Best in Show under Paula Hartinger. Breeder-owner Nancy Russell of Storm Kloud Kennels handled.   *Meyer*

Am./Can. Ch. Storm Kloud's Vvanilla Snoman, C.D., W.W.P.D., W.T.D., R.O.M. Owner, Nancy Russell of Storm Kloud Kennels. Handler, Jeri Russell.   *Lloyd W. Olson Studio*

Top show winner of all time, Am./Can. Ch. Williwaw's Sunbear of Targhee, R.O.M., won thirteen all-breed Bests in Show. Co-owners are Al and Mary Jane Holabach and Bill and Norma Dudley. *Fox & Cook*

enjoys being groomed and fussed over to the point that he forgets that all tables are not to be jumped upon for grooming. This kind of dog is a real pleasure to show and the kind that wins consistently. So how do you develop this attitude? First experiences of all the things associated with dog shows and going to a dog show must be pleasant ones. This is the cardinal rule.

TRAVELING

For example, do not make your puppy's first ride in the car a trip to the veterinarian for shots. He will then associate a car ride with an unpleasant experience. Instead, take him to the Dairy Queen for an ice-cream cone, to the country for a romp, and to a friend's house for lots of petting and attention. A few trips like this will establish an association pattern of pleasant experiences of a ride in the car, and you will have a dog eager to travel.

CRATE TRAINING

A show dog must consider his crate his home. This way, he will be content wherever his crate is placed. Adjusting to new places readily is a natural characteristic of the Malamute since the Eskimos were nomads and home was wherever the dogs were staked for the night. So now you only need to introduce your pup to his crate in such a way that he feels this is his home. Place comfortable bedding, food, and water in the crate, leaving the door open so the pup can come and go as he pleases. Praise him for going in it to sleep and eat, and never scold him in the crate. After he is using the crate without reluctance, start shutting the door for short periods, gradually increasing the time he is left in. Choose a word such as "kennel" or "crate" and use it as a command for entering the crate. Always praise him for obeying. Take his crate along when you visit friends, to training classes, on a picnic, etc. Have him spend time both in and out of the crate. Do not use the crate as a form of punishment. His crate must be his security and his home.

GETTING ACCUSTOMED TO OTHER DOGS

As soon as your puppy has had his vaccinations, begin exposing him to other dogs. Even if he is too young to participate, take him to conformation or obedience classes to observe. Alternate between having him in and out of his crate. Encourage people to go over to him and pet him. Although it would be unusual for a young pup to be aggressive toward other dogs,

90

Ch. Ceili's No Doubt About It is a Best in Show and Top Twenty winner, and was bred and is owned by Pat and Florence Muchewicz. *John L. Ashbey*

Am./Can. Ch. Beowulf Beau Dehr jyk, bred and owned by Beth J. Harris and handled by Gary Zayac, is a multiple Best in Show winner. *Vernon*

Ch. Onak's Tuggerenhell was in the Top Ten in the nation for five years, breeder-owner-handled by Wendy Corr. She is also the dam of four champions. *Fox & Cook*

Ch. Princess Nikkita Sno-Kloud is a Best in Show winner and was the top ranking bitch in 1985. She is owned by Mike and Julie Butler and handled by Mike.

Martin Booth

Am./Can. Ch. Beowulf Thamaia Oheneah won the 1983 AMCA summer Specialty from the Veteran Bitch Class. Although over ten years old, she defeated more than a hundred Malamutes at this show. Breeder-owner-handler is Beth J. Harris. *Fox & Cook*

discipline him if he shows any signs of aggressiveness such as growling, snapping, or excessive barking. Of course, don't forget to give assurance and praise for proper behavior.

Do not be alarmed if your puppy who has always loved the world one day suddenly growls at the nearest dog. Usually, this occurs between eight months and a year of age. This is a sign he is leaving puppyhood and is trying to establish his place in the pack. The pack instinct is very strong in the Malamute and the more dominant dogs will try to establish their superiority over the others. This leads to the aggressive behavior too frequently seen in the show ring and elsewhere. You must teach your dog this is not acceptable behavior. So be ready for that first growl. Make the punishment so quick and so severe it will leave a lifetime impression. If you are strong enough, pick him up by the ruff, shake him, and shout, "No!" If not, then hit him under the jaw with your fist, hard, and shout, "No!" at him. Let him know you are really upset by this behavior. If you administer the discipline properly, once or twice will be all it takes. From then on a firm "No" will bring his attention back to you, and he soon learns it is much more pleasant to just ignore other dogs.

Think of it as comparable to a small child who runs out in the street. You run out, grab him, scold him, and administer physical punishment because you realize that if he continues this action he'll very likely be killed or severely injured by a car. A dog whose aggressive traits are not controlled by his master has about as much chance of surviving in the show ring, on a sled team, or as family pet as the small child who plays in the street.

LEAD TRAINING

I find that leash training is the most difficult lesson to make enjoyable for the puppy because it does require restraint and discipline. However, if you are generous with praise and treats, the pup will soon associate the leash with pleasant experiences at the same time that he learns to respect it and your commands. I start a young pup on a $3/16$-inch flat Resco show lead. Place the lead right where the neck and skull join, with the lead coming up between the ears. First, let the pup go wherever he pleases and just hang on to the end of the lead. Continue this until he seems accustomed to having the lead on. Then as you are walking along with him, call him, change directions, giving a slight tug on the leash, enough to turn his head in the direction you are taking. At the same time, start coaxing him to come. If he does, give lots of praise or even a pat if he comes next to you, but keep on going. Repeat this procedure until he has learned that a tug on the leash means he must change directions.

The next step is to teach him to walk beside you on a loose lead. This is similar to teaching a dog to heel in obedience, only you command the dog

Am./Can. Ch. Barrenfield Rocket Torpedo was awarded the AMCA Specialty Best of Breed by judge Lester Mapes. The dog was breeder-owner-handled by Jerry Musyj. *Ludwig*

Am./Can. Ch. Maltrail's Champagne Edition. *Booth Photo*

Ch. Windrift's Nakoah, bred and owned by Richard and Barbara Brooks, was a multiple Best in Show winner.

Ch. Trillium's Bull Moose Party won the AMCA Top Twenty competition at Louisville, Kentucky. Owners are Mike and Val Littfin. *Booth Photo*

to stand when you stop and you work your dog on the right side as well as the left side. Corrections are always made with a sharp jerk, release, and lots of praise for correct response. Talk to your dog in an encouraging, happy voice. Convince him this is fun. Make left and right turns and complete turns at a walk until he responds properly and happily. If you are teaching an older puppy or an adult dog who pulls constantly, use a slip collar and leash until he has learned to walk with you on a loose lead. Although this may sound exactly like obedience training for heeling, there are some slight but important differences. First, you do not want your dog to gait looking up at you. This will cause him to throw the outside elbow outward or perhaps even cause side-winding. You want him to look straight ahead. Therefore, you should make a habit of moving slightly ahead of him. This way he can watch you for changes in direction and pace without turning his head. Also you do not let the lead drop down beside the dog in the typical obedience loop.

A loose lead in conformation means only that there is no tension on the lead which would interfere with the dog's movement. Unfortunately, not all dogs in the show ring have been properly trained, and if another dog should run up on your dog from behind or attack him by the time you reel in your extra lead, they would be into a fight. If you have the proper tension on the lead, you will be able to feel a growl through the lead, a shift in weight or even a tensing of the muscles in the neck. This gives you time to anticipate your dog's action and intercept it. For instance, if a dog is going to move his left foot, he has to shift his weight to the right one.

When gaiting, have only enough lead out of your hand to allow your dog to move in the proper position without interference from you or the lead. The excess lead is folded up in the palm of the hand nearest the dog. Flexion of the wrist should be all that is necessary to tighten the lead. This gives you good control of your dog. He will know you have control and pay attention to your commands.

As soon as you have your dog walking with you in the proper position, gradually increase your speed until he is trotting. Practice the turns as before and practice with the dog on both the left and the right side. If your dog drops his head, correct with a sharp jerk upward and at the same time say enthusiastically, "Heads up" or "Let's go." The leash must be directly behind the skull, not down on the neck, to make an effective correction. Don't be afraid to talk to your dog while gaiting. A happy dog moving out freely is a beautiful sight.

GROOMING TABLE

Grooming should always be an enjoyable time for both puppy and master. It is also an excellent way to accustom the pup to being handled.

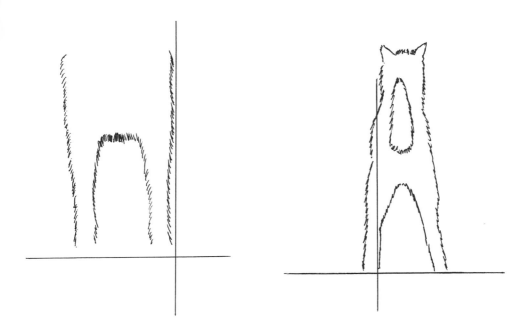

Figure A.   Figure C.

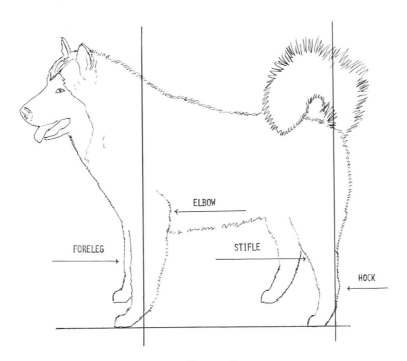

Figure B.

Illustrations of Nancy Russell's instructions in this chapter on how to pose the Alaskan Malamute for show.

If you do not have a grooming table, then get a rubber mat or other nonslip surface for any table at a comfortable height for you. The first time on the table may be frightening for the pup, so play with him, admire and pet him. Don't start grooming until he has lost his fear. Since a full-grown Malamute standing on an ordinary grooming table is too high for comfortable grooming, also teach him to lie down on the table.

Never let him jump off the table except on command. And teaching him to step down to another object and then to the ground can eliminate possible injuries from jumping onto slippery floors or uneven surfaces. Also teach him to climb or jump up on the table. A full-grown Malamute is no fun to lift on and off the grooming table.

POSING THE DOG

Once your pup enjoys the grooming table, it is a good place to practice posing him (also known as stacking). At first, just be satisfied with getting the pup accustomed to having his legs moved and getting him to leave them in that position for a few seconds. Gradually increase the time you require him to stay. This is where being on a table helps, as he is less inclined to move around. Always give lots of praise for standing as posed. While he is posed, go over him as a judge would: checking teeth, picking up the feet, checking testicles, etc.

The Malamute is set up square. Viewed from the front, the outside of the front legs should be a perpendicular line from the side of the body to the ground, feet pointing straight ahead. Viewed from the side, the foreleg should be perpendicular to the ground. A common mistake is to set the front feet too far forward. Practicing in front of a mirror will help you to see this error immediately.

The rear legs are placed so that the hocks are perpendicular to the ground and the feet point straight ahead. Viewed from the rear, the legs are usually placed so that if a line were dropped to the ground from the widest point of the pelvis it would come along the inside of the hocks. Viewed from the side, the hocks are perpendicular to the ground and a line extended upward would touch the rear of the pelvis. Understand this is merely a guideline and should be varied according to the individual dog. Set your dog in varying positions in front of a mirror until you find the one best suited to your dog. Don't forget to view from front and side and rear.

To set the front legs, hold the dog's muzzle in your right hand. Reach over the body and grasp the left leg at the elbow to move it into position. At the same time, turn the head slightly to the right. Change hands on the muzzle, moving the head slightly to the left, and place the right leg as desired by grasping it at the elbow. To set the rear legs, either hold the muzzle in the right hand or hold the leash at the base of the skull. Control

World's most titled dog may well be Ch. Storm Kloud's Follow My Dream, with twenty-six Bests in Show, five Reserve Bests in Show and forty Group Firsts. Titles included are U.S., Canadian, World FCI, Italian, and from Monaco. He is shown by owner Gloria Urbani, Genoa, Italy.

South African Best in Show winner Ch. Storm Kloud's Ffjor Midnightsun, owned by Wolfgang Horlacher.

Best in Show winner and three times world international champion—Italy, France, Hungary—is Ch. Sugar River Foxfire, owned by Gloria Urbani of Genoa, Italy.

Italian and World International Champion is J-Len's Blue Ice Spirit, owned and shown by Gloria Urbani.

Australian Ch. Dane Olympus Cochise's sire and dam were imported from the United States with Cochise in utero. Owners are Ron and Delia Wells of Southern River, Western Australia.

100

of the head is important in order to keep the dog from moving. Reach under the body and grasp the left leg at the stifle joint and lift and place in position. Place the right leg by grasping either the stifle joint or hock joint to move into position. Bring the tail up over the back, but do not flatten it down. The tail should be a waiving plume.

Using commands such as "Stand," "Stay," or "Show" when teaching your pup to pose will be most helpful, especially if he will be handled by more than one person. And a well-trained dog will perform for any handler. Since our Standard specifically states that a Malamute is "not a 'one-man' dog," he should readily adjust to a new handler and will do so especially if trained to voice commands.

BAITING

Once you have taught your pup the words "Stand" and "Stay," you can now step out in front of him and entice him with a piece of liver or other treat. This is done to make him look alert. If he moves, do not treat him but scold with the word "No," replace the leg he moved, repeat the command "Stay," and try again. Reward with praise and the treat when he performs as requested. One obvious rule: Never teach a pup to sit or sit up for food.

Next try baiting him into a show stance. Gait your dog and, as you slow down, give the command "Stand" or "Stay." At the same time, turn to face him with a piece of bait in your hand. Discipline him for not stopping on command or jumping for the bait. And, of course, reward for proper behavior. A dog which walks into a show stance is most impressive.

CONFORMATION CLASSES

Make every effort to attend conformation training classes. They are designed to simulate show conditions and are therefore the ideal place to train your dog. The people there understand the necessity of discipline for a dog. They like dogs and know how to approach a strange dog and examine him as in a show ring. They can teach you the gaiting patterns used in the show ring and help you to become familiar with some of the judge's hand signals. They can help you discover the best speed at which to gait your dog and the most advantageous way to pose him.

And if you are willing to listen and observe, you will gain valuable information about all phases of dog shows. What you learn, you can teach your dog. If you love it, so will your dog. And that makes a winning combination!

Am./Can. Ch. Maltrail's Champagne Edition is a Best in Show winner in both countries. Breeder-owner-handler is Monika Terryn of Norijo, Ontario. *Alex Smith Photography*

15

Alaskan Malamutes in Canada

EARLIER IN THIS BOOK, we pointed out that the fame of the dogs bred by the Malemute people had spread across Canada. Since the Malamute dogs were large, around eighty pounds, and were famous for their great pulling strength, it came about that any large sled dog might be called a Malamute. Often, local names were attached. Thus, in an area along the Mackenzie River there were large freighting dogs which were called Mackenzie River Malamutes, or sometimes Mackenzie River Huskies. In 1925, Freeman Lloyd wrote in the *American Kennel Gazette* that James River Malamutes were being crossed with German shepherds to give them greater pulling strength. This experiment apparently failed.

The concept of a purebred race of large freighting dogs did not develop until about 1928. Earl and Natalie Norris, Alaskan breed pioneers who are still active, once told one of these writers, "The Alaskan Malamute breed developed 'outside,' that is, in the United States."

It was the gathering together of the dogs for the first Byrd Antarctic Expedition at Wonalancet, New Hampshire, in the kennels of Arthur Walden which started it all. There Milton and Eva Seeley first saw Rowdy of Nome. And it was shortly after that they got Yukon Jad from Leonhard Seppala. Walden had a bitch of similar type, Holly, and the Seeleys were on their way.

The worldwide publicity given to the Byrd Expeditions created interest elsewhere, and other people began to collect dogs which they felt to be of Alaskan Malamute type. Captain Alan Innes-Taylor, in charge of the 157 dogs on the second Byrd Expedition, called them "Yukon Malamutes," but the best of them had come from the Seeleys. One area which developed a large concentration of the dogs was Wisconsin.

The real thrust to promote the breed was delayed for a long time. First, many of the best of the Seeley dogs went to the Antarctic, never to return. Some were killed in accidents. Others were deserted as the explorers scrambled to get safely out of the breaking ice. Another Seeley team was lost in training for World War II, and it was that war which truly held back the development of the breed.

Gripp of Yukon was the first Alaskan Malamute to be registered in the United States, July 1, 1935, by the Seeleys. In Canada, Lorna Jackson's first dog was Lorn-Hall Klondyke M'Loot. He was bred in the United States by Paul Voelker, whelped January 1, 1947, and registered in the 1950–51 Stud Book. In those days, Canadian Kennel Club registrations were made through the Canadian National Livestock Records. The dog was by Mikiuk, a son of Tobuk out of Vixen M'Loot. Mikiuk was a well-known stud dog in his own country.

Lorna Jackson then imported Lorn-Hall Oogorook M'Loot. He was a son of Gentleman Jim, a son of Dude's Wolf. His dam was Noma M'Loot, a daughter of Silver King. Lorn-Hall Oogorook M'Loot was whelped July 27, 1945. He, too, was registered in the Canadian Kennel Club Stud Book of 1950–51.

Lorn-Hall Oogorook M'Loot was the first Alaskan Malamute to win a championship in Canada. He was the first white champion, and indeed one of the very few whites ever to win a championship. He weighed 80 pounds and was 24½ inches tall at the shoulder.

The dog made history in another way. He had been police-trained, and when Toronto suffered a disastrous hurricane, Lorn-Hall Oogorook M'Loot was used to locate trapped and injured people in the wreckage of homes and buildings. He was also used to locate the bodies of those who did not survive.

His champions under the Lorn-Hall prefix were Lorn-Hall's Nordic and Lorn-Hall's Yu-Kon. The latter sired Ch. Lorn-Hall's Nootka.

The most famous of all Alaskan Malamute kennels in Canada is that of Dr. T. K. R. Bourns of Lambeth, Ontario. As of January 1, 1975, there were nineteen Canadian champions carrying Dr. Bourns's Boru prefix. Ch. Boru's Guy sired five champions, and Boru's Chilcootin Cub, a nonchampion, four. Boru's Elaitutna, leads all Canadian bitches as the dam of five champions. In addition, Dr. Bourns has been a North American leader in the fight to stamp out dwarfism and the Malamute eye syndrome. He is also chairman of the breed standard committee of the Alaskan Malamute Club of America.

Can. Ch. Lorn-Hall's Yukon, owned by Lorna Jackson, Canadian breeder and professional handler.

A top Canadian sire, Am./Can. Ch. Keikewabic's P'Tis N'Ours, bred and owned by Maureen Anderson of Dryden, Ontario.

Keikewabies P'Tis Guy starts toward his title. Handler-owner, Maureen Anderson.

Future Best in Show and World Champion is Trillium's Charlie's Angel, shown by Nancy Russell, owned by Gloria Urbani of Genoa, Italy.

Barry Freedman Photographer

Future champion Kanangnark's Windsong was shown by Lynda Birmantas for owners Marilou Cockrell and Lou Pleuchell.

Birmantas

106

Today Canadian-owned or -bred Malamutes are a force to be reckoned with in the conformation ring. Canadian Malamutes are now placing with consistency at the group level, both north and south of the border. In the obedience ring, the number who trial their Malamutes is small, but gradually increasing. It appears most are ecstatic just to receive their degrees, so few go on to compete for top obedience rankings. It takes skill, dedication, and a dash of courage to trial a Malamute. All those who venture into an obedience ring with a Malamute deserve the highest accolades.

Dogs in Canada magazine has been keeping Top Conformation Statistics since 1963 and Top Obedience Rankings since 1974. The winners are:

	#1 MALAMUTE IN CANADA— CONFORMATION	#1 MALAMUTE IN CANADA— OBEDIENCE
1963	Igloo Koyuk of Cold Foot	No Statistics Available
1964	Am./Can. Ch. Kodara El Toro	"
1965	Misquah Hills Shinook	"
1966	Ch. Eldor's Little Bo	"
1967	Ch. Boru's Guy	"
1968	Ch. Boru's Erkloonook	"
1969	Am./Can. Ch. Rippleridge Sun Dance	"
1970	Ch. Turner's Tuk Tuk	"
1971	Am./Can. Ch. Glacier's Storm Kloud	"
1972	Am./Can. Ch. Misquah's Magasowin	"
1973	Am. Ch. Eskimo's Charlie Brown	"
1974	Am. Ch. Sno Falls Thor of Silver Frost	Icefoot Shanwonnick
1975	Ch. Skyfyre's Chimo	No Malamutes Qualified
1976	Ch. Naksala's Kiskayo Mistaya	Naksala's Atka Star
1977	Am./Can. Ch. Skyfyre's Chimo	Naksala's Atka Star
1978	Am./Can. Ch. Inuit's Sweet Lucifer	Tote-Um's Falika, C.D.X.
1979	Am./Can. Ch. Inuit's Sweet Lucifer	Cheboukinero Barnak, C.D.
1980	Ch. Storm Kloud's Canadian Club	C/C. Ch. Tamorok's Yukon Sugruk Aklak, C.D.X.
1981	Ch. Keidun's Sikku	Ch. Amik-Barnak, C.D.X. and Am./Can. Ch. Tamorok's Yukon Sugruk Aklak, T.D.
1982	Am./Can. Ch. Farouk de Chabek	Ch. Sparkling Sweet Daniel Webster, C.D.
1983	Am./Can. Ch. Farouk de Chabek	Partner of the North
1984	Am./Can. Ch. Malhavan Follow My Shadow	Oopik's Country Bumpkin, C.D.X.
1985	Am./Can. Ch. Malhavan Follow My Shadow	Malhaven Stormy August Dusk, C.D.X.
1986	Am./Can. Ch. Farouk de Chabek	Storm Kloud's Hustlin Hanna, C.D.
1987	Am./Can. Ch. Malhavan Follow My Shadow	Malhaven Stormy August Dusk, U.D.

Best in Show winner Am./Can. Ch. Barrenfield King's Excalibur, owned by Barrenfield Kennels, Amherstburg, Ontario.   *Alex Smith Photography*

Sharon Cupples showed Am./Can. Ch. Fire n' Ice Hegemony to Best in Show at Oronocto, New Brunswick.
Dennis Photography

A Canadian victory under the late Fred Young made Kimberly Meredith's Nizhoni Atanik's Platnum Plus a Canadian as well as an American champion. She also won C.D. titles in both countries. "Koona" was nationally ranked four years, and won thirteen Bests of Breed.   *Vernon*

108

Ch. Kiekewabies Tikki Taboo,
owned by Laurie Andersen and
Laurie Savage.
Stu Wainwright

Am./Can. Ch. Keikewabies
Lady Tora.
Paw Prints, Inc.

Ch. Keikewabies Scarlett O'Hara,
a red bitch handled by Leslie
Broeneman. *Mikron Photos Ltd.*

CLUBS IN CANADA

Through the courtesy of Michele Loucks, archivist for the Alaskan Malamute Club of Canada, we present this brief history of the clubs and activities special to those people and Malamutes north of the border.

The Alaskan Malamute Club of Canada

The Alaskan Malamute Club of Canada was formed late in 1973 and obtained official Canadian Kennel Club recognition in 1980. Like many organizations, over the years the Alaskan Malamute Club has not been without its tribulations. Persistence and dedication has enabled the club to now boast numerous accomplishments.

Through the persistance and hard work of dedicated members, the Alaskan Malamute Club of Canada hosted its first National Specialty in Calgary, Alberta, on February 12, 1982. Since then, six other National Specialties and one AMCC Regional Specialty have been held. Area Boosters have been held since 1975. The National Specialty Best of Breed and Best of Opposite Sex Winners are as follows:

Calgary, Alberta February 12, 1982	BOB:	Am./Can. Ch. Kiwalik's Taolan Quilleute	R. & G. Pohl
	BOS:	Am./Can. Ch. Skookum's Mika of Tugidak	A. Holabach
Winnipeg, Manitoba December 2, 1983	BOB:	Ch. Keidun's Sikku	E. P. Haas
	BOS:	Ch. Oopik's Northern Light	C. Calvert
Toronto, Ontario December 15, 1984	BOB:	Am./Can. Ch. Farouk de Chabek	A. Lepine
	BOS:	Ch. Barrenfield's Guinevere's Angel	A. & G. Cooper
Vancouver, B.C. February 2, 1985	BOB:	Am./Can. Ch. Malhavan Follow My Shadow	N. Lumsden
	BOS:	Ch. Malhavan Poetry in Motion	K. Ibbitson
Calgary, Alberta February 1, 1986	BOB:	Am./Can. Ch. Malhavan Follow My Shadow	N. Lumsden
	BOS:	Am./Can. Ch. Chukchi's Taolan Mystique	R. & G. Pohl
Regina, Sask. November 14, 1987	BOB:	Am./Can. Ch. Malhavan Follow My Shadow	N. Lumsden
	BOS:	Am./Can. Ch. J-Len's Taolan Tamisan	R. & G. Pohl
Montreal, Quebec April 10, 1988	BOB:	Am./Can. Ch. Storm Kloud's Better Than Ever	N. Russell
	BOS:	Ch. Keikewabic's Lady Tara	M. Anderson

Maureen Anderson of Dryden, Ontario, showed group placing Am./Can. Ch. Keikewabies Nitchee.   *Mikron Photos Ltd.*

Ch. Keikewabies Buck won a group placement at Winnipeg under judge Maxwell Riddle. Leslie Broeneman handled. *Barry Freedman Photographer*

Ch. Keikewabie's Sh'Boom won a Group at fifteen months old. He is owned by Maureen Anderson, his breeder, and Rose and Robert Markewich. Handled by Joanne Faulkner.   *Barbara Gauthier*

The Canadian Award of Merit

In 1987, the membership of the Alaskan Malamute Club of Canada instituted the Canadian Award of Merit (CAM) to recognize top producers. It is based on more than just the number of champions produced, because it rewards those kennels which also produce quality. Progeny and get earn points, which are credited to their particular sire and dam. The first point is earned by obtaining a Canadian Championship. Additional points are awarded for placements at Group and Best in Show level. To date, the following have acquired the right to add the letters CAM after their names:

Dogs	*Bitches*
Am./Can. Ch. Bigfoot's Field Artillery	Am./Can. Ch. Alcan Mate to Arte
Am./Can. Ch. Glacier's Storm Kloud	Am./Can. Ch. J-Len's Taolan Tamisan
Am./Can. Ch. Inuit's Sweet Lucifer	Keikewabic's Shebandowan
Am./Can. Ch. Keikewabic's P'Tis N'Ours	Can. Ch. Knik-Knak's Kincora Kween
Am./Can. Ch. Kiwalik's Taolan Quilleute	Can. Ch. Malhavan Alaskan Diamond
Can. Ch. Storm Kloud's Canadian Club	Can. Ch. Naksala's Shangrila Black Monk
Am./Can. Ch. Tote-Um's Black Warrior	Can. Ch. Polar Pak's Munchkin
Can. Ch. Mohawk of Wilinda	Can. Ch. Tao Silver Mist
Can. Ch. Malhavan Chasing Rainbows	Can. Ch. Tote-Um's Black Mischief
	Can. Ch. Barrenfield's Autumn Smoke
	Can. Ch. Valsun's Frosty Fox
	Can. Ch. Storm Kloud's Quintessense

The Alaskan Malamute Club of Edmonton and District

The founding board and members of AMCED were the driving force which brought about the AMCC's first National Specialty. The experience and enthusiasm of the AMCED Board convinced the Canadian Kennel Club that their group should have the right to hold the first Malamute Specialty in Canada. Many of AMCED's members were also active within the Alaskan Malamute Club of Canada. The Specialty was held on October 3, 1980, with Ch. Keidun's Sikku going Best of Breed. Subsequent AMCED Specialties were held April 15, 1983 (BOB—Ch. Keidun's Sikku) and April 18, 1985 (BOB—Am./Can. Ch. Malhavan Follow My Shadow). By 1985, the national club had hosted three of its own Specialties and was well on its way to assuming the lead role. An oversight in the paperwork department caused AMCED's membership with the Canadian Kennel Club to lapse. The Edmonton club, deciding it had served its purpose, disbanded shortly thereafter.

The Working Alaskan Malamute Club of Manitoba

WAMM is an extremely active, cohesive regional club with a current membership of about forty. They are most busy in the winter months, but do organize activities all year round. Winter camping trips, picnics, races, and weight pulls are just some of their activities. They also participate within the community, putting on displays in malls and at one time held obedience and handling classes. They are combined with regional Siberian and Samoyed clubs to hold Sanction Matches and have held one Specialty, on December 7, 1985, with Best of Breed going to Am./Can. Ch. Taolan Fancy Colours.

WAMM encourages owners to be active with their Malamutes and to interact with other Mal owners. "For Work, Show, and Play" is the club's motto, and it appears to apply to both Mals and their owners.

Arthur Olmen took this picture of puppies he bred out of Am./Can. Ch. Timberlane's Good Karma.

16

The Personality of
the Alaskan Malamute

THE PERSONALITY of the Alaskan Malamute is as complex as a Rubic's cube. They are the essence of simplicity and directness, a breed of dog totally without guile. Concomitantly, there is an inherent duplicity to the personality of the breed, found most often in those dogs that exhibit evidence of a strong sense of humor.

This may be the most diversified breed of dog known to man, excelling in a wide variety of talents beyond that of being most simply a superior companion animal. They are draft dogs beyond peer (being able to pull the heaviest load, over the longest distance, on the least amount of food); hunters; and fishing dogs (some will even dive under water briefly). They have been known to excel in performances in obedience at all levels, including one breed representative that earned the title of Obedience Trial Champion. Conversely, they have brought tears of frustration to their owners' eyes for their comic antics in the obedience ring, and despair to obedience instructors.

The Alaskan Malamute is known as a gentle and loving family dog. They are known to be inordinately fond of small children and will follow them anywhere—even a child foreign to them. Some few of the breed, however, are stand-offish with children and show a total disdain for their company. Usually, dogs of this latter type have simply not had experience in meeting "little people."

Am./Can. Ch. Trillium's Bull Moose Party rests between shows. He is owned by Michael and Val Littfin of Kennewick, Washington.

Ceili's Kanon at seven weeks old. Owners are Dan Peacock and Irma Rivera.

Some few Alaskan Malamutes have earned a reputation as ferocious fighters and, in rare instances, for being vicious. These few dogs, very much in the minority in the breed, have done great damage to the breed's reputation as a whole. Quite a number of Alaskan Malamutes have been raised on farms or ranches with valuable livestock and have been known, in these places, for being protective, especially as "alert dogs," informing their owners if danger to the home or livestock is nearby. And yet, apparently, others are so indiscriminately affable that their owners swear these dogs will invite a burglar in and show him where the silver is kept.

The Alaskan Malamute is, as a general rule, never happier or more content than when pressed up against some portion of its owner's anatomy—or sitting in someone's lap! Conversely, others are known to be regally aloof or even wary of strangers. For the vast majority of the breed, however, we find that the word "stranger" is foreign to their vocabulary.

As hedonists, Alaskan Malamutes are total gluttons, whether it be for pleasure or for food. Some dogs will eat anything in sight, from shoes to furniture, or even radial car tires! Some are first-class thieves, stealing from closets and countertops, and even pots from stovetops without a telltale spill. While some few of the breed will eat their way through bags of food until they bloat, others are finicky eaters, driving their worried owners to distraction, deigning to eat only enough to keep body and soul intact.

This breed has the desire to be especially close to mankind, to those deemed as "master." They have developed uncanny abilities to communicate: humor, boredom, love, danger, eagerness to work and to play, candid honesty (being unable to "lie" when they have done something wrong). They are proficient as working sled dogs, fishing and hunting dogs, as well as companions. All their abilities and emotions are easily communicated to those who are willing to take the time to learn the "language" of these magnificently regal canines.

Among those who do not take the time to understand the breed, they have earned the reputation of being intractably stubborn. For those who do understand them, they are inordinately sensitive to their owners' moods and well-being. They are dogs whose very mission in life is to be openly affectionate, humorous, or compassionate when the owner is feeling depressed. They can be protective of their owners and their owners' belongings as "alert dogs" if they deem the situation warrants it. And they are unflaggingly loyal, courageous, and seemingly tireless in their energy output while working on a job, or while playing.

There is a remarkable intelligence reflected in the openly friendly, inquisitive dark brown eyes. Well known by the most loving and attentive of owners, this breed of dog has more comedians per capita than perhaps any other of the canine kingdom. Too, these dogs have an undeserved reputation for extreme stubbornness by those who fail to recognize the etiology of the breed, how it *evolved,* and so importantly, *why.* Without this

Dane Olympus Tikani, owned by Lynne Fenton of Southern
River, Western Australia, tries the owner's swimming pool.

A five-week-old puppy reaches out to touch its sleeping mother, Trillium's Princess Thia, owned
by Michael and Val Littfin. This is an illustration of "aunty behavior" between a puppy and an
adult.

understanding, an owner will fail to be a master, and an obedience instructor will fail in his professed field of expertise.

What then is the real personality of the Alaskan Malamute: scoundrel or canine saint? The answer lies somewhere between the two poles. It is not a man-made breed of dog, but one whose exact ancestry lies enshrouded in the mists of prehistoric times. This is a highly adaptable breed of dog which can be found living from Alaska to Israel, South America and Japan to throughout the Western Hemisphere and Europe: from farms encompassing hundreds of acres to urban apartments. These are dogs that love to race the wind, and who will as readily adapt their steps to the halting ones of tiny masters as to those who no longer enjoy the spry state of their youth.

Ch. Sno-Pines Oomenak gets a workout. He was Best in Show at the 1987 Goldfield's South Africa show. He is owned by J. Marquis.

17

Alaskan Malamutes— Sled Dogs with a Versatile Heritage

THE ALASKAN MALAMUTES whose company we enjoy today have a myriad of complex characteristics, among which is the innate, driving will to pull. Pulling dogs have been known to help mankind for thousands of years. Who has not seen grade-school textbooks with pictures of Indian dogs pulling laden travois as their Indian masters migrated in search of game? Like the Indian dogs, the Malamute type of dog has been known to man in the subcircumpolar Arctic regions for thousands of years as well. Indeed, there is strong archeological evidence that by 1800 B.C. Eskimos used sled dogs, the progenitors of our present-day dogs, to pull toboggan-like sledges.

Fridtjof Nansen, in his two-volume history of Arctic exploration *(In Northern Mists),* quoted the fourteenth-century Arabian chronicles of Ibn Battuta, who was a businessman trading near what is now known as Kazan in Russia. This man dwelt with great appreciation on sled dogs, noting that the "journey is made in small cars drawn by dogs. For this desert has a frozen surface, upon which neither men nor horses can get foothold, but dogs can, as they have claws."

The original sled dog was essentially a hunting animal. As hunters, the northern dogs are instinctively efficient. Gontran de Poncins described in his volume *Kabloona* how the dogs were used to locate seal breathing holes out on the ice. Each Eskimo would walk with two trained dogs on long leashes out onto the snow-covered surface. The dogs would sniff along, questing for the breathing hole that a seal had made far below the surface of the snow in the ice. When the dogs began circling excitedly in one spot, they would be taken back to the sled, located a goodly distance away and downwind. The hunter, prodding with his harpoon, would confirm the existence of the seal's hole. Then man and dogs sat back to wait for the seal to return.

There are some rare accounts given of primitive hunts where the native, upon taking his hunting dog back to the sled and team, would kick the dog over the heart to make it "lie down." Upon passing out, the dog would then lie quietly. The remainder of the team supposedly followed the leader's example of resting quietly during this time. This barbaric practice shortened the lives of many good hunting and lead dogs.

Not only did the Arctic dogs pull, they packed as well during the summer months. Supplies would be loaded into two pouches, tied together, one on each side of the dog. Some pouches were enormous, almost dragging the ground. At a walk (which is all many of the animals thus laden could accomplish), a dog could carry a pack "equal to his own weight all day long." One early prospector said that he would load his dog up "until his back sagged and his knees began to buckle" and by this measure he would know that the dog's load was heavy enough. Being far more humane today, it is suggested that a dog be packed with no more than one-third of its body weight. Thus a dog which weighs ninety pounds will backpack but thirty pounds of "dead weight."

Simply put, those dogs that showed a willingness to work lived to procreate. Those animals which did not show such a propensity for pulling were, through necessity, quickly eliminated. Indeed, the lifespan of the Arctic dogs was at best a brief one, lasting but about four years on the average, after which time the dogs were destroyed.

During the season of winter migration in search of game, the Eskimos' dogs lived principally on seal and walrus meat obtained by the native hunters. They also, however, would eat anything else in sight, as the earliest explorers soon discovered. Not only would the dogs eat meat of any kind (fresh or decomposed), but they would in addition eat garbage, offal, harnesses, boots, skin kayaks—literally anything that could be gnawed upon, frozen or otherwise.

Under the best of normal conditions, the dogs were fed approximately two to three pounds of meat daily. When times were good, the dogs were fed every evening. When rations were scarce, the dogs would be fed either half-rations, or every other day . . . when available. Under the worst of conditions, when the natives would be faced with starvation themselves, the dogs became the food. During these winters months, the oldest dogs would be killed swiftly by a crushing blow to the skull. Then they would be skinned and the carcass allowed to freeze. A frozen carcass carries no scent and the surviving dogs, if any, would then partake of the dead teammate as would the Eskimo masters.

During those times of such dire privation, it was not uncommon for the skins of these dogs to be used for making clothing in lieu of other types of skins. It was also a fairly common practice for surplus puppies to be killed and utilized in such a manner. Once skinned and frozen, the newborn whelps could be fed back not only to the other dogs, but additionally, to the dam.

During the winter months, the Eskimos were as solicitous of their dogs' welfare as conditions would permit, feeding them with as punctilious regularity as conditions would allow. Having the dogs in the best condition possible allowed them to travel and hunt far more easily.

The summer months, however, dictated radically different conditions for the dogs. It was during this time of the year that no effort was made to feed the dogs. In those areas basically devoid of wolves, and either singly or in packs, the dogs foraged widely. They would obtain refuse around the settlements (including eating offal), or hunt, bringing down small game such as birds, lemmings, mice, shrews. They followed the seacoast and river- and streambeds for mussels, shrimp, fish, and even cast-up aquatic carcasses in their seemingly tireless and endless search for food.

The harsh conditions of livelihood for the masters brooked no sentimentality. If a driver had a favorite dog that he was loath to part with once the dog's prime working years were concluded, then that dog was often kept by the driver in the form of adornment on the man's clothing. Thus, it was not at all unusual for the early trappers and explorers to find an Eskimo "wearing" his favorite dog either as gloves (the pelt of the head was used for these) or as a portion of the parka itself.

Thus developed the Alaskan Malamute, a dog that evolved to work, a true freighting animal born to pack or pull heavy loads under harsh conditions that only the relentless northern latitudes provide. The best of the breed, the true working Alaskan Malamute, is a dog that can pull the heaviest loads over the longest distances, on the least amount of food. Such was the mandate of their hardy ancestors. We find today, however, that our hardy Malamutes are affable family members, helpers who are capable of hauling a sledge or a child's sled, a cart or toboggan loaded with firewood, or happily backpacking necessities and equipment into the wilderness as readily in any of the "lower 48" as did their progenitors in the North.

Dogs were a premium for prospectors and other hardy adventurers of the Pacific Northwest during the gold rush of the late 1800s. It was not an uncommon occurrence for a good dog, either a trail leader or an outstanding wheel dog, to command prices of $1,000, or even more at times. It was during this period that the hauling of freight by dog teams became a big business. The dog drivers became known as either "freighters" or "dogpunchers." These dogpunchers would haul equipment overland to prospectors and miners. They also hauled building equipment, tents, stoves, food—anything that would be of a premium interest to these remote people and satellite businesses. Sometimes they would be hired to carry out gold dust or nuggets from claims.

The native dogs were those which brought the greatest demand due to their ability to withstand the rigorous cold, for their ability to work the longest distance with the heaviest load on the least amount of food (thereby taking up less payload). From the Malamuit tribe (later known as Malemute Eskimos) who lived along Kotzebue Sound and the mouth of the Yukon, we obtained our hardy Alaskan Malamutes.

"Eskimo" is the modern-day spelling of the Algonquin Indian word meaning "eaters of raw flesh." This word was first put in print by early French trapper-explorers who spelled it "Esquimau."

The earliest sleds were actually toboggans made of birch bark strips that were lashed together with sinew, and held together by crossbars. The front of this narrow toboggan was raised in a curl, reminiscent of the Russian troikas (sleighs drawn by horses, reindeer, or dogs) in shape, and obviously influenced by the first explorers in the area now known as Alaska, the Russians who had pushed eastward from northeast Siberia.

Over a period of time, and through necessity, the shape of the vehicle changed from that of native toboggan to iron-shod sled, which became known as "Yukon sleds." Not unlike those sleds used by the U.S. Army during World War II, the Yukon sleds measured some seven feet in length, but were only sixteen to twenty inches wide, being essentially a twenty-inch-wide bed with runners. These sleds were both braced and shod with iron and weighed approximately eighty pounds.

The first teams were normally composed of four or fewer dogs and were not known as "teams," but rather as "dog trains." If more than one "dog train" was a part of a convoy, then the group was known as a "dog brigade" by the early English explorers. The lead dog was simply the "foregoer" and the wheel dog (the dog directly in front of the sled, sledge, or toboggan) was known as the "steer dog." This latter dog had to be the strongest in the team, as it was this animal's job to keep the toboggan on the trail when moving between rocks, around trees, or traversing a hillside.

The most enterprising dogpunchers ran up to as many as three Yukon sleds, hitched together with cross-chains, one behind the other in train fashion. The first sled, that being closest to the dogs, would be loaded with as much as 600 pounds of payload. The swing, or middle, sled carried approximately 400 pounds, and the rear sled, being the farthest away from the dogs, would be the lightest, holding about 200 pounds of payload. Thus, a single team of but six to eight strong dogs would haul payloads of approximately 1200 pounds.

We know our dogs of today as having generally very affectionate dispositions, who can also be, at the same time, jealous of attention given elsewhere, such as to another dog. The early explorers, trappers, and then gold prospectors and dog drivers found that sled dogs as a rule can be very quarrelsome among themselves, with fights ensuing with the least provocation. Newcomers to the North quickly learned that normally one dog in each group would fight its way to supremacy, bossing or bullying the rest of the pack. If it was a good dog, they attested, he would enforce "discipline" among the other dogs, thereby becoming invaluable to that owner. The "greenhorns" also found that the introduction of a new dog to their pack was most difficult, as the new animal, if left to its own devices, would have to take on all the others at the same time in a fight—and stood a strong chance of not surviving.

Contrary to popular mythology, the driver did not ride behind the dogs, standing on the runners of the sled, snapping his whip over the animals' heads as he shouted out instructions of direction. Rather, the earliest dog drivers throughout most areas broke trail for their dog brigades by walking on snowshoes in front of them. (The exceptions to this would have been in those areas of the high Arctic where snowshoes could not be utilized.)

Almost everyone has heard the familiar expression "Mush!" yelled at Hollywood's version of sled dogs. The word "Mush" is an Anglicized version of "Marche en" (go ahead), which the earliest French explorers would call out to their dogs. The first Englishmen who heard the French trappers thus direct their dogs misunderstood the French and came up with "Mush!"

At the right-hand ("gee" side) of the leading sled was a six-foot sapling lashed at a 45-degree angle to the ground, called a "gee pole." This gee pole extended forward from the runner to about the height of an average man's shoulder. The driver walked in front of the sled, a towline between his feet, and the gee pole in his right hand. He used the pole's leverage to steer the heavy sled, keeping it upright on slanted trails and over bumps and hillocks. The gee pole was an aid in swinging wide around corners and breaking the sled loose when the runners became frozen, or helped in braking when descending small hills.

The earliest harnesses were primitive, according to our standards today. Made most commonly of moosehide, they had a heavy round collar to which were attached by buckles side-lines, also known as "traces." These traces were attached to wide leather bands called "tapis." These tapis completely encircled the girth of the dog, not unlike a harness for a horse.

Some dog brigades were decked out by their proud owners with brass bells that were attached to the tapis. Each dog brigade then had its own unique sound, which could be heard as the dogs approached a settlement or factor's outpost, alerting those within as to who exactly was on the trail, friend or foe. Some additional enterprising dogpunchers also bedecked the harnesses with ribbons or embroidery that they had sewn into the collar piece.

Am./Can. Ch. Hill Frost's Dream Maker, W.W.P.D., shown pulling 1,000 pounds to win pull that day. Owners are John and Laura Swire.

18

Weight Pulling

WEIGHT PULLING may have been first romanticized by Jack London's *Call of the Wild,* in his account of the indomitable dog Buck. Numerous other stories have been told over the years, of dogs hauling miners' grubstakes for untold miles over trackless terrain throughout Alaska and the Yukon Territory. It was not an uncommon practice for men of the North to challenge each others' dogs to pull loaded sleds, the runners of which had frozen fast to the snow or ice during a stop. The dog which was first able to break the sled free and pull it a given distance in the briefest period of time was acclaimed the winner. Not confined solely to Alaska and the Yukon, stories also abound of challenges along Greenland and New-foundland coastal areas. There dogs were used to haul logs and driftwood out of the ice, onto the beaches. It is easy to imagine such challenges of pulling occurring anytime there are two or more competitive owners of strong dogs in the same place at the same time, vying against one another.

The sport of weight pulling began as an event concurrent with orga-nized sled dog racing. Originally, drivers would enter their best dogs in a weight-pulling contest after the day's race, in order to see which dog was the strongest and fastest. This was essentially the case as recently as a few years ago, where weight pulling as an event was an adjunct to racing.

By 1978, there was sufficient interest in weight pulling to organize it as a separate event. At this time, an interested group of ISDRA (Interna-tional Sled Dog Racing Association) members drafted a set of regulations, making the activity of weight pulling a sport in itself. Within a year, the sport grew sufficiently to require revision. As it continued to grow, new rules were required again in 1981. At this time, recognition was first given to those dogs which achieved the top three placings in their weight divisions. Thus, by 1982 ISDRA for the first time awarded certificates to those outstanding top-placing dogs in each weight classification.

Weight pulling as a separate event saw a real surge of interest between the end of 1982 and the beginning of 1983, most particularly in the state of Montana. At this time, an advisory committee to the ISDRA weight-pull chairman was established along with the establishment of the formation of the ISDRA medal program for weight pullers. The result was equitable nationwide competition for the first time. While there were no breed requirements (in that any dog, of any breed, or combination thereof would be eligible for competition), the dogs in competition had to be a year old and vaccinated for the basic diseases and viruses which afflict dogs. Focused by a strong goal and the chance to vie the best dogs against each other nationally, region by region, the program once again grew. The number of people involved in all phases of planning and pulling appeared to increase by geometrical proportions, augmented by Montana's Treasure State Weight Pull Circuit of 1983.

It was about this time that those who were deeply involved with weight pulling under the strict auspices of the Sprinters International Association felt it was an opportune moment to establish an organization devoted to, and strictly focused upon, weight pulling alone. Thus was born in the summer of 1984 the International Weight Pull Association (IWPA). It was through the efforts of this latter group that the public in general was introduced to weight pulling as a one-person, one-dog sporting event. Held in shopping malls, as exhibitions and competitions at certain dog shows, and as fund-raising promotional events for various charities such as the March of Dimes, spectators and dog fanciers alike have been introduced to this sport of brawn and heart.

SELECTION OF A WEIGHT-PULL DOG

The selection of a dog for weight pulling (or the selection of a puppy to train for eventual weight pulling) is dictated by the required essentials necessary for an animal to do well in this field: basically sound conformation and superior movement. A massive dog weighing 120 pounds does not stand a better chance of becoming a weight-pull champion than does a strong, athletic dog of 65 pounds, given the various classifications of today's contests. The preferred dogs by veteran drivers are those which tend to be smaller in size and more lithe, rather than large and ponderous. Whether or not the dog is a purebred is irrelevant to the function of the animal as a potential competitive weight puller. As long as a dog of any ancestry has the conformation and movement, in addition to a strong desire to pull for the owner, it has the potential to be trained as a competitive animal.

Because dogs must pull with more than just their heart, have more than just a desire to pull, an objective evaluation of each animal's potential is required before placing it into a weight-pull training program. Not unlike climbing a corporate ladder, the dog is evaluated from the ground upward.

The dogs must have thickly padded paws with well-arched, tightly fitted toes. The shape of the paws should be round and large. Just like those dogs used on the trail, the feet of the weight-pulling dogs also take abuse in training and competition. The shape and length of the pasterns are of equal importance to the shape and depth of the paws. It is imperative that the dogs have good strong straight pasterns, neither too long nor too short; any deviation from this is indicative of weakness in the pasterns and will eventually lead to severe joint problems.

"Moderation" is the key word of the "assembly" of the ideal weight-pulling dog. The canine requires a certain depth of chest (ideally about to the elbow) and a moderately broad front to work "into" (push) the harness. The shoulders should have a moderate layback. The topline should slope moderately from the shoulders to the hips. A solidly strong back is also required. A dog that is too long in the back (usually the loin area), will be a weak-backed animal and will be unable to work effectively either as a weight-pulling animal or a running dog (effective sled dog).

The rear angulation also needs to be moderate: that is, neither too straight nor too much angulation (bend of stifle). A dog which is moderately angulated will be able to lower himself in a line with the load, thereby having the ability to exert a formidable forward thrust. The broad, moderately square hindquarters, which match the forequarters, allot an efficient energy transfer as the dog drives hard. If the dog to be used in weight pulling is without basically solid conformational soundness according to the guidelines above, then that dog cannot build and condition the required muscles for heavy weight (and other) pulling.

Those dogs which exhibit a certain amount of fearlessness, who exhibit a focus on what they are doing (single-mindedness), and who have a driving desire to pull in addition to all the other necessary requirements, will make good weight-pulling dogs. Without any doubt, the dogs concomitantly must have a strong desire to please their owner. For some dogs, this is affection—a strong sense of bonding and of respect for their owner and the owner's requests of them. This desire to please the owner helps immeasurably to make a good pulling dog. A number of other dogs less closely bonded with their owners have, nevertheless, such an indomitable will to pull commensurate with the desire to win (and the dogs do know), that they make no less fierce competitors.

When the hour has grown late, the dog has already made succeeding heats (rounds) successfully, the track of the pull has grown sticky or rutted, and the weights are increased, it is those dogs who are able to remain focused, working until the job is done, giving it everything they have, which are the dogs with the true working temperaments.

WEIGHT-PULL TEMPERAMENT

How is a potential puller chosen from a litter? How does one find that elusive puppy who, as an adult, will develop into a first-rate working dog? How are those puppies culled that do not have the heart for pulling? Every litter will contain a variety of engaging personalities. There may be puppies which are outgoing; aggressive; friendly; slow-learning; shy; "vacant between the ears" (brainless); brilliant; inventively playful. Not every litter will contain a puppy of each personality type. Nor is it that out of parents excelling in the field of sled work every puppy will be a fine puller.

The search for the "perfect puller" may begin when the puppies are still in the whelping box. Considerable time is spent observing and evaluating the puppies' individual behavior. Breeders have the best opportunity to observe the puppies' individual behavior. Therefore, reliance on the ethical, knowledgeable, and reputable breeder for analysis of the puppies will benefit the prospective owner.

A few breeders are able to begin evaluating and projecting puppy personality types at a few days of age, through having had long experience in observation. For others, however, the search begins later, when the puppies are three to six weeks of age—when they have first discovered that there really is a life beyond the walls of the whelping box. Close observation of the puppies at this time is helpful, noting particularly how they react to their newly expanded horizons.

Watching how the puppies interact with each other is very important. At three weeks of age, there is not too much generalized interaction, but there are usually one or two puppies that are more adventuresome than the rest—those who explore their world thoroughly, who chew on siblings and mother, and who have discovered that the funny noise they have been listening to comes from their own mouth! It is humorous to watch this latter discovery. When the puppy discovers that it has a voice, it will often test its range, from "barking himself backward" to tremulous howls to growling in its most "terribly terrifying" manner.

Those puppies which are real explorers and discoverers, and which react positively to the large world around them, are worthy of close observation. Those puppies which are assertive (not necessarily aggressive) and obviously dominant to the littermates are those which bear the most careful scrutiny. Other characteristics to look for beyond assertive leadership are intelligence and natural curiosity. The ideal prospect should exhibit signs

130

Sasha Serenade, owned by W. C. Adams of Bitteroot Kennels, shows great weight-pull form. Dog has W.W.P.D.X. 2 degree.

Sasha Serenade, W.W.P.D.X. 2, makes a winning pull of 1,650 pounds in the Budweiser Cup Series.

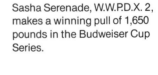

Sue Fuller of Mountain Home's Kennel, Twisp, Washington, coaxes and encourages Mountain Home's Yukon, W.L.D., W.W.P.D., into making a winning pull of 2,415 pounds.

131

Ch. Whitewater Bitteroot Shuyak, W.W.P.D.X. 1, is the only group-placing show dog to win an ISDRA medal in weight pulling. Owner is Cynthia Adams.

Bitteroots Inuit Teeyan, W.W.P.D., was major-pointed with Cynthia Adams owner-handling.   *Missy Photo*

Ch. Bitteroot Shuyak's Kachemac, W.W.P.D. The dog is owned by Cynthia and William Adams, Bitteroot Mountain Kennels. *Rinehart Photo*

of independence, and the capacity to be away from mom and siblings. The ideal puppy, while being dominant in addition to the other characteristics, is one that is not stubborn. Those puppies who, while showing some hesitation in reactions to new things, nevertheless explore them first—these are puppies that should be kept under the closest observation as potentially fine workers.

Some veteran sled dog drivers wean their puppies as early as three or four weeks of age. The vast majority of breeders will agree, however, that it is unwise to wean puppies before they are six or seven weeks old. Early weaning can have a deleterious effect on the temperament of puppies (with the possible exception being those puppies so treated by experienced dog drivers). Not only do puppies derive much-needed nutritional benefit from staying with their dam (in addition to the breeder's supplementation of solid foods), but they derive as well other positive benefits from continued close association with her. Among these is her continued emotional nurturing.

Once the puppies are out of the whelping box and becoming "real little Malamutes," the litter is observed more closely than before, while eating, sleeping, and at play. (Those puppies which dream actively exhibit signs of superior intelligence.) This close observation of the litter (in particular those puppies which have been singled out as potential sled dogs), is a search for those specific characteristics indicative of a good working attitude. Puppies that possess all of these attributes have the potential for being able to ultimately survive well the stress of a competitive weight puller or sled dog.

An advantage that many dog-driving breeders have is their ability to keep multiple puppies which they are considering adding to their teams. (This is expensive, and older puppies are often difficult to sell.) These puppies are normally socialized with older dogs whose characteristics they want the puppies to acquire, such as socially acceptable behavior in a pack environment.

Bill and Cindy Adams (Bitteroot Kennels) have enjoyed much success with their teams and weight-pulling dogs. They have developed a method of testing those puppies under their consideration. At six months of age, they give the puppies what they call a "harness test." This allows them to find with some certainty those dogs which are potential workers.

Initially, the puppies are placed in harness and their reactions observed. Puppies in the "A" category continue about their business as if nothing had occurred. The "B" category puppies are disturbed by their harness. They bite at it, try to wriggle out of it, and vocalize their complaint. The final category, "C," encompasses those puppies which are totally submissive to the process and lie down, "waiting for it to go away."

The Adams's next step is that of securing a tow line between the puppies' harness and a Volkswagen tire that weighs about eighteen pounds. Again, the reactions of the youngsters are noted. The "A" class will exhibit some eagerness for moving into the challenge. The "B" pups may stand patiently and mildly confused. The "C" puppies may lie down, roll over, cry, or any combination thereof.

The next step they employ is that of actually calling the puppy and giving encouragement to work into the harness. The "A" puppies will take off eagerly without looking back. Puppies categorized as "B" require additional encouragement and reassurance. The "C" puppies are frightened of the load, of having something "following" them. They require help in pulling the load, to give them reassurance and confidence.

As the final test, the Adamses increase the load slightly, or place the load where it is slightly more difficult to drag. Again, the puppy is called. The "A" puppies exhibit their eagerness by trying to work the load almost before the command has been given. They are not daunted by the added weight or difficulty. The "B" puppies are initially stymied by the increased load. They may try to "figure out" what is required and need additional encouragement from their owner. The last puppies, the "C's", have no idea what is expected of them. They may lie down and cry or simply stand in dejected confusion. These puppies need the owner to pull the load with them until the load is moving smoothly.

Puppies which are consistently "A" puppies are those which have exhibited the ideal innate ability to work. These puppies need little more in their lives other than conditioning. The "B" category puppies are those which show promise, but require more confidence. And finally, the "C" category puppies, according to the Adamses, if they are to make a sled dog at all, must be taught everything. Most dog drivers do not have the time or patience to waste upon a "C"-type puppy and will neuter them and give them away.

The puppies which score well in the "A" (and sometimes "B") categories have the capacity to become outstanding pulling dogs, given the proper training and conditioning. The "C" class puppies, however, will never be team members. Puppies in the "A" and "B" categories will, with training and experience, earn Working Weight-Pull and Working Sled Dog certifications.

EQUIPMENT

A properly fitted harness is the first item of equipment that must be obtained before any dog may begin training. Harnesses which are purchased through the mail are inexpensive. The better mail-order vendors require exact dimensions of the dog in order for the harness to fit well. Many newcomers to the sport of sledding or weight pulling have difficulty in taking accurate measurements due to their dogs' thickness of fur. If when measuring they do not firmly compact the dog's coat, they end up with a harness which is far too large. An ill-fitting harness will discourage a dog from working.

Harnesses come in two basic types: freight and racing. They are comparatively easy to construct. The freighting harness is considered to be an all-around harness and is usually the first to be made or purchased. Once the owner has gained experience in dog driving, he may wish to try a racing harness for his other dogs. Once the owner-driver is working more than one dog, racing collars for each dog should be acquired.

When two or more dogs are being trained, a training cart or sled becomes a necessity. A training cart may be made from a stripped-down electric golf cart or scooter. A training cart may be built by purchasing three wheels, welding a frame, and improvising a front castor. Training carts may also be purchased through a mail-order catalog.

MAKING A WEIGHT-PULL HARNESS

A weight-pull, or freighting, harness is a requirement for training a dog to weight pull. Basically, the two types of harnesses are identical. Many freight harnesses, like weight-pull harnesses, have a whiffletree (spreader bar), which prevents the harness from closing in and rubbing hair off the dog's flanks while working under a load. However, unless the dog is to do a *lot* of freight running or weight pulling, the spreader bar may be omitted. It is very important that the harness be very well padded around the neck and shoulders to help prevent the dog from being severely chafed.

A weight-pull harness may be made by those who have some manual dexterity. The average Malamute weight-pull harness requires approximately twelve feet of webbing one and a half to two inches wide, and about four feet of one-inch-wide webbing. Initially, the webbing should be either tacked or stapled while experimenting for a perfect fit. Place the webbing under the dog's chest, between the forelegs, in front of and around the shoulders, then pass it over the back at the point where the neck meets the withers (directly over the shoulder blades). Take the end of the webbing and complete the loop just below the last rib while pulling it tight to compress the dog's coat. Allowing room for a spreader bar and the attachment of a steel ring, pull the harness loop back tightly (while making sure that the loop is still in place on the "model" dog), and mark with chalk what will become the center of the harness. Allowing sufficient material to make a second loop, cut the webbing to length.

An identical but opposite-hand loop is now made at the open end of the webbing. Slide the steel pulling ring onto the harness before once again fitting it onto the dog. Place the first loop onto the dog, then the second loop—this will naturally fit over the first loop, crossing in two places. Pull the harness tightly from the rear, compressing the dog's coat. Then attach both loops where they cross, beginning approximately at the point of the dog's breastbone and finishing even with, or just slightly past, the elbows. (This last step is very important to prevent the harness from chafing the

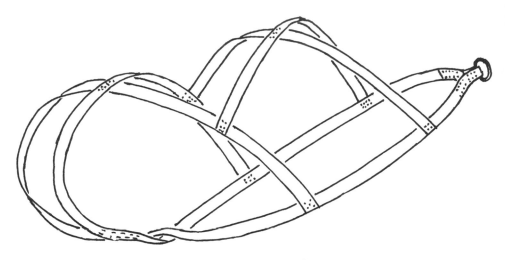

Basic freighting harness sewn together, ready for padding and spreader bar.

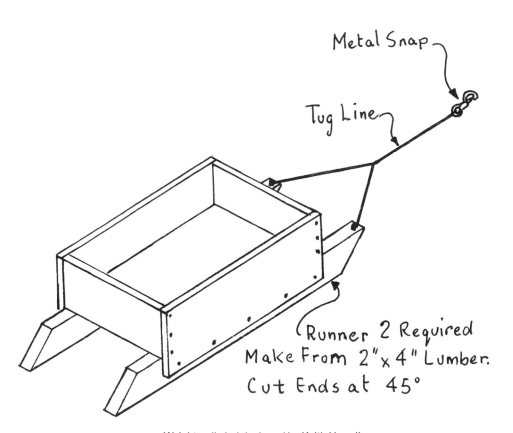

Metal Snap

Tug Line

Runner 2 Required
Make From 2"x 4" Lumber.
Cut Ends at 45°

Weight-pull sled designed by Keith Hurrell.

inside of the forelegs.) While keeping the two loops pulled tight (at approximately a 90-degree angle to each other), the two loops are crossed and attached where the neck meets with the withers. At the harness's rear center point, sew the steel ring into place and reinforce with four inches of webbing.

The two support straps may be one inch wide. Their sole purpose is to support the harness. One strap is attached at approximately a 90-degree angle to the loop webbing, on each side of the harness, midway between where the two harness loops meet over the shoulders, and where the webbing ends, closing the loop. After the harness is fitted once again on the dog, cross the support straps over the dog's back and attach them at the point which will support the harness at the correct level. Sew the straps together where they cross over the dog's back. Using a good strong nylon or dacron thread, double-stitch all the joints ("They take an awful beating," according to veteran driver Keith Hurrell). A spreader bar may be added to the harness. The harness is now completed.

MAKING A WEIGHT-PULL SLED

A person with some woodworking experience may make a weight-pull sled by building a box and mounting it on runners. The box should be capable of holding at least two hundred pounds of weight (such as sacks of dog food, cement blocks, training weights, or rocks). An advantage of training with a sled rather than a wheeled cart is that it is easier to make and requires less weight. It may be used on either dirt or snow and the pulling effort is almost continuous, not diminishing appreciably once the weight begins to move.

TRAINING THE WEIGHT-PULLING DOG

Once the dog has been fitted with a harness, he is ready to be introduced to its use. Most weight-pull trainers possess a selection of harnesses ready to fit different dogs as they grow. Some successful weight-pull trainers begin training their puppies at five to six months of age by putting them in a suitable harness and attaching a towline with a light weight. It takes a puppy only a few minutes (through a few startled starts and stops as he looks behind, puzzled by the noise and drag of the "thing" following him) to realize he will not be harmed. At this point, many experienced owners get out in front of the puppy, calling it to them, then praising the puppy effusively as he pulls the load.

The better pulling puppies quickly learn what is expected of them.

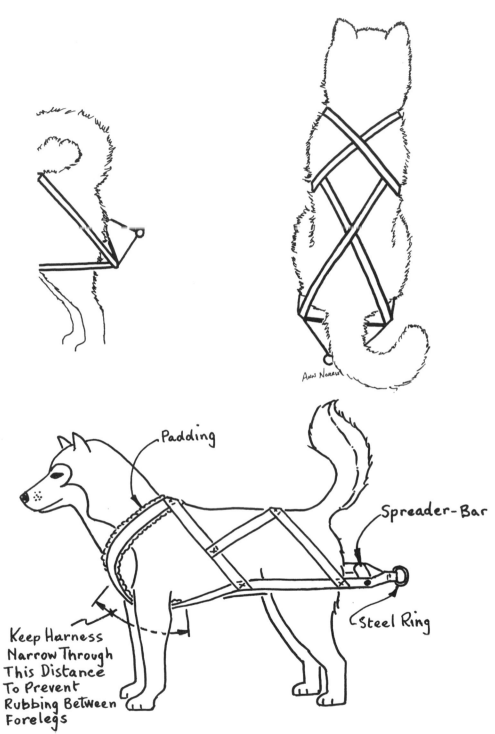

Padding

Spreader-Bar

Steel Ring

Keep Harness
Narrow Through
This Distance
To Prevent
Rubbing Between
Forelegs

Ann Norris

Freighting or weight-pull harness.

138

They quickly learn to enjoy this new challenge. Some puppies, however, never take to pulling. A trainer who holds the collar or harness and drags both the puppy and the weight together will accomplish nothing whatsoever in the way of training the dog. Indeed, such actions will quickly teach the dog to resent or fear the harness. Alaskan Malamutes have the innate desire to pull—or they are born with nothing in the way of desire and heart. A desire to pull (which most Alaskan Malamutes have) is an innate characteristic: it cannot be trained, coerced, or otherwise "put into" a dog.

At about one year of age, a dog may be hitched to an empty sled, thereby building up his muscles without excessive strain, and getting him used to the feel of an object dragging behind. One may encourage the dog by having him pull the empty sled twenty or twenty-five feet to his dinner. The dog's dinner may be divided into five or six helpings, thus giving the dog experience of five or six pulls. A special treat, such as a dog biscuit, may be substituted for the dinner as a reward.

When a dog is eighteen months or older, and after several (successful) sessions in the above manner, a small amount of weight may be added to the box. The weight is increased slowly, over a period of weeks, until the dog is pulling hard, but *never unable to move the weight alone.*

A word of caution is advisable. *No* dog should pull a heavy weight of any kind before it is eighteen months of age, otherwise the youngster may suffer irreparable injury, such as a stress fracture, through what constitutes real physical abuse. Many of these dogs do not mature until well after two years of age. Nor should most dogs of eight or more years of age be requested to pull. The few exceptions to the latter would be those rare veteran dogs which have not been neglected, having been kept in an optimum physical condition. A veteran which has remained in peak form may still pull at ten or eleven years of age. These latter dogs are, however, exceptional.

When the dog has reached the food or treat, the tug line is pulled forward to release the tension. At this point, the dog is given the treat or allowed to eat dinner. If the dog is fed a treat only, training may continue safely. If, however, the dog has been fed its dinner, training should cease for the day. If training continues at this point, the dog and sled are turned around, and the dog pulls the same distance in the opposite direction.

Some sleds are constructed bidirectionally—that is, both ends appear to be the same. With such construction, the dog and tug line are moved to the opposite end of the sled. This is far easier when a small person is doing the training.

Each time the dog makes a successful pull, in addition to the reward of food, he is praised effusively with happy-toned "Attaway"'s and given a hug or is petted. Eventually, the reward of food is eliminated. The dog will have learned by then to work no less hard for the owner's obvious delight in the dog's newfound ability and desire to please.

Every training session with the dog should be ended with a successful pull. There may be starts and stops, commands to "Hike!" and praise, several times along each way. ("Hike!" is a sled dog driver's term meaning "Go!") It is recommended that the dog make no more than six pulls at a time, otherwise it could become bored by too much repetition. No dogs bore more quickly than Alaskan Malamutes. A bored dog will not work, having lost the challenge and thrill.

Although not a prerequisite, a few trainers precede weight training by constructing a "weight-pull lane" as an established site for all training. The site, they feel, allows the dog to get acquainted with a regulation type of lane so that when in competition he will not be distracted. The site should be approximately twenty-five feet long by eight feet wide. Barriers which are present at regulation pulls may also be used in training. These may be made out of low, portable, slatted fencing, or even more simply, bales of straw. While such barriers help to keep the dog focused, their main purpose at a pull is to keep the bystanders and other dogs from interfering with the working animal.

It is also helpful in training and conditioning the dog to make the course a challenging one by grading it with a slight upslope. The surface should be moderately soft. This helps condition the dog through the creation of an additional resistant force while being easier on his feet.

It appears that the majority of people train their dogs by calling them from a position in front of them. Others train by driving the dogs from behind. They give the dogs commands such as "Come!" and "Hike!" (and "Gee" or "Haw" as required), interspersed with a lot of encouragement. Driving the weight-pulling dog (working from behind with vocalized commands only), appears to work best for those dogs which have been run on competition teams. Those dogs driven from behind must rely solely on their master's voice for commands of direction and encouragement. A dog which is called from ahead is able to see the owner as well as hear him. This dog can be given directional hand signals along with the vocal commands.

"Gee" and "Haw" are vocalized directions given to animals such as horses, mules, or dogs that are driven. "Gee" indicates a right direction while "Haw" is indicative of a movement toward the left.

When a dog is brought to the pull site and the harness is attached to the towline of the sled or cart, the owner then gives the dog a command to stay, either by voice or hand signal. When everything is ready, the owner then gives the dog the command to pull. The well-trained dog will then begin his pull with a low forward lunge toward the finish line. Those dogs which back into their harness only to lunge forward again, or those which leap directly into the air, or to the side, waste energy and strength that should be applied to the pull. A dog which backs up one or two steps before lunging forward, however, should not be confused with inefficient animals.

Outstanding weight-pulling dogs utilize two basic techniques when

Freight/weight-pull harness.

Freighting harness made by Keith Hurrell has no spreader bar and is made from 1¾-inch-wide nylon webbing with 1-inch-wide back support straps.

initiating a pull. In one technique, the dog backs up slightly and then *throws* himself forward into the harness, moving first to one side and then the other to break the load loose, starting its forward momentum. Instinctively keeping his head down, the dog moves the load to the finish line. An old or poorly made harness will "blow apart" under the dog's impact with this method.

The second method is somewhat controversial for moving a very heavy load. Here the dog stands on his rear legs, leaning into the harness, letting his weight plus the strength of his rear legs slowly initiate the forward momentum. The dog then lowers his head and pulls the load to the finish line. This latter method is useless for moving a heavy load stuck in snow. Such a load must be broken loose using the "Gee! Haw!" method.

Teaching the dog to concentrate on the pull is not hard. Nor is it hard to teach the dog to begin the pull in the proper position—that of the head lowered for the tremendous exertion of the initial forward thrust. Some owners get in front of their dogs, and, crouching down, call the dog to them while holding out their hands just above, or while patting the ground. These actions by the owner will aid in bringing the dog's focus downward. The dog will, by lowering his head while under restraint, be in the correct position to begin the pull.

Another method of early training is that which utilizes obedience commands and a lead. The dog (in harness and hitched) is placed in the "down" position with the lead attached to the collar and the owner out in front of the dog at the end of the lead. The chosen command—"Hike!"; "Come!"; "Pull!" for example—is given.

Some dogs are born with the genetic imprinting of how to pull properly. There are those dogs, however, which start a pull by leaping or turning aside to run. At this point, the lead is given a forceful correction (quick strong jerk). This rectifies the movement in error, bringing the dog's energy and focus back to the owner who is in front of him.

From the very beginning in training, the dog is taught that once the load begins to move, he must continue to the finish line. During this time, the owners need to encourage the dog with excited tonal qualities and, if the dog is called and not driven, by gestures as well. When the training sessions take place under snow and ice conditions, the dog must also be taught not only to lunge forward ("buck the harness"), but to lunge first to one side (and/or then the other); to break the frozen load free.

"Bucking the harness" is a dog driver's term applied to that action the best dogs use when initiating a difficult pull. This movement, not unlike the bucking of a horse, prompted the term.

Training for weight pulling should be alternated two or three times weekly with a running-conditioning program. The emphasis early in the training program should be on running to strengthen *all* of the dog's muscles, thereby increasing his stamina and lung capacity. Training is only done in cool weather. *Never* train a dog when the temperature is over 60 degrees Fahrenheit or the dog may end up suffering from heat prostration. This format of a running-conditioning program is necessary to keep the dog balanced in its development (i.e., that the forequarters stay proportionately developed with the hindquarters). As the date of a competition pull nears, the focus of training then shifts to more of the weight-pull practice sessions.

Turning a dog loose in the yard (or acreage) by itself, or even with other dogs is not enough to condition the animal properly. Some trainers condition their animals by running them alongside a bicycle or a car (in an area where there is no traffic and the footing will not damage the dogs' feet, muscles, or ligaments). By using a vehicle, the trainer can keep the dog at a constant speed, clocking him to make him work hard. (When a vehicle is utilized for training and even with the dog on a long line, there is always the danger of exhaust inhalation.) Eventually, the days of running are alternated with days of pulling only.

The length of ground covered for running-conditioning does not need to be overly long. If the dog is being road-worked, two to five miles at a gait will suffice nicely. A moderately mature dog of eighteen months can be hitched to a tire that is weighted down with cement. As the season progresses, cinder blocks or bricks may be added to the tire. The resistant drag factor that is created by a weighted tire (up to seventy-five pounds for a medium-sized Malamute) pulled over a short distance, such as one-third of a mile, is quite formidable. No dog, however, should be asked to perform this feat early in training or conditioning.

No young puppy should be trained on as strenuous a program as just outlined. Youngsters should be trained in moderation. Because strenuous running or weight pulling can cause damage to hips (such as stress fractures), this type of program should not be engaged in until the puppy is about eighteen months old and after hips have had a preliminary radiograph. No puppy should be placed in competition before this time. Also, too much training, pulling too many loads (even if only over a very short distance) too often, becomes boring and will cause the puppy to sour on this work.

Any dog which is to pull without sustaining injury must be in prime physical condition (no adipose tissue). The fact cannot be ignored: The process of conditioning and training a weight puller is challenging for both the owner and the dog. This form of training requires a *dedicated* owner. The work involved in training a world-class or otherwise competitive puller simply cannot be skimped upon, nor skipped from time-to-time.

Occasionally, a competitive dog will lose the joy of pulling. Like people, they too can suffer from burnout. While they know the commands and routine, they lose the will, the desire, to pull. At some point, these dogs have realized that they cannot be "touched" for the sixty seconds, the allotted time of a pull's start. There is nothing that can be done to put that

Am./Can. Ch. Hill Frost's Dream Maker, W.W.P.D., has an indoor weight-pulling record of 2,714 pounds. Hill Frost Kennels are at Traverse City, Michigan.

Dick and Diana Alverson

A Fontana, California, Christmas parade included Beverly Turner taking her grandchildren for a ride behind Ch. Tikiluks Kalaska Red Lobo, C.D., T.T. 6.

desire back into the dog. He has just let the owner know that it is time for his retirement. Asking or demanding that a dog pull if it has reached this critical point (or is beyond his prime, or out of condition) would be cruel to the dog. It would show that the owner had no regard for the animal as a sentient being.

Rules of the Sport

The Alaskan Malamute Club of America adopted the following rules for indoor and outdoor weight-pulling events. Effective as of March 15, 1984, the rules are written with a heavy emphasis on safety, while preserving the breed's genetic heritage as well as its original function.

I. General

   A. The pulling area must be at least 10 feet wide and 20 feet long with an open end toward which the pull is made. There shall be a physical barrier separating the crowd from the pulling area.

      1. The outdoor area shall be as level and hardpacked as conditions permit.
      2. Indoors, the area shall be of dirt, sod, carpet, or runner.
      3. The dog does not need to achieve traction on the same surface as that on which the vehicle rides.

   B. Three officials will supervise the event. One will be designated Chief Judge. A majority ruling will be the deciding factor.

   C. All entrants are responsible for the conduct of their dogs and handlers before, during, and after the contest. Unmanageable dogs will be barred from competition. Unsportsmanlike conduct in the weight pull area or on the weight pull course will result in disqualification.

   D. All dogs shall be kept in a designated holding area behind the starting line while they wait to pull. No dogs shall be allowed in the general area ahead of the starting line except for the dog that is pulling.

   E. All dogs must be under physical control, on lead, except when hooked to the weight pull vehicle.

   F. No female in season may be used in a weight pull or brought into the weight pull area. Other unentered dogs and family pets are also excluded.

   G. No dogs shall be brought from a kennel where Parvo, Brucellosis, Hepatitis, Distemper, Leptospirosis, or any other contagious canine disease exists, nor shall any equipment be brought from said kennel.

   H. All persons, or dogs, capable of baiting the dog pulling must be no further forward among the spectators than the starting line. Any violation of this rule will result in the disqualification of the involved dog.

I. No handling or bait is to be allowed. Handling is to consist of anyone touching the dog, his harness, the pulling vehicle, or any other part of the equipment or load except to stop the dog after completion of the pull. Baiting consists of the use of anything to influence the dog other than hand signals or voice command.

J. During the pull, the use of whips, noisemakers, leashes, muzzles, or any form of baiting is prohibited.

K. This event is open to any Alaskan Malamute that is *at least* one year old. For non-AKC sanctioned events, this event may be opened to other breeds, at the discretion of the judges.

L. Entries close ½ hour before pull starts.

M. The sponsoring club, or judge, may reject any entry for due cause. No medication to stimulate the dog's pulling ability may be used.

N. Cruel or inhumane treatment of a dog is strictly prohibited and will be cause for disqualification.

II. Weight Pulling Divisions
   A. There shall be four divisions in the contest.
      1. Dogs weighing less than 80 pounds.
      2. Dogs weighing 80 to 100 pounds.
      3. Dogs weighing 101 to 120 pounds.
      4. Dogs weighing 121 pounds and over.
      Divisions 3 and 4 may be combined, but each dog's weight must be recorded on the finish report.
   B. After a dog has won in his particular weight class, it shall be the prerogative of the owner and/or handlers of the lighter weight dogs to request to compete in a heavier division.

III. Equipment
   A. The dog must be fitted with an adequate freighting or weight pull harness. The judge will determine whether or not the harness is proper and safe for the dog. If any part of the harness or other equipment breaks, the contestant will have another chance after repairs are made.
   B. Carrying capacity of weight pull vehicles.
      1. Sled should be capable of safely carrying a load of 2700 pounds.
         a. Sled should have runners 2 to 4 inches wide, and 7 to 10 feet long, curved at the front end in a reasonable manner for a sled.

Ch. Traleika of Tundra strains to the task at Grandby, Colorado.

Three-dog weight-pulling champions at the North American races, Fairbanks, Alaska. The dogs pulled 3,700 pounds over sixty feet, driven from behind, not coaxed, with the temperature at ten degrees. Taaralaste Naki Nein, Tote-Um's Littlest Hobo, and Taaralaste Vosa Villem are from Roger Burggraf's Taaralaste Kennels, Fairbanks.

147

        b. Report of the pull should indicate whether the vehicle runners were shod with steel or plastic.

    2. A wheeled vehicle must be capable of safely carrying a load of 3,000 pounds.

        a. Wheeled vehicle can be of a three or four wheel design, with wheels in a fixed position so they track in a straight line.

        b. Report of the pull should indicate whether the vehicle was equipped with solid or pneumatic tires.

        c. The use of a car as the pulling vehicle will result in invalidation of the contest.

  C. Tug line.

    1. Shall not exceed 6 feet in length when a sled is used, with minimum of 3 feet.

    2. Shall not exceed 10 feet in length for a wheeled vehicle, with a minimum of 6 feet.

    3. No shock line is to be used as any part of the tug line in weight pulling events.

  D. An adequate supply of pre-weighed, inert material suitable for safe, stable stacking shall be provided.

  E. Provision should be made for attachment of a 16 foot rope to the rear of the pulling vehicle for stopping the vehicle at the end of the pull and preventing injury to the pulling dog. The rope is then used to pull back the vehicle to the starting point, and can serve as an accurate measure of distance traveled by the vehicle.

IV. The Contest

  A. Each dog must pull a qualifying weight, as determined by the judges, at least once during the pulling season. This is to insure that each entrant has had adequate training and will not prove to be a nuisance or embarrassment during the contest.

  B. Each dog must be weighed in at least once during the season. If a dog is within 5 pounds of a class division, it must be weighed before each contest.

  C. The starting weight in each division shall be at least 300 pounds including the pulling vehicle. There shall be approximately 100 pounds increments. This increment can be reduced, or raised, if the majority of contestants agree.

  D. During each pulling effort, the handler must be in one of two positions.

    1. No further forward than the front of the pulling vehicle when the dog is commanded to start the pull.

2. No closer than the dog's finishing line if the dog is being called.

E. The finishing line is a measured 16 feet from the front of the vehicle, and the pull is completed when the vehicle reaches this line.

F. The pull is started by the timer when the handler calls his dog or commands him to start.

G. A dog has 60 seconds to pull the weight 16 feet. If the weight is in motion when the time expires, the dog will be allowed to complete the pull without disqualification provided the weight has been in continuous motion. Unless the weight is pulled the full 16 feet the dog will not be credited for that pull.

H. The judges must make sure that the pulling vehicle is properly lined up before each pull and that the runners or wheels are not frozen or wedged.

I. If a dog becomes entangled in his harness or lines, the judges may declare a repull. The pulling vehicle will be returned to its original position and the clock reset. One repull only will be allowed at a particular weight.

J. Contestants may pass no more than two consecutive turns at a time. They may not request that the load be lightened at any time.

K. The judges may stop a pull at any time if it appears that the dog may injure itself.

L. The maximum load, including the vehicle's weight, pulled by each dog the entire distance of 16 feet, together with the time required for the pull, will be recorded and reported. If two or more dogs pull the same maximum load, the fastest time determines the winner. A lighter dog may continue competition in heavier classes but may not receive more than one trophy.

M. Weather conditions should be reported and should include the following:
1. Temperature at start and end of contest.
2. Snow conditions if applicable.
3. Rain, sleet, or freezing rain, if applicable.

N. Type of surface under dog and under vehicle when pull is made should be recorded.

O. For any infraction of these rules, the judges will impose a warning or disqualification.

P. Any person wishing to protest any violation of these rules must do so immediately following the contest. The protest may be verbal, but must be followed by a written statement

Little Delta, owned by the Tuglu Kennels of Larry and Mary Ann Breen of Winnipeg, was a noted weight puller.

First place in the weight-pulling contests at the Chicago International K.C. show for five years in a row was Sugar River's Tundra Boy and owner, Jerry Winders, Durham, Illinois.

Ritter

citing the circumstances and particular rule or rules involved, within 20 minutes of the end of the contest. The individual against whom the protest is lodged shall be entitled to notification and a hearing before a decision is rendered.

Q. The judges' decisions are final.

Eva "Short" Seeley drives a team which she has trained. *Dick Smith*

19

Good Sledding

GOOD SLEDDING is the result of a synchrony of driver, dogs, and equipment. Each must be of high quality and each must be suited to the other components. For example, even an experienced driver who does not know the team will find rough going regardless of the terrain. In this chapter, we present the essentials for everyone to know the true meaning of "good sledding."

LEARNING TO DRIVE

Driving a dog team can be one of the greatest thrills of your life, no matter how many times you do it. The unexpected comes up on almost every trip. There are two major rules. Learn and obey all the rules for safety, and live with your dogs and observe them closely so that you know each dog intimately. These are the foundation rules for sledding with dogs.

The first thing you need to know are the basic commands by which you make the dogs obey. These are the same commands used for centuries by American farmers in controlling their horses. "Gee" means to turn right, "Haw" means to turn left, and "Whoa" means to stop.

Let us assume that you own a puppy. It should not be put into harness until it is at least six months old. You can, however, use a leash and teach it the basic commands. You can walk it through woods and in places where

Recreation Harness   *Artist: Ann Norris*

Keith Hurrell designed and built this three-wheel cart for night training. It has a steering rope rigged with a headlight and a motorcycle battery.

there are dogs and cats and where you can teach it that it must obey in spite of such temptations.

There is another and easier way to teach the puppy, although it may not be available to you. If there is a sled dog club near you, you may be able to find a member who has a retired lead dog. You can use such an "instructor" dog to guide your puppy.

Be careful not to be too strict with a puppy. He may get bored, or you may cause him to lose his spirit. You should try to meet with experienced drivers. They can tell you the type of harness to use. And they can show you how to measure your dog for harness.

Be careful of secondhand harness. Stiff webbing, or any elastic material, can bruise the shoulders and back of your dog. In measuring your dog, see to it that the harness falls correctly around the neck, between the windpipe and chest, so that your dog will not have his wind cut off.

Novice dogs get very excited and tend to waste their energy before they start. Try to keep your dog quiet. A good rule is to require your dog to be quiet for at least five minutes after being harnessed and before you start. You should require five to ten minutes at the end of the trip before you unharness your dog.

Once your puppy is six months old, you can start teaching it to pull. Some of the sledding families have started their small children with puppies hitched to skis, or to a child's sled or wagon. Sleds and wagons should have brakes, of course. Also, there are one-dog sledding events at many of the racing meets.

You should banish all thought of racing until you have fully learned to drive. You and your dog, or dogs, must learn first that sledding is for pleasure, and only later for racing.

Even thoroughly trained dogs need regular exercise, and this can be given to them the year around. Maxwell Riddle once went out with the great Kit Macinnes when she was training for the Anchorage Rendezvous. Although it was late November, there was little snow. Mrs. Macinnes was using a converted ice-cream vendor's wagon.

Several advertisers state that three-wheel gigs are safe for summer work or when there is insufficient snow for sleds. Many feel, however, that these three-wheelers are unsafe, and the New England Sled Dog Club recommends against them. Many drivers feel that the four-wheel carts are safer, and that they have better balance. In teaching your dog to pull, you should use a type of harness known as "draft." You should ask an experienced driver to show you how to use it. The so-called Siwash type does not fit well unless one uses a high draft arrangement on the sled.

You must never take your eye, or your concentration, off the team. The unexpected can happen, and you may find yourself in a snowbank while your team trots merrily on. Also, a team may have a mischievous dog which will await an opportunity to rush off after a cat or other animal and get your entire team in a tangle.

Always carry a kit bag tied to your sled or summer cart. This kit bag is your emergency outfit, your first-aid kit for sled, harness, and even dogs. The kit should contain two collars; one length of a hitch; an ice remover such as a paint-remover tool; matches in a wet-proof container; and a wax candle. The latter is for waxing runners.

Never begin a trip without first checking the gang line and harnesses. Unless you are clever at making loose hand ties, it is better to use sport snaps. However, these sometimes freeze and come undone. Tie a snub line onto the back of your handlebars, but string it through a large ring fastened to the sled.

It does not matter whether you are using one dog or twelve, always snub (fasten) the line to a stationary object. It is the same, winter or summer—always snub the line. This will prevent the dogs from bolting. Moreover, using the brake to hold the dogs before starting often makes them very nervous.

We have assumed that you began with a single puppy. Now you have acquired a team. If you have been wise, you will have bought older and experienced dogs as well as youngsters. Some dogs are slow to learn, others too eager. Some are shy and have to learn to go with other dogs. Older dogs will have more patience if a learner travels beside them, so always place a learner with an older dog. Also, young dogs should be placed in the middle of the team. If you have a team of five, use three with experience.

Tangling is a frequent occurrence, and it can be a difficult situation to handle if you are alone. Some drivers use the brake, but it is far better to snub your leader to a tree or to some other immovable object while you are untangling. You may have to overturn your sled if snubbing is not possible. When your dogs get tangled, do not lose your patience, and do not blame the dogs. Just work quietly and swiftly.

Conditioning your dogs' feet is a must. Sore feet can result if your dogs' pads are too hard. Your veterinarian can supply you with a product to moisten the pads, and there are toughening products available. The mileage you travel should be governed by the progress of the dogs. Gradually lengthen the distance as the dogs strengthen their muscles. Observe your dogs, and do not make them travel farther than they can go without severe effort.

Practice in turning around should be one of the first lessons. Commands must be understood by your leader, by your two point dogs, and if five, your wheel dogs. Your wheel dogs are those directly in front of the sled, and they control the movements of the sled.

The best drivers of the past have had an important saying, or rule: If you can make five dogs obey you, and go anywhere you ask them to without effort, you have the nucleus of a team. But too many beginners see drivers with up to fifteen dogs and double sleds and think this is the way for a beginner to learn.

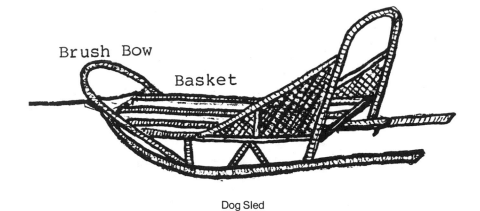

Dog Sled

Brush Bow

Basket

Bull Snapp

Swivel Snap

Necklines

Necklines

Swivel Snap
Lap Link
Neck Line

Bull Snap

+ — 5 Ft. — — 5 Ft. — — 5 Ft. —

Rod

Laplink

Laplink

Laplink

Rod

Picket line design by Bob White.

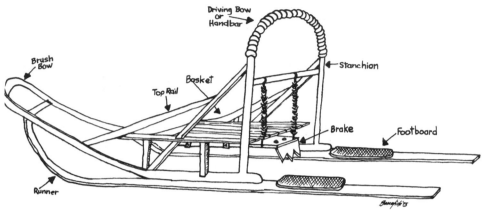

Chinook sled designed by Arthur Walden.   *Jackie Bonafide*

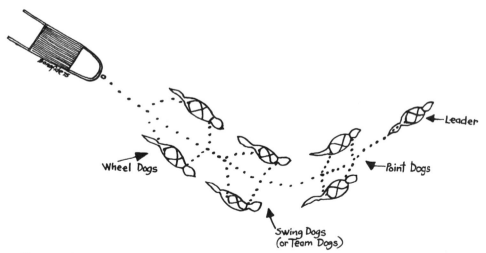

Diagram of a gang hitch and placement of dogs.   *Jackie Bonafide*

Short Seeley said it took one year of winter learning to drive nine Alaskan Malamutes. Their strength and eagerness could have caused many accidents had they not been taught absolute obedience to commands as a unit.

Here are some of the commands and terms traditionally used in teaching and in driving sled dogs:

Gee!	Turn right.
Haw!	Turn left.
Whoa!	Stop.
Brake:	A device to slow the sled.
Lead dog:	The leader of the team.
Wheel dogs:	Dogs directly in front of the sled.
Snub line:	Line by which the sled is tied to a stationary object.
Snow hook:	Hook jammed into the snow to hold the team briefly.

MAKING A SLED

Making a sled is a difficult undertaking. It requires a solid background in woodwork skills, and the purchase of high-quality, straight-grained wood, such as ash, birch, maple, or oak. The latter is the wood preferred by veteran dog drivers. Any one of these selections may be properly steam-bent. Wood-bending forms, however, must be made, borrowed, or, if possible, purchased. The joints of the sled require precision tooling. They are lashed together with dampened rawhide which, as it dries, tightens to such a degree that the joined pieces appear to have been carved out of a single piece of wood. Once the basic form of the sled has been completed, either steel or high-density plastic runners are attached. The completed sled should not be stiff, but should have a certain degree of flexibility to it in order to corner well in tight places.

For the novice driver, or even one who is experienced in running a team of novice dogs, a protection plate may be added to the brush bow. This will prevent the brush bow from shattering should the sled hit a rock or a tree.

However, to avoid headaches, it is far easier, less time-consuming—and may well prove less expensive—to purchase a reliable sled from an outfitter of good repute.

Sledding equipment cannot be considered complete without a snow anchor and a stakeout chain. The stakeout chain's purpose is twofold. It keeps the dogs restrained when at a training or running site, and out of harm's way. It teaches the dogs who step over lines to untangle themselves safely. The latter is a very important procedure for any running dog to learn. It helps to teach the dogs how to prevent becoming tangled in the

159

traces while running. And this problem is a very real one for novice dogs and drivers.

The main chain is intended to be stretched tautly between ground stakes, trees, or even truck bumpers. The overall chain length is six to ten feet, plus five feet for each dog to be chained thereon. Neck lines made of lighter chains two feet long which end in a strong swivel snap are attached at five-foot intervals along the main line. A strong swivel is necessary to keep the dog from getting tangled up and possibly strangled. Neck lines longer than two feet would allow two dogs to get tangled up, and this could allow a panic-induced fight, or strangulation of a dog.

TRAINING THE LEAD DOG

Today it is hard to envision a sled dog team of any merit without at least one, if not two, leaders at the fore. In historical perspective, lead dogs are a relatively new phenomena. Formerly, dogs were hitched, when crossing vast expanses, in a fan formation with the dogs of the team having tug lines of varying lengths. In those areas where the going was rough or wooded, the dogs were most often hitched single-file rather than tandemly. The dog "driver" would then walk out in front of his team on snowshoes, breaking the trail. Occasionally, a loose leader was employed not only to break, but to find the trail (best way of going) as well. Today, however, such methods of transport by dog team are considered antiquated and drivers run behind, or "pedal"* with their dogs.

Great, or even good, lead dogs come with a "set of designer 'genes.' " A lead dog of a large team may be as much as fifty feet out in front of his driver. A lead dog must have the innate ability to work in this position. Not every dog can be trained as a leader. He must be one of the fastest and strongest members of the team. This dog must have a strong sense of responsibility. He must, at all times, keep his tug line tight. He must be able to take verbal commands from the driver. He must have a sense of "trail": having the innate ability to *find* the trail in a blizzard, a whiteout, or when the trail has been covered with a powdering of snow. The lead dog, when in an unmarked area, must be able to find the best path, footing, or other way of going for the team. This is a dog which can take the extreme pressure that the responsibility of leadership puts upon him. Being in the position

---

*In pedaling, the driver stands with one foot upon the sled's runner and "pedals", not unlike how one pedals while riding a scooter. When the driver tires of pedaling with one leg, he then uses the other. Pedaling when running a team offers the dogs a great deal of assistance, although not as much as when the driver runs behind the sled, holding onto the handlebar. When the team is moving fast, it is not possible, of course, for the driver to run behind, and pedaling gives the team assistance for speed.

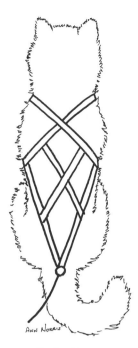 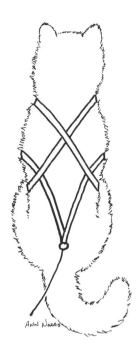

Racing Harness
Artist: Ann Norris

Racing Harness
Artist: Ann Norris

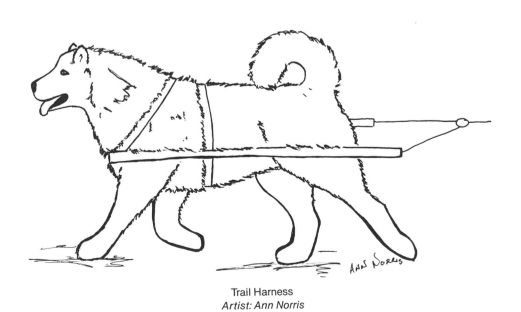

Trail Harness
Artist: Ann Norris

161

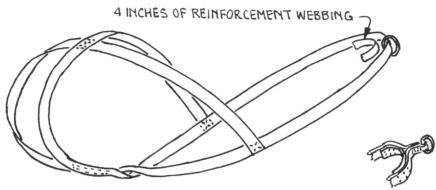

4 INCHES OF REINFORCEMENT WEBBING

HARNESS SHOWING TWO LOOPS
FITTED TOGETHER

HARNESS RING WITH
REINFORCEMENT SEWN
IN PLACE

Recreation Harness

Artist: Keith Hurrell

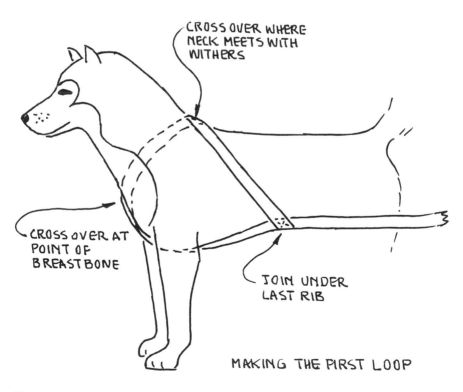

CROSS OVER WHERE
NECK MEETS WITH
WITHERS

CROSS OVER AT
POINT OF
BREASTBONE

JOIN UNDER
LAST RIB

MAKING THE FIRST LOOP

Making the First Loop

Artist: Keith Hurrell

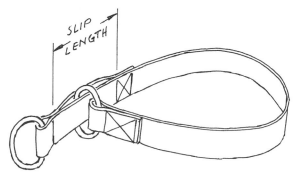

Semi-Slip or Racing Collar

Artist: Keith Hurrell

SLIP LENGTH

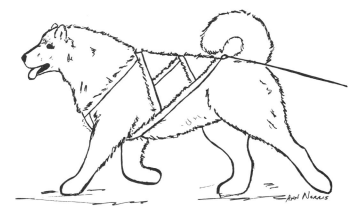

X-Back Racing Harness

Artist: Ann Norris

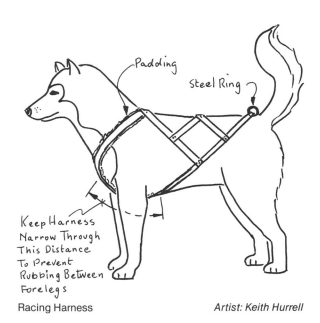

Padding

Steel Ring

Keep Harness Narrow Through This Distance To Prevent Rubbing Between Forelegs

Racing Harness

Artist: Keith Hurrell

of working out in front of the other team dogs, the leader is in effect "chased" by the other dogs.

The characteristics of a lead dog are then: responsive tractability for working with the driver; an uncanny sense of trail; a sense of duty; and incredible courage (what is known as "heart" by drivers)—courage to continue when the going is rough or precarious. A dog would be a possible candidate for training as a lead dog that exhibited these characteristics in addition to being moderately independent (independent enough to work out front).

Some drivers praise leaders which are "push-button" dogs. These are dogs which, when given a command to move in a certain direction, will do so with alacrity: unhesitatingly and, concomitantly, without thinking. Alaskan Malamutes in general have a tendency to think, to figure out what needs to be done. This is an innate characteristic trait of the breed which *must* not be lost through poor breeding practices. These are the dogs of fable which bring injured drivers and team members to safety. The best of these dogs find safe passage through broken leads, unmarked trails, and across hidden snow chasms. The refusal by these dogs to obey a command has saved a team and driver on more than one occasion.

There are a variety of methods to train a lead dog, once the lead dog prospect has been found. Sometimes finding a lead dog can be done (particularly for someone new to the sport) only through trial and error: trying out one dog after another from the team, until the "right" dog is found—if there is one. The owner's physical condition will strongly determine which method of training is employed.

At the selected training site, the owner attaches either a long lead, a lunge line (such as that used for training horses), or a rope to the harness's pulling ring. A sled dog's training is *always* performed with a harness and *never* with a collar. If the trainer is in good condition, he encourages the dog to move out ahead of him while holding onto the end of the line. Providing a small amount of drag, he helps to teach the dog to keep his tug line tight at all times. Given the verbal command to go (such as "Hike!"; "Let's go!"; or whatever the driver chooses), the dog is encouraged to move out ahead of the owner enthusiastically at a brisk pace. Quietly toned encouragement such as "Attaway" or "Good dog" is given as the dog responds. If the dog slows, the owner should give additional verbalized encouragement to keep it moving along at a brisk pace by saying something to the effect of "Pick-it-up, pick-it-up," to which rhythm many dogs will react positively. Other drivers may "cluck" in the cadence of the desired pace—the same as the sound used on a horse.

At an intersection (of the training trail or even street), the dog is given a directional command for right, left, or straight ahead. The dog is taught only one turn command at a time. As soon as he learns one *well*, he may then be taught the other direction. During early training, these commands

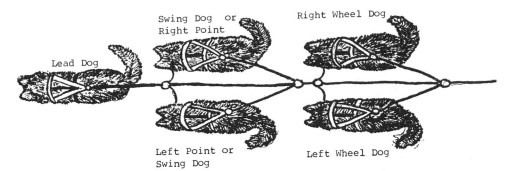

The Gang or Tandem Hitch Formation

Artist: Daniel Grant Jenkins

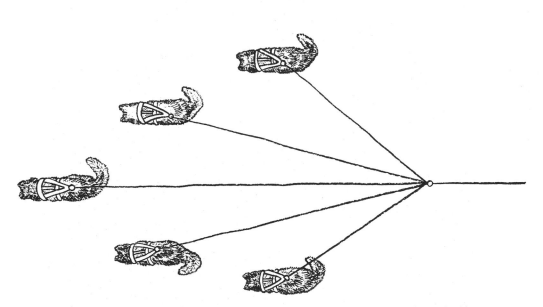

The Fan Hitch Formation

Artist: Daniel Grant Jenkins

165

Dogs in action, showing how hitch works.

Dick Smith

may be given by a combination of voice, arm signals, and/or pulling on the line to indicate to the dog which direction it is to travel.

Verbal directions vary a lot from driver to driver. Most will use English commands such as "Gee!" for turning right, "Haw!" for turning left, "Easy now!" to slow the dog down, and "Whoa!" for stopping. Among the most common starting commands are "Hike!"; "Hike out!"; "Let's Go!"; or even plain old "Yahoo!" Almost no one, and certainly no driver of any repute will say "Mush!" to their dogs, which is the Anglicized "Marche!" that was first used by the earliest dog-driving explorers, the French trappers.

The method of running behind the lead-dog-in-training is hard for a driver. Such a method requires that the driver have strong legs and the stamina of a genuine athlete. After all, the dog was given four legs upon which to move, while man was given but two. This form of training works the driver twice as hard. The driver definitely becomes conditioned while giving his dog incentive to move at a fast clip. Training by such a method is not for every person, especially not for one who merely wishes to run a pleasure team rather than to race competitively.

As an alternative to extended periods of running, a trainer may prefer to attach a lightweight drag to the line. If the dog is instinctively an avid puller, or has been run on a team, this method will not slow him down any appreciable measure. As the dog advances in its training (responding to the directional commands, including those for slowing down and speeding up), he may then "graduate" to working on a lightweight training cart (with a brake)—if no snow is available for a small sled. Initially, the trainer will continue to run behind the dog until he is sure of the dog's responses to the given commands. At that time, he may ride to continue encouraging the dog to maintain its speed. Some Alaskan Malamutes, while smart and responsive, are nevertheless somewhat lazy in putting forth any great effort.

After only a few training sessions, the driver is able to ascertain if the dog is learning well and enjoying the challenge of this type of work. If necessary, the trainer can revise the routine as required until the dog is able to follow directions well. Once the dog is responding *totally* to vocal commands, one other dog may be added to the sessions, working of course behind the new leader.

A good team is built up *slowly,* with dogs being added one by one over a period of time. The driver must ascertain each new dog's position and objectively evaluate its performance as a reliable team member before considering the addition of another animal to the team. Only when the newest team member is working steadily with the others should another dog be placed in the team. Concomitantly, the lead dog must continue to exhibit that he is able to handle the added pressure each additional new member brings. Once the team has three dogs, the driver, too, must familiarize himself, and be totally comfortable with, driving such powerful dogs which are extended a distance out in front of him.

It is unfair to a lead dog once trained to place a number of untrained dogs on the team behind him (more than one at a time). The leader will be unable to keep his tug line taut with a number of large novice dogs behind him bouncing and jumping over the towline.

Whenever either training or racing, always have an extra person on hand to hold the lead dog's harness from behind by the pulling ring. This assists the leader in keeping the towline stretched tautly. The leader should *never* be held by his collar while the team is being hitched together, or while waiting for the "countdown."

The Oopik all-champion Alaskan Malamute team is shown in action during the winter of 1982–83. The team raced for Lorna and Gareth Muir.

20

Women in Sled Dog Racing

by Eva B. Seeley

VERY EARLY in the history of sled dog racing, women began to play an important part. While it is true that many of them drove Siberians, and in one case Eskimos, a few drove mixed teams and some used Alaskan Malamutes. It seems fitting, therefore, to tell about some of these early women drivers and to remind readers that women can get as much fun out of driving teams of Alaskan Malamutes as can their husbands and children.

The New England Sled Dog Club held its first race during the winter carnival at Newport, New Hampshire, in 1924. Two young women had come from Cambridge, Massachusetts, to spend the winter at Wonalancet Farm. There they fell in love with the dogs, and both learned to drive. They decided to enter the race at Newport.

The two were Clara Enubuskie and Carol Peabody. Clara later became the wife of the late Richard Reed, and Carol married Frederick Lovejoy of Concord, Massachusetts. At the last minute, Carol decided not to race. This particular race was of six miles only, and it was designed for novice drivers. Clara Enubuskie started with her team, but the dogs got hopelessly entangled on the course, and she was unable to finish, yet she gained the publicity needed to inspire other women to become drivers.

After Leonhard Seppala had set up his kennels at Poland Spring, Maine, his partner, Mrs. Ted Ricker, now Mrs. Kaare Nansen, learned to drive. She first raced at Lake Placid, and she entered the first point-to-point race sponsored by the New England Sled Dog Club. This type of race was called a "long mileage race." Teams came from all over New England, and overnight housing was arranged for all drivers and dogs at the towns along the three-day event. Mrs. Ricker's team once got tangled up with a stray dog. But she finished the race, and within the minimum time limit. Eva Seeley was at the Laconia Tavern when she arrived there, and she became convinced that she would someday drive also.

When Milton and Eva arrived at Wonalancet Farm in 1927, they had a son of Arthur Walden's Chinook, called Nook. Walden had trained him for them, and he became their lead dog. Before long, Eva was driving as many as eleven dogs in the team. The first race was at North Conway, New Hampshire.

One of the earliest woman racers was Florence Clark of Milan, New Hampshire. She drove a team of matched Eskimos. All had white bodies and black ears. But they were addicted to fighting, and also it was most difficult to get them to obey under all circumstances. For these reasons, the team had been barred from some races, but the team did well enough in other events.

At the time of the Olympic trials held by the New England Sled Dog Club, Florence Clark drove her team from Woodstock to Wonalancet. She had to climb over the treacherous Sandwich Range that leads into Wonalancet, and because of a mighty storm, she was forced to spend the night in the open. When the team arrived at Wonalancet, neither she nor the dogs were in fit condition to race. They were taken home by truck.

The Lake Placid Club set up an invitational race for sled dogs and both Leonhard Seppala and Mrs. Ricker entered. Seppala finished first, and Mrs. Ricker second. In another point-to-point race, Mrs. Ricker drove a Seppala team. But a stray dog got tangled with her team and the team escaped. Spectators helped her to catch it. As far as racing time went, she was disqualified, but the incident again helped to spark interest in women as drivers.

Another sled dog club was formed at Laconia, New Hampshire, and this club still holds a race which is billed as the world championship of sled dog racing. Both Mrs. Clark and Short Seeley entered. Mrs. Clark was forced to drop out, but Mrs. Seeley finished the three-day event of twenty miles each day.

Lorna Demidoff also entered racing at this time. Both she and Mrs. Seeley won races, and Lorna Demidoff became one of the best known women drivers. She used a team of matched gray and white Siberian Huskies.

Natalie Jubin of Lake Placid drove a dog team for passenger rides in order to earn money for her college education. She majored in sociology at Syracuse University. When Milton Seeley died in 1945, Natalie and Marga-

Sue Fuller, Mountain Home Malamutes, takes a pleasure spin with son Jesse in her backpack. Kennel is at Twisp, Washington.

She may live in Brooklyn, New York, but Janice Dougherty has time to train and work her Hook-Tooth Alaskans. Here Jude Travars gives a ride to Benny Heredia during the Winter Carnival at Bear Mountain State Park. Lead dog is Icefloe's Hook-Tooth Talisman. Right Wheel is Hook Tooth Jessie. Left Wheel is Hook Tooth Jabberwocky.

Sally Heckman drives a three-dog team at Tamworth, New
Hampshire, in 1975. Her dogs: Rowdy, Teeko (left), and Wolf.

Eva Seeley, only woman driver in the 1933 Olympics, with, l. to r., Wendy of
Kotzebue, Finn of Yukon, Gripp of Yukon, and Kearsarge of Yukon.   *H. I. Orne*

ret Dewey of the Lake Placid Club went to Wonalancet to take care of the dogs while Eva Seeley underwent surgery. Natalie took the dogs out daily, even in the worst blizzards.

After college, she planned to go to Juneau, Alaska, to teach. Mrs. Seeley had given her a letter of introduction to Earl Norris. She arranged with Earl to take four dogs to Alaska, two large dogs from Chinook Kennels and two Siberian Huskies. Natalie met and married Earl Norris, and their partnership in both Alaskan Malamutes and Siberian Huskies has lasted ever since. Natalie Norris was an early winner in women's championship races in Alaska, the first of which was held at Anchorage in 1953. She won in 1954.

Jean Bryar went to Alaska with her husband for the races at Fairbanks and Anchorage. She won twice at Fairbanks. Her teams, driven by Richard Moulton, also compete in Canadian and U.S. professional circuit races.

Perhaps the greatest record made by a woman driver is that of Kit Macinnes of Anchorage. She won the world championship at Anchorage four times, in 1955, 1959, 1960, and 1961. Barbara Parker and Shirley Gavin have won three times each. Rosie Losonsky, an Eskimo and always a strong competitor, won in 1957.

Editor's Note: There are great women drivers today, even in the most grueling races, such as the Iditarod. The 1980s saw Libby Riddles become the first woman to win that great Alaskan race, soon followed by Susan Butcher, a multiple Iditarod winner and one of the most consistent winners in that race's history.

However, neither Alaskan Malamutes nor Siberian Huskies are now used in the great Alaskan races including the Iditarod. Instead, a newly developed breed called the Alaskan Husky has taken over.

21

Backpacking

NOT EVERY PERSON is interested in training and working their dogs for sledding. Some people, while they thoroughly enjoy their dogs and would like to do "something" with them, have a lifestyle which precludes the rigorous commitment required for such endeavors. Happily, Alaskan Malamutes are highly adaptable dogs. They are content to spend pleasant hours just sharing their owners' time.

Backpacking as an alternative to sledding-type endeavors has proven to be a form of recreation that the one-dog owner can enjoy just as readily as the owner of multiple animals. Nor does backpacking call for large investments of either money or time for training—no extensive training program is needed. All that is required is a healthy dog of an age to backpack and an owner who enjoys walking with the dog.

When many people think of backpacking with a dog, they think of strenuous day-long hikes (or longer treks), through rugged mountainous areas. While such excursions are highly enjoyable for the athletic and adventuresome, backpacking can be enjoyed by any ambulatory person. One can simply backpack around the block to a neighbor's home; backpack on a picnic; backpack on a nature trail; or for the hardiest, backpack for several days in the wilderness.

Ready-made backpacks can be purchased at backpacking or mountaineering stores, or through mail-order catalogs. In general, the best backpacks for Malamutes that will be doing extensive trekking are found through those mail-order vendors who specialize in sled dog equipment.

A lot of satisfaction can be gained also by the "do-it-myself" person, one who desires to have a custom-fitted, custom-made backpack for his dog. Kits which contain all the necessary material (including instructions for assembly), may also be purchased through these mail-order vendors. As another alternative, an inexpensive, yet reliable and sturdy backpack can be constructed from two surplus army packs and three 1½- or 2-inch-wide lengths of webbing to join the two packs across the dog's back, and several quick-release buckles for fastening. These latter items are available through most backpacking retailers. Some people have used Velcro tape when making their dog packs. Most experienced backpackers who have tried this method of construction have found that while such tape makes the construction of a canine backpack easier, over a given period of use it becomes clogged with hair and undercoat, thereby rendered basically useless as a fastening agent. Whenever fitting the dog to a pack properly, it is important to be sure that the pack rides securely on the withers and upper back only.

An important addition to any backpack is the attachment of a "D-ring" which must be strongly secured directly over the center of the dog's shoulders. This is where the leash is attached, allowing the owner to control the dog while walking. When moving up steep grades, the dog is concomitantly able to help pull his owner up. Conversely, when walking in deep snow conditions, the owner is able to take some of the weight off the dog, allowing it to regain footing after breaking through the crust.

TRAINING THE BACKPACKING DOG

When the suitably fitted dogpack has been acquired and the dog has had some time to adjust to this "contraption" (the owner has praised the dog for wearing it until the dog is comfortable and does not try to remove or get out of it), it is time to put some light weight into the pack. Initially, the pack is loaded bilaterally with plastic or paper bags of either sand or dry dog food. The dog is then exercised on lead to allow him to become used to the feel of the pack with some weight. The owner must be certain that *each side of the pack weighs exactly the same amount.*

For the first week, the dog should carry only five pounds of weight. The following week, the weight may be increased to ten pounds. The weight is then increased gradually, in equally small increments each week until the dog is comfortable carrying up to one-third of his actual body weight.* If the dog is out-of-coat when training or actually working in the backpack,

*Most dog owners are unable to accurately "guesstimate" the weight of their dog. If their veterinarian does not have a canine walk-on scale, a walk-on scale may be found at any freight terminal (truck or air shipper), or at some feed (not pet) stores.

Dog pack is made from two army surplus packs attached by two-inch-wide nylon seat-belt webbing. Adjustable chest and loin straps are made from one-inch-wide webbing with plastic quick-release buckles. Made by Keith Hurrell.

Gina Hurrell, 13, and Shadak's Arctic Sonrise, C.D.X., and Hall of Working Fame, returning from a backpacking trip to Palisades Glacier in the California Sierras.

a heavy towel or baby blanket should be used under the pack, not unlike the use of a saddle blanket on a horse. It is *very* important to the dog's mental and physical comfort that the towel or blanket does not crease under the pack while on the dog. This can cause severe chafing ("saddle sores").

In addition to being physically conditioned for backpacking, the dog should also have some successful obedience work: heeling on- and off-lead; stand-stay (for putting the backpack on or taking it off without the dog leaping everywhere in its joy); and down-stay for rest periods. The dog must learn to: walk quietly by its owner's side; out in front; or behind without bumping the owner. By virtue of its size alone if nothing else, an Alaskan Malamute carrying a pack and running loose could easily knock a person literally off his feet, thereby causing a serious accident.

The dog will also need to learn to refrain from chasing any wildlife. Aside from the fact that a pack and its contents are easily damaged by bashing against a tree or a rock, a dog loose in the wilderness or country is a *totally unprotected* dog, one that could easily become injured.

BACKPACKING TIPS

After conditioning, a dog as young as six months should be able to carry 15 to 20 percent of its weight for a day's outing: a fully-mature adult should be capable of carrying 30 percent of its weight in camping gear or provisions. Historically in the North, it was not unusual for a dog to carry 50 percent or even more of his weight on a daily basis.

Some people when outfitting their dogs will have them carry their own food. Thus, as the journey progresses, and stops are periodically made for meals or snacks, the dog's pack becomes lighter. While this may not make a great deal of difference to the adult animal, it can make a difference to a puppy.

To prevent some sharp object from jabbing the side of the dog (even a cereal box corner can become an irritant after a period of time), the smart owner places softer items such as a groundsheet or towel between those objects and the dog. The placement of water-sensitive items inside zip-lock packages will keep them safe when streams are to be forded during the trip.

If making an excursion into a wilderness area, it is wise to examine a topographical map. Consideration should be given to the terrain to be covered. If there will be sharp rocks (such as lava or pumice), or the possibility of sharp ice underfoot, then the dog should be prefitted with sturdy dog booties which protect not only the pads, but the delicate areas in between. Booties can be purchased through any mail-order vendor that specializes in Arctic dog materials.

Bob Aninger, Clicquot (Kleeko), and Fancy Tail (Arnuk), doing their thing as "Sargent Preston" and "King" and his mate.

22

Search and Rescue

ALMOST EVERYONE is familiar with the St. Bernard breed originally named for Saint Bernard of Menthon, an eleventh-century Savoyard churchman who founded the Alpine hospices in both of the St. Bernard passes. These animals were the first, perhaps, to have gained fame in the search-and-rescue work of weary or lost travelers through these Swiss mountainous areas. It has been only in more recent times, however, especially during the past one hundred years, that dogs have actually been trained worldwide for use in search-and-rescue work.

While snow may be the most unstable substance known to man, the St. Bernard's ability to scent victims of avalanches may prove to be the most crucial aspect of developing prompt avalanche response. Dogs in general are estimated to have olfactory senses some four hundred (and in some breeds more) times more acute than that of man. An avalanche victim's chances of rescue and survival are therefore greatly increased by the use of these animals.

When dogs are not used in search-and-rescue work, then chances of the victims' survival may become minimalized, whether the person is merely lost and exposed to the possibility of hypothermia (the loss of vital body heat) alone, or lies buried beneath what can be at times tons of snow. As a result of an avalanche, fatalities can occur not only from colliding with trees and rocks or the avalanche passing over a cliff, but also from suffocation and hypothermia. It has been estimated that an avalanche victim's chances of survival are only about 50 percent within the first half-hour of being buried, and then decrease by approximately ten percent each half-hour thereafter.

The amount of time a victim lies buried therefore becomes the critical factor between life and death. The victim's warmth may melt the snow a small amount that is in direct contact with the body. The warmth of the person's breath will melt a small portion of snow directly surrounding the face also. As the victim's body temperature begins to drop with the onset of hypothermia, the snow refreezes, encapsulating the person, or at the very least and most dangerous, encapsulating the face in ice which will cause suffocation. The critical nature of the time factor in rescue cannot be stressed too much in the discovery and retrieval of a victim.

In the coming years, the ideal dog for avalanche and other search-and-rescue work in cold climes may well prove to be the Alaskan Malamute. The ideal dog is one which has a double coat, protecting it from severe weather conditions over many hours of arduous work. Heavily furred webbing between the thickly padded toes enable this breed to stay on the snow's surface in all but the most finely powdered conditions. These paws developed over eons, enabling them to withstand subzero temperatures for hours on end.

The most effective avalanche rescue dogs have, too, the keenest development of the olfactory sense, along with hearing ability on the same level. Directly as a result of the Alaskan Malamutes' historical development, the breed has evolved not just to be keen of sight rivaling those powers found in any sighthound, but have extraordinarily highly developed scenting ability, rivaling those of many scent hounds.

Their keen eyesight allows them not only to focus on birds soaring high in flight, but to clearly see a snow hare motionless, white, against the pristine protective background of a snowfield. Their hearing developed to be keen enough to listen to the stealthy, almost silent underground movement of lemmings, mice, and shrews upon which they customarily fed themselves during the summer months.

During times of antiquity, the breed was used by natives to help locate seal breathing holes in the ice, which are normally hidden from view by a light powdering of snow. They were also used to aid in the location of caribou and musk oxen, among other large game. They alerted their owners to the presence of wolves, wolverines, and bears. And perhaps most importantly, they had to alert their drivers to the dangers of a hidden snow chasm or a broken lead. Commensurately, they had to locate and follow the trail home during raging, blinding blizzards that created a condition known as a "whiteout" which erases all known landmarks to a driver.

Literally, through survival of the fittest, those animals which were able to sustain themselves successfully as able hunters and wily enough to keep their "prizes" of food from the jaws (and gullets) of stronger dogs, are we able, therefore, to enjoy these unique combinations of characteristics in our present-day pets. While content to lie at their masters' feet quietly for long hours at a time, the Alaskan Malamutes nevertheless contain the almost tireless energy of their hunting and working forebears. This trait of seemingly limitless energy coupled with their almost uncanny ability to focus intently upon the job until it is done, and working with incredible swiftness, allows them to cover well an avalanche site.

Last but not least, those dogs used in avalanche and other search-and-rescue work must be inordinately people-oriented. Again, the historical evolution of the Alaskan Malamute makes this breed perfectly ideal for this form of work. These dogs carry the genetic imprinting of their forebears, which were usually raised, as small puppies, within the confines of a dwelling by their Eskimo masters and family. Indeed, it was not at all uncommon for the early explorers to find, upon entering such a domicile, Malamute puppies tumbling about the fur-blanketed floors with the infants and other young children of the family. Also documented by these early intrepid historians are their accounts of finding, upon more than one occasion, a native woman, suckling at her own breast, an orphaned puppy or the puppy of a dam that was working. Thus, the breed developed its uniquely close relationship with mankind over thousands of years.

Linton and Kay Moustakis of Kee-Too Kennels, longtime residents of Alaska, have been successful breeders and exhibitors of Malamutes since the early sixties. This success has included not only numerous champion progeny from their breeding program and several Best in Show winners, but has included as well, the distinction of having lovingly owned and trained the first Alaskan Malamute in the breed's history to have been certified as a Search and Rescue Dog. Their female Kee-Tah garnered further recognition from the Alaskan Malamute Club of America during 1983, by having been awarded the first Search and Rescue Certificate offered by this parent club. This national recognition of those efforts between Mr. Moustakis and Kee-Tah initiated this new classification of award for the breed.

According to Linton Moustakis's experiences with their dogs, and notably Kee-Tah, he became convinced that "the Alaskan Malamute would be ideally suited for cold-climate search and rescue, and avalanche work." Prior to Mr. Moustakis's involvement in this area, the breed had not been considered ideal for this strenuous work due to a generalized concern about the unknown temperament of these dogs under stressful conditions. Dogs which are suitable for search-and-rescue work must prove themselves to be virtually unflappable under the most adverse of conditions: they must prove themselves in training to be totally reliable, trustworthy, and capable of handling this arduous form of endeavor.

The Alaskan search-and-rescue group D.O.G.S. (Dogs Organized for Ground Search) was first formed about 1975. The group's main objective was to be available at all times, in all types of weather, to help locate and recover individuals who were lost in the Alaskan wilderness, or who had become avalanche victims.

Kee-Too's Silver Frost Kee-Tah, trained for search and rescue by Linton Moustakis. Here Kee-Tah believes she has located the victim.

She begins to dig and search.

Further digging yields stronger sensory clues.

Proof emerges.

We're halfway there!

Another successful rescue
mission completed by
Kee-Tah.

Training sessions for search and rescue begin, the same as any other education, on a "grade-school basis" and advance both the handler and dog through a "college" level. The initial test used by D.O.G.S. begins with the owner leaving his dog with an instructor and walking away (while in obvious sight of the animal) approximately fifty yards, to an area thick with brush. The owner then turns and, facing the dog, calls it tersely before dashing (while hunched over to minimize size) another five or ten yards into the brush. Here, the owner remains totally motionless and silent. At this point, the instructor releases the dog with the verbalized encouragement "Go Find!"

Initially, a dog will race directly toward the last sighting of the owner, using only the instinct of affection and companionship for its master. When the dog reaches the area of the last glimpse of its master, it is then forced to utilize its powers of scent to find its hidden owner. Once the dog has made his first "find" in this most basic training session, the owner heaps lavish praise upon the dog. Often in the early training stages, the owner will offer the dog a favorite treat as well.

The training experiences of Linton Moustakis proved to be memorable on more than one occasion. One instance in particular aptly demonstrates the trust which develops bilaterally between the Alaskan Malamute and its handler. Some of the training sessions include obstacle-course work. Here the dogs must learn to have total faith in their handler's commands. (Those dogs that do not learn this are quickly eliminated from the program.) The Moustakises' Kee-Tah proved herself to be one of the most apt pupils in her group, learning to climb ladders, walk along planks suspended high off the ground, and to squeeze through long tight culverts with implicit confidence in her owner's requests. One day this bond of trust that so strongly developed between Kee-Tah and her owner-handler brought her to the test exercise of crossing a dangerous, fast-moving stream. While the majority of dogs in the class refused, Kee-Tah unhesitatingly waded into the rushing water and was immediately swept a good distance downstream before she was able to gain footing at the other side. Such bonding, such a demonstration of implicit faith in the owner-handler, cannot fail to impress even the most skeptical.

Training continues through multiple sessions, each becoming more remote geographically, and far more difficult in nature. As the training advances, the dog quickly learns to forgo the use of sight, learning instead that the "victim" is found through both ground- and air-scenting.* By the time the dog progresses to this stage of training, the owner has become the handler. A total stranger to the dog is used as the "casualty," thereby training the dog to locate any person within the search-and-rescue area.

---

*Malamutes are generally noted as an air-scenting breed by many tracking experts.

Initially, Mr. Moustakis began training a mother-daughter team for rescue. However, he quickly found that the two would not work efficiently as a team in a given area. Once again, the evolutionary aspects of the breed were revealed, instincts which demanded that there be but a single "leader dog."* He discovered that the daughter fell behind the mother during the searching portion of the exercise, backing her up, but without any attempt to demonstrate her own proven abilities.

D.O.G.S., like other search-and-rescue organizations elsewhere in the world, work together with all other emergency groups, such as the Air National Guard, the Air Force, and state and local law enforcement agencies, to find missing persons. As a result of this, the dogs are required to prove their stability in a variety of unusual situations. The dogs in Alaska, for example (and other places where used in snow conditions), are required to learn to ride on toboggans (known as "ahkios" in the native Alaskan tongue). They must also learn to board and disembark from crates strapped to the outside of extremely noisy helicopters with, at the very least, a modicum of equanimity. The Malamutes proved to perform well, and as expected, are easily able to survive the extreme temperatures of an exposed helicopter ride in Arctic conditions without frostbite or other mishap.

Advanced training sessions require that the dogs practice simulated avalanche rescues which, in Linton Moustakis's experiences, involved travel with the D.O.G.S. group to the primitive Chugach mountain range. Such avalanche rescue training requires that the volunteer "victim" be buried beneath several feet of snow. There is always the possibility that the "casualty" volunteer could panic or become short of oxygen and actually pass out, thereby becoming a real victim. This portion of the training requires extreme caution throughout the entire procedure and should never be undertaken, therefore, without a *qualified* team of instructors present.

In the advanced training sessions, it is not uncommon to have real avalanche debris strewn around the sites of the volunteer victims and elsewhere in the training-field locale. This debris is the type that could be indigenous to an area where a dog might encounter it during genuine search and rescue. Debris may consist of rocks, tree limbs, skis, backpacks, snowshoes, and wearing apparel (boots, gloves, hats, jackets). At times in training, these articles are strewn around sites where no "victim" is buried, thereby honing the dogs' sense of dedication to work in searching for real avalanche victims. Normally, these articles will not contain enough scent to hold the dogs' concentration for more than a brief period of time.

---

*As a direct result of the evolutionary process in the breed, a number of variable "leader" types developed which include, but are not limited to: scenting leaders, song leaders, hunting leaders for point and rear (such as when holding a moose or bear at bay), trail leaders, and simply, boss leaders.

PREPARING THE TRAINING SITE

An avalanche "casualty" is created through the following method. A large hole is dug, usually five to six feet deep. A tarpaulin to protect the "victim" is then placed at the bottom. The volunteer then lies upon the fabric and is covered with a second tarpaulin. The "victim" then props an arm and an elbow over his head to create an air space while the hole is then filled with the snow that has been removed by other volunteers. Once the "victim" has been buried, these other volunteers then clear the surrounding surface area of any obvious signs of "burial," leaving the site as virginal as is humanly possible.

These advanced training sessions demand that every precaution be taken for the safety of the volunteer "victim." The "victim" will carry with him an FM* frequency CB transceiver. Some training groups also use a rescue beacon affixed to the "victim's" clothing. The beacon emits a signal to a receiver, aiding the instructors in the location of a volunteer "casualty," should a rescue-dog-in-training become confused and work off-site. Other groups, such as D.O.G.S., prearrange coded signals. Merely by "keying" the microphone, the monitors above are alerted and thereby kept informed of the "victim's" condition. These precautions are used to overcome the possibility of the volunteer being unable to speak, feeling faint, or getting snow in his mouth, for example.

The distance to be covered in some training sessions, from the drop point of the handler and dog to the "victim," may be more than a mile! Thus, speed, focused concentration on the matter at hand, and dedication to the work, along with all the other criteria, become absolutely imperative characteristics for a good sound search-and-rescue animal.

Neither the handler nor the dog is ever permitted to know beforehand the site of the buried volunteer "victim," nor, in the most advanced training, the sites or numbers of multiple "victims." The handler is therefore unable consciously or subconsciously to influence the dog's direction of endeavor.

When the team of man and dog arrive at the avalanche field site, the dog's lead is removed, allowing the animal full freedom for quick search and rescue. It is at this time that the dog is given the command "Go find!" Ignoring all the people that may be milling around on the snow's surface (thereby making it even more difficult for the dog-in-training, but emulating realistically a real event), the dog concentrates its efforts at the snow level.† It is a truly remarkable and emotionally stirring experience to witness the trained dog react with total urgency and purpose to this briefest of com-

---

*The FM band has the tightest, strongest signal, which carries clearly over a longer distance than the more commonly used and less expensive AM-frequency radios.
†Human scent rises through layers, through multiple feet of snow, thereby enabling the dog to scent it, to home in at the proper site of the victim's "burial."

mands, to quickly locate the "victim." Obviously, dogs which are able to perform this lifesaving task must have the keenest sense of scent and an abiding focus on the work.

Many of the dogs used are actually able to dig for their "victim" faster than people are able to shovel snow. These dogs are able, therefore, to reach the "victim" in a lesser amount of time, establishing far more quickly the lifesaving airway. The Moustakises' Malamutes showed an immediate and correct response to this life-threatening situation when, upon having located the "victim," they quickly lowered their heads to the snow's surface, avidly sniffing to determine the position of the "victim's" head, and then began sniffing without cessation to first uncover this most vital area. One of the dogs worked with such intensity and strength upon one occasion that once the tarpaulin covering the "victim's" head was exposed, she backed out of the pit with not only the tarp clenched firmly in her teeth, but also some of the volunteer's hair! While this had caused the volunteer some discomfort at the time, it was obvious that the dog had reacted properly to free the buried person in as brief amount of time as was possible. This makes all the difference between life and death in such potentially life-robbing situations.

There is no reason why more Alaskan Malamutes cannot be successfully trained for search-and-rescue work. While some Malamutes are better at being lead dogs or fishing dogs, there are also those dogs that demonstrate the aptitude, willingness, and dedication for this specialized and rewarding endeavor. Those dogs which show a somewhat independent attitude, that are intelligent as well as being lovable and tractable, that have steady and calm temperaments, could prove to be fine candidates for search-and-rescue work. There is no doubt that the physique of the Arctic dogs gives them the real advantage in cold-climate rescues. Such training for the owners will undoubtedly prove to be the most soul-satisfying and rewarding of all trials undertaken with these magnificent dogs.

Ch. Sena-Lak's Beowulf Thorjhawk, Am. and Can. C.D., shown with owner-trainer Beth Harris. Thorjhawk is a winner of Highest Scoring Dog in Show and is lead dog in a sled dog team.   *Lawrence Jenkins*

Beowulf Thosca of Snow Foot, Am., Can., Bermuda, Mexican F.C.I. international champion, and Am. C.D.X., and Mexican C.D.; top winning bitch, 1970, owned by Beth Harris.

190

23

Alaskan Malamutes in Obedience

ALASKAN MALAMUTES have extraordinary innate intelligence. Quick to learn, they possess sharp reflexes. Concomitantly, they become bored rapidly. Whenever training a Malamute, it is best not to repeat the same exercises, in the same order, time after time and day after day. Once a lesson has been learned, lavishly praise the dog and stop for the day. Because the dogs are so intelligent and learn so rapidly, training and discipline may be started at a very early age. A young dog has the capability of learning positive (rewarding) behavior just as easily as poor behavior (which can only net them negative reinforcement from the owner).

Whenever training, whether it is for obedience work, sledding, backpacking, or any other endeavor, teach the dog *only one category* of training at a time. In other words, if training in obedience, stick with that and do not confuse the dog with alternating obedience work and sledding—that would be highly conflictive work. In sledding, the dog is out in front and pulling with all his heart. In obedience work, the dog *must not pull,* and must at all times remain by the owner's side.* Whereas a sled dog is required to keep his tug line tight at all times, a pack dog and/or an obedience dog must accept a variety of roles: walking at heel either on- or

---

*The exceptions for remaining by the owner's left side are: the "stay" exercises (sits, downs, and stands); the utility hand-signal exercises; and tracking.

The first winning obedience brace in Malamute history are both champions. They are Cliquot of Husky-Pak, C.D.X. (right) and Husky-Pak Fancy Tail, C.D. Here they demonstrate the Long Sit. Owner-trainers are Mr. and Mrs. E. Z. Aninger of Somers, Connecticut.

Ch. Taimani Inunnunaktuk at Onak, C.D., bred by Wendy and Randy Corr. Wendy handled him to Best in Show and a C.D. Title. *Cook*

Beowulf's Degen, C.D., T.D., is the youngest Tracking degree Malamute in breed history. Owner-trainer is Debi Bliss, who co-owns the dog with her husband Monte.

Sena-Lak's Cheeno of Bringham, U.D., owned and trained by Lloyd D. Mazur of Gates Mills, Ohio. *Axel Studio*

Ch. Tote-Um's Tongass, C.D.X., owned and trained by Wendy Aronsen, practices the bar-jump for the coveted U.D. title.

off-lead; walking in front or behind on narrow trails; on steep trails, the dog may be expected to pull the owner from his backpack "harness"; and walking behind the owner in deep snow conditions (the footing is better in the owner's snowshoe tracks).

Obedience trials are a test of man and dog and their bonding, how well they are able to perform a prescribed set of exercises together. Each dog enters the ring with a perfect score of 200 points. As the dog and handler progress from one set of exercises to another, points are deducted for any deviations from the ideal performance. Few dogs ever achieve a perfect score of 200 points. Each exercise must be passed with more than a 50 percent score or the dog is disqualified. A minimum total of 170 points out of the perfect 200 must also be achieved if the dog is to pass for that day. It is possible, although rare, for a dog to earn 170 points total and still not qualify. The average dog will earn a score of about 185 points.

Each qualifying score a dog achieves toward an obedience degree is called a "leg." It takes three legs to attain an obedience title. The only exceptions to this are the Tracking Dog (T.D.) and Tracking Dog Excellent (T.D.X.) titles wherein a dog must complete a successful track just one time in order to add the titles to their names.

A dog's suitability in conformation has no bearing on its ability to compete in obedience. Dogs which would be disqualified in the show ring under a breed's Standard are eligible to compete in obedience trials. This includes bitches which have been spayed and dogs which have been castrated.

Obedience competition is divided into three levels, each with an "A" and a "B" category (excepting tracking trials). Each successive degree is more difficult than the one preceding. The three basic levels are Novice (Companion Dog, C.D.); Open (Companion Dog Excellent, C.D.X.); and Utility (Utility Dog, U.D.).

The Novice work is at an "elementary-school" level, embracing the basics which all dogs should know if they are to be good companion animals. Open obedience work is at a "high school" level. Utility work is the most difficult. It may be equated to pursuing an education at the "college" level.

The rules and regulations for obedience trials are essentially the same from one country to another in the Western Hemisphere. Thus, a dog which is trained well enough to be competitive in any of the above categories in the United States will be sufficiently trained to perform competitively in other countries, such as Canada, Bermuda, and Mexico.

Dogs must be smart to make the grade as a team member. A smart dog will easily recognize the difference between an obedience collar and a mushing collar, between a lead and a harness. They are able to make the transition easily from one field to another by recognition of the equipment they wear.

Jackie, first Alaskan Malamute to win an obedience title, was owned and trained by Louise Lombard in 1940.

Ch. Coldfoot Oonanik, Can., Am., and Mexican U.D.T., owned and trained by Andre Anctil, won Best of Breed handled by George Heitzman. Nikki was the first Malamute in the world to earn a U.D. title.

Ch. Fire 'N Ice in Conclusion, C.D., is owned by Linda Ball and Janet Edmonds of Manchester, England, but he was bred and taken to his titles by Linda Dowdy and Sharon Scholl in Minnesota.

In the past, common myth had it that obedience work of any kind for a sled dog would ruin it, taking away the dog's spirit. In recent years, it has been found that at the very least some obedience training is a necessity for a good sled dog. Even purist dog drivers have found their job of driving easier if the team dogs have had some training, such as a sit-stay or down-stay. Such commands are invaluable to the driver and team when, for example, resting a team along the trail or untangling a dog that has become caught in its traces.

The numbers below demonstrate considerable obedience activity among Alaskan Malamutes since Louise Lombard's Jackie got the first Companion Dog title. A dog named Boots won a C.D. title in 1954, but no one has been able to identify its sex or the whereabouts of its owner.

There have been 422 males and 426 bitches—plus Boots—which have won C.D. degrees; 24 dogs and 33 bitches have won C.D.X. titles; 4 dogs and 5 bitches, U.D. degrees; 8 dogs and 5 bitches, T.D. titles; and 1 dog and 1 bitch, T.D.X. degrees. That means for the breed 849 C.D.'s; 57 C.D.X.'s; 9 U.D.'s; 13 T.D.'s; and 2 T.D.X.'s.

Additional information about the foregoing may be obtained by requesting free copies of Rules and Regulations applying to Dog Shows and Obedience Trials by writing to the American Kennel Club, 51 Madison Avenue, New York, NY 10010.

24

Emergency First Aid

SOME BASIC KNOWLEDGE of emergency first-aid treatment is essential for all dog owners. Such knowledge may prevent complications of an injury; such knowledge may alleviate some of the animal's pain; such knowledge could possibly save the dog's life. Outlined here are initial steps only, to be followed *immediately* by veterinary care.

Dogs can get into as much inventive trouble as can any child—or adult. Problems that may be encountered in the lives shared by dogs and owners are shock, poisoning, broken bones, cuts (bleeding), heatstroke, porcupine or skunk encounters, to name but a few.

Smart dog owners will have at least some degree of preparation for administering to an injured dog. All owners should know how to immobilize a dog, apply temporary splints, apply a tourniquet, and have some basic knowledge of CPR (cardiopulmonary resuscitation).

A simple means of restraint is necessary to handle any injured dog. Even the most lovable and tractable pet can become frenzied or panic-stricken after being injured and while help is being given. A dog in great pain or one that is panic-stricken may not recognize its owner—and it may bite. A muzzle is the quickest and easiest way to prevent other injuries (such as to the owner) from occurring.

Providing the dog has not sustained a head or jaw injury, a muzzle can be made simply out of a two-foot (approximate) piece of rope, a belt, stockings, or gauze strips, for example. Practice tying a loose knot in the middle of the "muzzle," leaving a large loop, and slip it over the dog's muzzle. Pull the knot tight over the nose. Bring the ends down under the chin and tie another knot. Then bring the ends around behind the head, in back of the ears, and tie yet another knot. The muzzle will not interfere with the dog's breathing (provided it has not sustained a head injury).

A dog which has been injured needs to be transported to the veterinarian's with the least additional trauma possible. The ideal carrier is a large flat surface, such as a piece of plywood. Maneuver the dog carefully onto a blanket or a sheet, supporting as much of the dog as possible while doing so. Then with another person, one at each end of the sheet, pull the blanket or sheet taut and lift the dog onto the board. (This method makes it easier to transfer the dog onto an examination table at the veterinary hospital.) If a board is not available, the blanket or sheet alone will suffice, although it is not the first method of choice for transport.

If the dog is injured in a place where no blanket or plywood board is available, such as a wilderness area, it can be transported by carrying it over your shoulders, around your neck, and holding the legs in front of you. This latter however, is a last-resort method of transport. It can be, in certain instances, critically important to keep pressure off the abdomen and chest to maximize breathing.

A puppy can be transported with one hand under the head and neck, the other hand supporting the chest. A small (young) puppy can also be transported safely by picking it up by the loose scruff of the neck, allowing the puppy to hang straight down. This method also keeps the spine straight while allowing for maximum breathing capacity.

Internal bleeding can bring on shock. It can occur following an injury such as being hit by a car or having fallen. A dog which may have internal bleeding requires extremely gentle handling. The moving should be performed as suggested earlier, the ideal being on a board with a blanket. The blanket should be large enough to also cover the dog, helping to maintain the dog's body temperature, which aids in the prevention of shock.

Internal bleeding is not always easily apparent. A suspect case must be transported to a veterinarian as soon as possible. Outward signs in extreme cases can be bleeding from the mouth or nose, and some amount of turgidness to the abdominal area. This is for a veterinarian to determine, however, not a layperson.

Visible bleeding from cuts or contusions may be controlled before the dog is transported to the veterinarian's. A pressure bandage can be applied to control all but the most severe bleeding site, and/or bleeding may be slowed moderately with a cold pack. Do not, however, apply ice or a cold pack directly to an open traumatized site. Nor should a cold pack be used if there is any possibility whatsoever that the dog is in danger of going into shock.

Severe bleeding from a leg wound can almost always be controlled by increasing the tightness of a pressure bandage. It is *not* recommended normally that a tourniquet be applied to a limb. Only when absolutely necessary, a tourniquet can be applied to help staunch major bleeding. The tourniquet will have to be loosened every twelve to fifteen minutes. If the veterinary service is farther away than twelve or fifteen minutes, this will prevent other trauma to the limb from occurring. The tissues of the skin are very delicate and tissue death will begin after twenty minutes *or less,* which creates the possibility of life-threatening gangrene occurring.

A tourniquet may be made simply with either a piece of rope, a belt, a stocking, or gauze strips. Traditionally, a loop is made around the limb a couple of inches above the site of the laceration. Place a stick, board, or even a pen or a pencil over the loop and make a second loop. Then twist the stick until the fabric of the tourniquet is pulled moderately tight—tight enough to help ease the flow of blood. Do not try to stop the flow altogether.

It is very important to time the period a tourniquet is tightened. Prolonged periods of tightness will not only staunch the flow of blood to the limb, but will with time cut off all circulation. A tourniquet should remain tightened for periods of twelve to fifteen minutes, followed by a period of three to four minutes when the tourniquet is moderately loosened before tightening it again.

A dog suffering shock will become completely prostrate. Its breathing may be shallow and rapid. The eyes may dilate (the pupils wide open), the pupillary reaction may be slow, and the eyes may have a rather glassy look to them. The mucous membranes, such as the gums, will often be pale.

If the weather is not hot, cover the dog with a blanket to keep it warm. If the weather is warm, cover the dog lightly with a lightweight blanket or a sheet. If the dog is injured during cold months, an emergency hot-water bottle can be made with a plastic bleach or detergent bottle filled with very warm (not hot) water. This should be placed next to the dog. A large dog can require several warm-water bottles to help prevent shock.

A dog suffering from shock requires *immediate* transportation to the veterinary hospital. If low blood pressure (shock) persists too long untreated, other often irreversible changes can occur.

Most fractures or dislocations are quite evident. Most dogs will not attempt to use a limb which has sustained such an injury. The sooner a fracture is set, or a dislocation attended to by a veterinarian, the less serious the aftereffects of such an injury will be for the dog.

If a leg bone is severely out of line, a temporary splint or support can be helpful to prevent further trauma to the injured leg. A simple splint can be made by wrapping two short boards or sticks in fabric such as cloth or gauze strips, and then placing these *carefully* on either side of the injury site and wrapping the limb *gently* with additional gauze or other cloth strips. (Stockings or pantyhose can be used in lieu of cloth or gauze.) The dog will require transportation to the veterinarian's as quickly as possible and in such a manner as to prevent further trauma to the injury site. Do not spend time worrying about a splint however, if the dog is in shock. Use the blanket-carrying method and transport the animal to the veterinarian *as soon as possible.*

Puppies and some adult dogs may be indiscriminate in what they ingest. Any dog with the propensity to eat anything and everything in sight could easily become poisoned. Treatment of poisoning cases presents special medical problems. It is *very* important to know exactly what has poisoned the animal.

If the poison is known, treatment with the proper antidote can be initiated immediately by a veterinarian. Unfortunately, many poisons have no specific antidote and can only be partially controlled. If the exact poison is not known, then the owner must become a "sleuth," helping the veterinarian to determine what possibly has affected the dog. Possible sources of poisoning are poisoned bait such as used for foxes and coyotes, mice and rats; paint; plant sprays and weed killers; and insect sprays. Certain plants are also poisonous to animals. Lists of these plants may be obtained through your veterinary hospital, a local university, an animal control agency, a poison center, or a state agency.

Warfarin is a common poison used for rodents, and a dog which has ingested this substance requires *immediate* veterinary attention. Within the past year, a new generation of warfarin has been marketed. This can require one month of daily vitamin K injections to prevent hemorrhage. Strychnine is often used for varmint population control and results in the dog's having rigid extensions of the legs and neck. **A dog which has been poisoned by the ingestion of a corrosive chemical should not be caused to vomit, as such a procedure can be extremely dangerous to the animal.**

If the pet has actually been observed ingesting a poisoning substance other than strychnine, causing the animal to vomit can be beneficial. Several teaspoons of salt placed at the back of the tongue may be enough to induce vomiting. A mustard and water solution, or a strong salt solution (six teaspoons of salt mixed with a glass of water), can also produce the desired effect. Directly after the dog has been caused to vomit it should be given either milk or egg whites. The dog should then see the veterinarian as quickly as possible.

Heat prostration or heatstroke may be one of the greatest causes of death in dogs. The most frequent cause in this category is from a dog being confined to an automobile on a warm day, or even in an automobile which is exposed to direct sunlight on a mild day. The metal of a car body acts exactly like an oven. Temperatures rise within *brief* minutes from double-digit to triple-digit figures.

The sign of heatstroke is dyspnea (difficult breathing, with very rapid and shallow panting). If a dog has reached this point, it is in a state of collapse and death can be imminent.

The dog's temperature must be reduced *immediately.* Do *not* wait to get the dog to a veterinarian's to initiate treatment. Time and quick reactions on the part of the owner are the most critical factors in initially saving the dog's life.

The dog's temperature can be reduced quickly by immersing it in a tub of cool-to-cold water; the dog can be hosed off thoroughly; or it can be placed in a shower stall to have cold water sprayed upon it. The dog can also be administered a cool-water enema. If a large dog, or one in extremis, several ice cubes can be inserted into the rectum. Towels drenched in cold water should loosely wrap the dog on the way to the veterinarian. The dog can also be packed in ice during this time; and ice applied to the groin area, around the ears, and between the forelegs ("armpits") as well. Elevate the dog's head and chest slightly during the ride to the veterinary hospital to facilitate easier breathing.

Once a dog has succumbed to heatstroke, it will be unable to regulate its body temperature for a period of time. It is critical that the dog be placed under veterinary care as quickly as possible. An animal can be prone to recurrence of heatstroke once it has suffered from this condition. Each year one hears about dogs (and small children as well) that die of heatstroke from having been left unattended in a closed car, or one that is inadequately ventilated.

There is no such thing as a fair fight, and few dogs are canny enough to win against a porcupine. Quills can become embedded easily anywhere in the dog's anatomy: legs, chest, neck, or head. Any dog suffering multiple punctures from a porcupine will become very distressed. If the quills become embedded about the mouth, face, or neck, it can become a life-threatening situation to the dog.

Removal of the quills is painful. Vinegar can be applied to the quills to soften them. Some people have experienced a good measure of success in quill removal by cutting (severing) the quills at the farthest point from the dog's body. The quills then partially collapse. This aids in their withdrawal.

The quills should be removed as carefully and gently as possible with hemostats or a pair of pliers, either of which gives a good grip on the quills. Quills have small barblike projections that act much like a fish hooks, making removal rather difficult. Many of the smaller quills may be totally embedded and can be felt under the dog's skin. These *must* be surgically removed. Most often the removal of quills will require veterinary care as the removal process is quite painful to the dog and the animal, already in pain, may further panic. In any event, the dog should be taken to a veterinarian after such an episode, as treatment with anti-inflammatory and antibiotic drugs may be necessary.

Undeniably, skunks are the most "popular" bane of dogs and their owners. Few dogs have the canniness and ability to become victorious over a skunk. Skunks are infamous for carrying diseases such as leptospirosis and rabies. Few things distress either an owner or a dog more than the dog's having been "hit" by a skunk.

The odor of a skunk needs to be neutralized as quickly as possible. The dog should be bathed (doused) repeatedly with tomato purée, then rinsed each time with water. After several repeated applications of the tomato purée, the dog should then be bathed with soap and water. Diluted tomato paste, tomato juice, catsup, or even tomato soup can be used as alternatives to tomato purée.

There are also a number of good products on the market today which aid in the removal of skunk odor, some for dogs and others for carpeting, clothing, and furniture. These are excellent for the first and final applications and, when used in combination with the foregoing, prove to be excellent in their results.

Alaskan Malamutes are infamous chewers. There is little that they will not try—at least once. They relieve boredom by chewing; puppies teethe by chewing; and adult animals often find recreation in chewing. The smart owners always have suitable chewing objects readily available to their pets.

Many dogs are known to swallow much of what they chew, if not all of the object. They have been known to swallow bones, golf balls, hard rubber balls, squeakers that pop out of toys, bells that pop from balls, entire pantyhose and bathmats! Straining to defecate, loss of appetite, a generalized lackluster air, and signs of abdominal distress are often indications that the dog has ingested foreign material. The dog may also try to vomit persistently.

First aid for this life-threatening condition consists of taking the dog to the veterinary hospital as quickly as possible. Sometimes emergency surgery is required to clear an obstructed intestinal tract.

The jaw power of Malamutes is veritably awesome. They have been known to shear off large pieces of bone, sticks, or other objects with their molars. On a rare occasion, an item can become lodged in the roof of the dog's mouth, between its teeth or jaws, or caught in the back of the throat. If an object is caught, the dog will attempt to dislodge it by pawing at its mouth, usually while holding its head slightly to one side. If the object can be seen, it can normally be removed with the aid of a pair of pliers.

The dog's saliva will make an object quite slippery, and using fingers alone can at times cause the object to slip dangerously toward the throat, possibly blocking the trachea (airway). Do *not* attempt to remove an object with your fingers alone, since even very tractable dogs may panic when an object is caught in its mouth, inadvertently biting the owner. Sometimes an object can become so firmly embedded that a veterinarian will have to remove it after giving the dog a mild general anesthetic.

Burns, while uncommon, are not rare to dogs. They can occur from hot grease, water, or simply from touching a hot object (such as a radiator, an iron, or a stovetop). A burn site should initially be flushed with cool-to-cold water. A syringe without a needle or a spray bottle can be ideal for flushing the site. Sterile ointment to protect the damaged area should be applied next. In lieu of a sterile burn ointment such as Furacin, products such as Solarcaine or an aloe vera compound will help to control localized pain.

A large burned area should have a loose gauze dressing applied to the area. This will give added protection against infection. In such cases, the dog will require antibiotics and should see the veterinarian as soon as possible. Infrequently, a dog may require additional veterinary support, such as intravenous or subcutaneous fluids, to help stabilize it.

A dog which is burned by acids or alkalis needs to have the site flushed *thoroughly* with a wash of baking soda and cool water (for the acidic burns), or a lemon juice and water solution (in cases of alkaline burns). The ideal vehicle for flushing is either a syringe (without the needle) or an adjustable spray bottle. Following this form of flushing, the burn site may then be treated as other burns with the application of a sterile (burn) ointment. Following this immediate emergency treatment, the dog requires veterinary follow-through care.

If the eyes are the site of a caustic solution type of burn, they must be flushed continuously for at least fifteen minutes with water. Following this initial emergency first-aid treatment, the dog will require immediate veterinary follow-up care to save the dog's sight.

Products like turpentine or kerosene as paint removers for a dog's coat will also produce a very painful burn. These should not be used for the removal of tar, grease, or paint from dogs. The best treatment for such burns is by copious irrigation of the sites possibly followed by an application of a vegetable oil. The area may then be washed with a mild soap and vegetable oil again applied. (Vegetable oil can be soothing in addition to healing.) Following such emergency first-aid applications, the dog needs to be seen by a veterinarian.

Veterinarians often have a list of products that can be used safely on a dog for the removal of paints, greases, and tar. If the affected area is small enough, the hair can simply be allowed to wear off, or it can be scissored without damaging the dog's appearance.

Burns can remain painful for long periods of time. They are prone to infection and are slow-healing. Any dog which has suffered more than the most minor burn should be seen by a veterinarian. If a large enough area of the dog is burned, or the burn is deep enough, the dog can go into shock. The electrolyte balance of a dog can also be easily upset by burning. In such cases, the dog will require immediate supportive electrolyte therapy.

Some puppies and adult dogs may attempt chewing on an electric cord. Normally, such an action will result in the dog's getting a severely painful jolt. A burn caused by the electricity can also occur. At the worst, the puppy or dog can get a bad electric shock, suddenly stiffening and falling over in a rigid manner. The animal may be unable to let loose of the cord and the shock may therefore be continuous. *Never* touch the dog first. The first response must be to pull the plug from the wall. If rubber gloves are handy, they would be advisable as an added safety precaution, putting them on *before* pulling the plug (and before touching the dog).

A dog which has suffered an electric shock may have an arrested heartbeat, and/or it may stop breathing on its own. Place the dog fully prone on its right side. Pull the left foreleg back toward the rib cage; the point of the elbow will be close to the site of the heart. Feel for the heartbeat. Watch the rib cage for a brief moment to note if there is involuntary breathing. If there is either no respiration or apparent heartbeat, *CPR must be started immediately.* If there is someone else nearby, have them call a veterinarian for additional instructions (as well as to notify him that you will be bringing in a case of cardiopulmonary arrest).

Cardiopulmonary resuscitation is best performed by two people. Although it can be effectively done by one person, it is harder—and riskier to the animal. CPR for a dog is best effected through the following method.

Check the dog's mouth first to make sure that the tongue is not in the way: pull the tongue forward to clear the air passage. With the dog prone (on its right side) on a *firm* flat surface, alternately depress its chest by pressing firmly on the rib cage just posterior to the fifth to sixth rib and release. Count in a rhythm as the dog is depressed and released. It is a three-part cadence: one for depression, two for release, and three for a brief pause before starting over.

The chest should be depressed and released alternately five times before "breathing" for the dog. Ideally, a second person is present to breathe for the dog. This can be performed, however, by a single person. Placing the hands around the dog's muzzle (to prevent air from escaping through the sides of the lips), and with the dog's neck extended, the person should envelop the animal's mouth and nose with their mouth and blow firmly with a moderately sustained flow of breath. Watch the rib cage for evidence of elevation, response to the blowing. Then repeat the depression and release of the chest five times before "breathing" for the dog again. This is repeated as necessary until the dog is breathing on its own.

If the heart has stopped beating, a quick thump over the dog's heart after clearing the airway (pulling the tongue) and before depression and release of the chest should be done. This too should be repeated until the heart begins beating or all hope is gone.

Resuscitation by these methods can take as long as twenty minutes or even an hour before the animal responds enough to have a steady heartbeat and breathe on its own.

In the ideal situation, two people will work on the dog while a third person drives all to the veterinary hospital. Even if an apparently normal heartbeat and respiration has been restored to the animal, it should still be seen by the veterinarian as quickly as possible. In cases where the heart has continued to beat and there has been no apparent respiratory arrest, but the dog was unconscious, aromatic stimulants can prove to be beneficial. In lieu of anything else, a small amount of ammonia can be used as a stimulant.

An uncommon occurrence in dogs is convulsions. Such an occurrence is more upsetting and dismaying to the owner than to the dog. An episode can be caused by a viral infection which has reached the brain, such as for example, distemper. Ear infections, epilepsy, certain parasitic infestations, in addition to other causal factors can also initiate an episode of convulsions.

If a dog is convulsing, make sure that it is out of harm's way, that it cannot become entangled in furniture or other objects, and that it is not up against a wall. If the dog is out of harm's way, *leave it alone.* If the animal is in a dangerous site, do not try to move it. Cover the dog with a blanket and restrain it from injury. Be certain to keep fingers and hands (and other portions of your anatomy) away from the dog's head, as dogs may bite actively while they convulse. Remember, a dog which is convulsing is totally oblivious to its surroundings, and while it will not attack anyone, or otherwise be vicious, it can inflict harm upon those who come too close to the head during such an episode.

Any dog which has convulsed requires veterinary attention to determine the cause. Dogs which have convulsed should *never* be wormed by their owners, as this may cause another episode under certain conditions. Owner-given treatments such as worming or other over-the-counter remedies can, in certain instances, even cause death to a dog which has convulsed.

If ever confronted by an emergency, the owner of the animal must respond quickly with a certain sequence of thinking in order to prevent further, possibly irreversible, damage or to save the dog's life. The dog's heartbeat and breathing response require the first attention. Bleeding sites should be checked next. And, finally, check the extent of the injuries.

Emergency first aid is just what is implied, the *first* aid only. Dogs which have encountered any one of these conditions (in addition to others) should always be seen by a veterinarian as quickly as possible. First aid never replaces the requirement for qualified veterinary attention.

25

Medical Problems and the Alaskan Malamute

CHRONIC OR GENETIC MEDICAL problems require the diagnosis and supervision of a veterinarian for either long-term cure or short-term alleviation of symptoms. It is essential that a proper evaluation of the condition be made as quickly as possible and that it be determined whether causal factors are environmental or genetic. It is important that animals with genetically linked medical problems be treated to improve their quality of life, and eliminated from any breeding program.

In this chapter, we will briefly discuss some of the disorders and abnormalities common to the Alaskan Malamute.

Anconeal Dysplasia

Actually an ununited anconeal process, what is known in lay terms as "elbow dysplasia." This condition is classified as a developmental abnormality that involves three small bones in dogs' elbows which unite as puppies grow. The exact cause of this condition is unknown.

Clinical signs of a suspected ununited anconeal process are a history of intermittent foreleg lameness that is progressive in its severity. This condition may affect either one foreleg or both forelegs, and it is not necessarily apparent that the conditions are continuous or simultaneous if both forelegs are affected. Signs of severe lameness usually occur following exercise. During exercise, the elbow is not fully extended as the dog moves.

There is almost always some swelling of the area between the elbow and the humerus. Crepitation is rarely evident until arthritic changes of the joint have occurred or there is a complete nonunion of the anconeal process. Radiographs are required to confirm a diagnosis of this condition.

Surgical removal of the anconeal process is the treatment of this condition, being the only manner in which pain can be alleviated and the dog's gait improved. Surgically placing a screw in the ununited anconeal process to the elbow bone can produce a better long-term repair if performed before arthritis occurs. Corticosteroids have proven to be of little or no value without surgical correction of this condition. Arthritic changes of the joint seldom occur after surgery.

Central Progressive Retinal Atrophy

Often called **CPRA,** this is a condition of central atrophy of the retina. Normally, the condition appears in affected dogs between four and eight years old.

Owners may report that affected dogs have difficulty in avoiding obstacles although their distant vision appears to be unimpaired. The pupillary light reaction of affected dogs is slow and incomplete when signs of reduced vision are noticed. Usually, a veterinary opthalmologist should make the determination.

It is believed that transmission of this condition is an autosomal recessive factor. As a result of the disease being inherited, any dog with this condition should not be used in a breeding program.

Chondrodysplasia

A hereditary condition found in Alaskan Malamutes. Commonly known as "dwarfism," affected dogs may exhibit a Basset Hound type of conformation. (Not all Basset Hound conformations are dwarfs. Such deformation can occur for other reasons, generally nutritional.) The mode of inheritance is Mendelian, that is, it is a simple recessive gene which produces this condition.

Bilateral stunting is most noticeable as occurring in the forelimbs and is variable in its severity. Stunting is accompanied by lateral deviation of the paw, enlargement of the carpals, and lateral bowing of the forelimbs. The topline of most dwarfs slopes forward. Diagnosis by radiographic examination is fairly reliable before the age of three months. After three months of age the characteristic red blood cell indices must be used, as radiographs are no longer definitive. Early definitive diagnosis is made by

Front view of a normal Malamute
puppy.   *Canadian Veterinary Journal*

Front view of a chondrodysplastic
puppy.   *Canadian Veterinary Journal*

Profile view of a normal Malamute puppy.   *Canadian Veterinary Journal*

Profile view of a chondrodysplastic puppy.   *Canadian Veterinary Journal*

radiographing one or both carpal areas of the forelegs. While an affected puppy is often lame for a day or two after a minor fall, mature dwarfs seldom exhibit such lameness.

Most dwarfs will exercise little, although those less severely affected are apparently as active as their normal counterparts. Occasionally, a severely affected animal requires euthanasia due to its inability to walk well. Although dwarfed in stature, some affected animals weigh as much as normal Alaskan Malamutes of similar age and sex.

The Alaskan Malamute Club of America through its Chondrodysplasia Certification Committee has compiled statistics and guidelines which all owners of purebred Alaskan Malamutes should follow in their breeding programs. Pedigrees are submitted to the committee for analysis. Dogs whose percentile ratings are greater than 6.25 percent should be test-bred either with a dwarf or a *known* carrier to determine if the suspect animal is a carrier, or they should be withheld from open breeding. Normal littermates to dwarfs will be carriers if either the sire or dam is a dwarf.

Affected dogs should *not* be used in a breeding program outside the test-breeding program established by the Alaskan Malamute Club of America's Chondrodysplasia Study Program. Suspect animals should be test-bred or, again, withheld from open breeding. Additional information about chondrodysplasia is available from the Alaskan Malamute Club of America's Chondrodysplasia Certification Committee.

Epilepsy

A condition in the dog not completely comparable to epilepsy found in mankind. It is a functional disorder of the brain and is characterized by symptoms related to the nervous system (which is structurally unaltered). Convulsions, hysteria, and unusual behavior patterns can occur in the dog as the result of parasitisms, exposure to toxic chemicals, as well as hereditary factors.

The clinical signs of the *petit mal* form of seizure are manifested by the dog convulsing for approximately two minutes, with or without the loss of consciousness. A history of the affected animal will often reveal that the dog has had one or more minor attacks several months prior to the current one; the dog appeared to be restless shortly before the seizure; and, if accompanied by unconsciousness (*grand mal* seizure), the dog was drowsy or unaware of its surroundings for several minutes after the attack. Dogs having suffered an attack will often appear to be very tired afterward, requiring a quiet place to rest.

Seizures will occur at decreasing intervals and will be of increased duration. A second attack may not occur, for example, until some six months after the first, a third after a period of four months, and so on. Recurrent episodes will often increase in frequency with increasing age.

The disease is not progressive. The dog will not harm itself during a seizure provided it is in a "protected area," one that is open and away from furniture or other objects which could harm the animal. Nor will the dog harm a person provided it is left unrestrained during the period of convulsions.

Medication has been proven to be helpful in the control of seizures and is normally dispensed during stressful times (such as thunderstorms). The owner of such an animal should notify the veterinarian of each seizure. A good working relationship of open communication and information between the veterinarian and owner will help to establish the proper level of medication in the dog. Some owners become so highly aware of their pet, they are able to prevent seizures by recognition of the prodromal behavior and administering the anticonvulsant medication in a timely manner.

Dogs which have exhibited a history of epilepsy should not be bred. Owners of related animals should be notified in order that they become aware of their dog's possible predisposition to this progressive disease.

Gastric Dilatation and Gastric Torsion Complex

A condition which may occur in any breed of dog, at any age. Commonly called **"bloat"** among lay persons, this syndrome is encountered most often in the large and deep-chested breeds, among which is the Alaskan Malamute. The complex results from the dog's inability to pass food (or other ingesta) through the stomach into the lower intestines, or lack of capacity for emesis (vomiting) if the torsion has occurred.

Dogs in which this complex has occurred (and which have survived) are highly prone to a recurrence of this condition. Studies of gas present in the stomachs of afflicted dogs suggest that a primary cause is accumulated swallowed air. The amount of air swallowed by dogs during eating and drinking varies greatly from one animal to another. Gulping "eager eaters" appear to swallow more air than the finicky, picky eaters. Exercise shortly after eating has also been associated with gastric torsion. Other factors which may produce gastric torsion can be: general anesthesia, abdominal surgery, traumatic injury, spinal injury, overeating, ingestion of foreign materials, whelping, vomiting, and malignant tumors.

The initial clinical signs of gastric torsion occur quite suddenly, normally within a few hours of the dog's having eaten. The dog becomes restless, may salivate excessively, and may finally have unproductive attempts at vomiting. As the abdomen continues to distend, the pain becomes manifested. The dog becomes reluctant to move, but at the same time will refuse to lie down. As the case advances in severity, the onset of shock quickly becomes apparent, with pale mucous membranes, a rapid heartbeat (tachycardia), and a weak pulse. Such a dog is headed toward a rapid and initially (before shock sets in) very painful death.

A recurrence of the complex due to dietary indiscretions is almost always inevitable unless the faulty feeding practices arc amended. The dogs should be fed light brothy meals from three to five times daily for at least two to three days before reestablishing a more normal diet. At that time, relatively soft foods should be offered several times daily over the period of an additional few days. When "normal" feeding is resumed, it is recommended that the dog be fed at least twice daily, and in small quantities each time. It has also been suggested that the raising of the food dish to a platform (about the lower chest level) helps to reduce the intake of air during feeding.

With gastric torsion, there are a few points which bear emphasis. The time factor in discovery and treatment by a veterinarian is critical because the dog's total collapse is imminent with these conditions. It is imperative that an *immediate* diagnosis be made by the veterinarian. **Rapid treatment must be initiated.** The sooner the distressed dog is found by the owner, the condition diagnosed and treated by the veterinarian, the better the prognosis for survival. Any delays in presentation, diagnosis, and treatment must therefore be avoided at all costs, or the condition will be fatal.

Once successfully treated, dogs can continue to lead normal healthy and productive lives if some small daily concessions are made. Animals which have suffered an occurrence of this complex should lead lives as stress-free as possible. They should be fed several times daily throughout the remainder of their lives. They should not be fed dry food alone, and kibble should be fed "wet." Dry dog food that does not swell once water and meat are added to it is recommended. Some dogs may, however, require a special diet which is available through a veterinarian.

Hemeralopia

Commonly known as "day blindness," this condition can be found in a few Alaskan Malamutes. It is genetically inherited and may be detected in puppies as early as seven weeks.

Some sled dogs found in the North have been said to be "night dogs," a title by which one suspects they may suffer from hemeralopia. Dogs which exhibit this condition can apparently see better in the predawn and dawn hours, in the evening, and at night. Indoors or in dim outdoor light (such as during an overcast or stormy day), the dog's vision is apparently as good as that of a normal animal. During daylight hours, however, these animals may have a tendency to bump into objects and be uncertain of distances. The condition does not worsen with time. A dog which is protected, one that has learned the positions and distances of all hazards (such as buildings, fences, trees, furniture, and vehicles), can lead a restricted but happy life. A strange environment can bring grief for the dog.

Dogs which are suspect should be checked by a veterinarian. Those animals found to be suffering from hemeralopia should be withdrawn from a breeding program. If the dogs affected have already been bred, owners of all offspring should be notified in order that their animals be checked for this condition. Owners of other related animals should also benefit from the courtesy of notification.

Dr. Kenneth Bourns, one of Canada's most successful Malamute breeders and chairman of the Genetic Research Committee, discovered this ailment in his own dogs. Working with the Ontario Veterinary College at Guelph, and at great personal expense, Dr. Bourns learned how to eliminate the fault in his own breeding stock.

His courage in making the problem public and his dedication and work in pioneering a method to eliminate it from breeding stock belong among the greatest services to dogdom. His still timely article on the subject appeared in *Dogs in Canada* in March 1968.

Hemophilia

Commonly known as the "bleeders' disease," hemophilia has been found in the Alaskan Malamute breed. The coagulation time of the blood is markedly increased, with a tendency to bleed following even insignificant trauma.

The clinical, hematologic, and hereditary aspects of hemophilia in dogs have been identical to those occurring in man. Apparently, females are carriers of this trait, with male offspring exhibiting the trait. Thus, hemophilia is an inherited sex-linked recessive characteristic.

Dogs which even slightly exhibit signs of prolonged bleeding following trauma should be checked for hemophilia by a veterinarian. Known dogs should be withdrawn from any breeding program. Owners of all offspring require notification for evaluation by a veterinarian.

Hip Dysplasia

An apparently hereditary condition, at least in part. It may also be caused traumatically. It is a condition in which the acetabulum (socket of the hip joint) is too shallow to maintain stability of the joint during movement. The head of the femur, upon radiological examination, may prove to have abnormal flattening in all but the most mild cases. The neck of the femur may also show a thickening of the area. Arthritic changes occur in time, and in cases of a more marked severity, arthritic changes occur early in the dog's life.

Controlled breeding programs offer the only means by which the incidence of hip dysplasia may be reduced. Corticosteroids and salicylates provide some relief for severely arthritic animals. In early-diagnosed cases, pelvic rotation surgery can be performed very successfully. Relief of the condition in severely affected animals may occur through surgery in which the head of the femur is replaced. In the most advanced cases an artificial acetabulum may also be implanted.

Hock Joint Instability

Found in those dogs without proper angulation. These animals generally appear to have a "straight" hind leg. They lack proper development in the stifle area: the lower portion of the thigh. When examined, such hocks will move forward in a double-jointed action under a very slight pressure. Such dogs are unable to perform satisfactorily either as good sled dogs or weight pullers due to the inadequacy of the hocks to withstand the great propelling pressures required of them.

Such improper development of the second thigh area may be eliminated from a breeding program by breeding to an animal with proper hindquarters. In any case of severe laxity of the hock (which is a physiological compensation for underdeveloped stifles), such an animal should be withdrawn from any potential breeding program.

Hypothyroidism

Manifested by a low metabolic rate among other clinical signs which can be determined only by a veterinarian. As comparatively "easy keepers" (requiring substantially small amounts of dietary intake relative to their size), Alaskan Malamutes in general are suspect for hypothyroidism.

Clinical manifestations may vary in intensity with individual cases. Affected animals have a dry, coarse, and sparse coat; narrow palpebral fissures; ocular discharge; enlarged epiphyses; pale mucous membranes; good appetite; normal or above-normal body weight; mental dullness; and an awkward, unsteady, and slow gait. Some manifestations are more apparent than others. Diagnosis is made through a blood sample. Treatment is effective in all but the most severe cases (where irreversible changes have occurred) through replacement therapy, with synthetic thyroid tablets given orally.

Clinical signs of this condition also often occur in older dogs. These signs include inactivity, obesity, sparse coat, and patchy loss of hair. Such dogs generally respond positively to thyroid therapy. *Any* dog with abnormal mating, heat, or gestation should be first checked for low thyroid.

Progressive Retinal Atrophy

A hereditary condition commonly and simply called **PRA.** Most dogs which are affected first exhibit clinical signs when they are about four to five years old, although younger animals may also exhibit signs of affect. The owners of affected dogs normally report that the dogs initially exhibit reduced night vision followed by a gradual loss of day vision. At the time of pupillary examination, the pupillary response to light is sluggish in the early stages, becoming incomplete or absent with the progression of the disease. At the ultimate stage, the pupil is widely dilated and fails to react to strong artificial illumination.

Cataracts are not uncommon in generalized retinal atrophy. Transmission of this condition is believed to be by an autosomal recessive factor. As a result, dogs which exhibit clinical manifestations of this problem should not be used in a breeding program.

"Wobblers" Syndrome (Cervical Spondylopathy)

A hereditary condition which appears to be a failure of proper support around the area of the vertebrae. Primarily large breeds are afflicted by this disease, although it can on occasion be found in smaller varieties such as the Basset Hound.

Wobblers is a fatally progressive condition affecting the spinal cord in the cervical area. The afflicted dog's head may shake with palsy. The dog's movement is a swaying or wobbling motion of the hind legs. The rear legs are very weak, supporting the dog minimally at best, and eventually not at all. Wobblers frequently is accompanied by considerable pain.

Signs of this condition are a slowly progressive lack of coordination in the hindquarters. Usually, but not always, the forequarters move normally. In the more advanced stages, however, the animal suffers in both the front and rear quarters.

The onset is normally between three and twelve months of age. The onset may, however, occur later and has been found on rare occasion in an animal as old as two years. Wobblers can occur suddenly, with the animal becoming quadriplegic within twelve hours of the onset.

While the exact cause of this condition is unknown, it has been suggested that the deformity and secondary displacement of the vertebrae is due to a long neck and rapid growth. Another possible cause which has been linked to the syndrome is *over*nutrition, especially from foods that are very high in protein, calcium, and phosphorus.

Skilled veterinarians are able to distinguish this anomaly from other skeletal diseases by radiology. Acute cases respond best to surgery. Those cases which have existed for a while respond less favorably to treatment.

Any dog diagnosed with Wobblers syndrome should be immediately withdrawn from any breeding program and owners of related dogs notified of this condition in the related animal.

More information about these conditions may be obtained through additional reading in *Ettinger's Internal Medicine* by Gary Ettinger.

26

Breeding Responsibility

$\mathbf{M}$ANY PEOPLE who breed dogs recognize their obligations. They are perfectly willing to accept the responsibilities assumed when bringing new life into the world. These people offer their brood matrons superior pre- and postnatal care. They have carefully researched the pedigrees of the dogs they have brought to a union. Conscientiously, they insured the sire and dam were radiographed (hips and elbows), along with being checked for other problems which afflict the breed.

These breeders carefully select the homes into which the puppies are placed. Once a puppy sale has been made, they provide detailed instructions for feeding and follow-up veterinary care. These dedicated people maintain a follow-up program, staying in touch with their puppy clientele. They insure that the puppies (and grown dogs) have good emotional as well as physical care. These responsible breeders are also prepared to take back (or help relocate), a dog of their breeding at any age, should the owners for whatever reason be incapable of keeping the animal.

There is nothing wrong with breeding and being a breeder per se. *Education* is, however, the key word for every person who contemplates such an activity. It does not matter if such contemplation is for a single litter or for an entire breeding program encompassing years of forethought. People who sell puppies which are surplus to a show and breeding program must be aware of those prospective clients who, during the interview process, disclose that they do not want to show, they only want to breed dogs.

But dog shows are, by their very definition, the place where the quality of a breeding program is proven.

All puppy clientele require adequate education. They need to be informed that it is far easier to place a puppy from champion parents, or parents that are working successfully on their titles, than it is to sell a puppy from untitled parents. A breeder should keep the concept of the breed's entire welfare in mind when making puppy placements. When a breeder is confronted by the type of purchaser who insists upon breeding alone, it is best, for the breed as a whole, not to make the sale to that person.

Most breeders carefully place their puppies in responsible homes. Through their silence, however, they may inadvertently condone the breeding of pet-only puppies by clients. Sales of pet-only-quality puppies without restrictions for *not* breeding them, is a real crime perpetrated upon the over-populated canine world in general. The truth is simple: Many breeders are uneducated about sound puppy placement practices.

Each day of the week, one can find in any newspaper numerous advertisements for puppy sales from "planned" breedings. Often these sellers panic because the buyers they anticipated did not materialize. Some of these "breeders" are people who by having purchased a registered animal feel they are "entitled to recoup" their expenses of the initial purchase and subsequent upkeep of the pet. As a result, they feel "entitled to breed just once."

These people do not realize the costs involved in properly rearing a litter: stud fees (and transportation costs to get to the stud dog); veterinary fees (radiographs, brucellosis tests, and artificial insemination if required); proper nutritional care for the dam and puppies; and advertising expenses. These people are only able to see dollar signs before their eyes with the arrival of each new puppy into the world.

When people call for a puppy, the first question to be asked by the breeder is, "Pet or show quality?" Many newcomers to the realm of the better-bred purebred are under the misconception that show dogs are not pets. They have no idea that the family dog which loves to eat ice cream and tablescraps (on occasion) can also be a fine show dog. They believe show dogs live in an emotional vacuum, an environment so sterile that the animal is allowed out of its kennel only to attend shows or to see the veterinarian.

These people need to be informed that champions are, after all, still dogs—and family members first. A show career, they need to be told, encompasses but a brief span of time in the lives show dogs share with their families. These people also need to be informed that show dogs may be eligible for a breeding program *only* if they are able to reproduce either their own quality or (what every breeder strives for) better quality (closer to the breed's Standard) in the "get" of each successive generation.

It is important to make it perfectly clear to a prospective client that the price of a puppy is *never* predicated upon the sex of the animal. It is up to you as the breeder to fully explain the differences between the show prospects and the pet-only puppies in the litter. Most importantly, it must be made clear without question that any puppy sold as a pet is *not* to be bred. Be a strong advocate of neutering such puppies by spay (ovarian hysterectomy) or castration.

Take the time to explain fully and in a positive manner that such irrevocable withdrawal from a breeding program does not affect the personality of the dogs. Nor does neutering cause a dog (male or female) to become fat and sluggish, as long as the proper nutrition and exercise levels of the dog are met.

One benefit derived from neutering is that castrated males will not chase neighborhood females that are in season; and conversely, a spayed female will not attract destructive neighborhood males. Another benefit is that many neutered dogs live longer and healthier lives than their unneutered counterparts, thereby giving their owners additional years in the pleasure of their company. Finally, some states offer price reductions in their licensing programs to owners of neutered animals.

These prospective clients are often only all-too-willing to neuter their pet puppy in return for a price reduction, or the possible difference in price between a pet-only and a show prospect. These people can be proud of their choice of a puppy and the breeding behind it. They have the added bonus of feeling good about the fact that their new family addition has come from a dedicated breeder, a person who so evidently cares strongly about the breed's general welfare.

It is important to *educate all clientele.* This education should also include those who purchase show-prospect puppies. These latter people will be showing and possibly breeding eventually. If the courtesy of such information is correctly extended to them, they will in turn be able to carry on the tradition of offering proper information to their own clientele. The breeder who educates all clients is the real breeder of good repute.

By all means, let your prospective clients know that of course "papers" are available for pet-only puppies. Inform them that such dogs may be shown in obedience trials. It is highly important to make it perfectly clear to any client from the beginning why each animal being individually registered is not necessarily a candidate for a breeding program.

As prospective clients view the puppies, teach them the physical differences between a show prospect and a pet-only puppy. It may be any number of physical variables which do not closely meet the breed Standard's requirements that designate a specific puppy as "pet-only." Stress the fact that lack of any of these physical qualities does not affect these puppies' potential as marvelous pets.

It is important to disclose that while a pedigree may be offered for five or more unbroken generations of champions behind the puppies, that not all dogs have the characteristics of desirable "designer genes." While there has never been a dog bred that is perfect, some dogs approach perfection, being closer to the breed Standard than others. Take the time to explain the breed Standard fully. Let your clients know *why* it was written in the manner in which it appears, the history and purpose of the breed, and why deviations from the Standard are unacceptable for breeding.

Most people are reasonable and will accept such explanations. They will show evidence of acting conscientiously upon the dedicated breeder's advice. There are many people who want a well-bred purebred dog in their home as a pet, but who cannot afford to pay the price of a show prospect. These people can nevertheless offer a superior home, a loving and supportive environment to the pet-only-quality puppy.

During a prospective sales interview, introduce the subject of obedience training. Every dog, from the finest purebred to the "all-American-bred," at the very least, should have some basic obedience work. Most people will exhibit interest if given a brief background about the basic rules and regulations of obedience and how competition is judged. Offer information about the challenge and excitement of obedience training and competition. Let your clients know that bonding and communication with their dog is increased immeasurably by such training. This will last the lifetime of the dog. Bring forth the point that while anyone can breed a "pretty" dog, it is in the obedience ring where the owner and the accomplishments of bonding with the dog are all that matter.

The American Kennel Club's rules and regulations state simply that the offspring of purebred, registered parents are entitled to registration papers. At the time of this writing, the AKC is working out a system whereby breeders will be able to put "not for breeding" on the individual's registration application. This further insures that no issue of that dog (should there be any) would be registered with the American Kennel Club, unless the breeder should reverse the nonbreeding registration.

Some people are undecided about a name for their puppy at the time of purchase. Too often these people fail to submit their puppy's Application for Individual Registration form to the AKC in a timely manner. The breeder, upon signing the application, must make it perfectly clear to these clients that the dog is not registered until the application has been received in the AKC offices. It must also be made known to the new owners that should the application become misplaced or lost, a duplicate application would be extremely hard to obtain. In some cases, the AKC has refused to issue a duplicate, and the dog remains unregistered.

When interviewing prospective clients for puppy placement, stress not only the positive aspects of the breed but also the "no-no's" according to the breed Standard. Be honest about the breed's basic personality. Describe not only the best in the breed, but also the breed quirks—for example, that almost all Malamutes are world-class champion diggers. Certainly, it would not be wise to place a puppy with a family that takes great pride in a beautifully landscaped yard.

Be assertively positive while explaining the *whys* regarding neutering, and the lack of effect except for reproduction purposes. Present a positive and sincere attitude when offering information about all the opportunities available with the breed: the never-ending excitement of obedience work; sledding and weight pulls; backpacking; and when applicable, exhibiting.

If these basic guidelines of being a responsible breeder are followed in making placements of puppies into responsible homes, if you offer an educational program in addition to your careful breeding program, then you are indeed a "breeder" truly worthy of this title.

A puppy steps out into the world unaware of life's uncertainties.

27

The Alaskan Malamute Protection League

THE ALASKAN MALAMUTE PROTECTION LEAGUE (AMPL) is an organization formed as a communications support network. It assists those people who are establishing, or who already maintain, a rescue-effort chapter. The formation of such a national lost-and-found file has proven to be highly effective for many breed members.

Each state has coordinating members of this national organization. They not only keep a local file, but also keep the national file current. This is highly necessary, not only for lost or found animals, but also because of the rampant interstate traffic in stolen dogs.

The AMPL is dedicated to the welfare of the individual animals that come under their care, either through successful attempts to reunite them with their owners, or finding an appropriate new owner, one who can give the dog a new lease on life. The temporary foster homes provide the dogs with a safe environment, proper nutrition, medical care, and the understanding and affection of people who know the breed. These dogs are then placed with a "shielding" contract. This assures those who are active in foster placements that the dogs will not be placed in a similar situation again. The creation of these satellite organizations fulfills the feeling of responsibility for the breed. It also serves to let the public know there are numerous and widespread efforts by dedicated people on behalf of the breed.

The rescue chapters shoulder the responsibility for the breed, no matter how good or poor an individual specimen may be. They create an environment whereby these animals can learn to be good dog citizens. These dedicated people do as much for the breed as any breeder of multichampions. While their experience and expertise may be different, in many ways they know the breed best. Until one has experienced working with an individual under severe stress (such as the hapless lost dogs, or those put up for adult adoptions), one does not acquire a complete education in the breed.

Approximately 10 percent of all displaced dogs are owner turn-ins. Some of these are absorbed by responsible breeders who take the dogs back and either keep them for the remainder of their lives, or successfully relocate these animals in an appropriate environment. The balance are in humane organization shelters or animal pounds, or are strays.

AMPL maintains a list of available dogs which are in need of special assistance. Their availability and success stories will be published through a newsletter. Responses are referred first to the state coordinator, then to the rescue organization holding the dogs.

AMPL plans to publish a newsletter for all members of the national organization, and for all organizations within each state who are active in rescue work. The newsletter will keep these "satellite" organizations current on new legislation within each state dealing with pound seizure, dog fighting, and the disposition of stolen and stray dogs. This publication will help to unite the efforts of all rescue organizations so that they can learn from, and yet assist, others. The newsletter will also help to standardize the handling of dogs in need. Additionally, it will aid in providing stringent encouragement for the neutering and tattooing of all dogs thus placed in new homes.

AMPL itself does not conduct the actual rescue work. Rescues are performed by each organization or chapter within the individual states. These chapters always need new volunteers to provide rescue work, foster homes, or more simply assistance to those who do perform these functions. Also, volunteers are needed in other capacities such as member coordination and keeping local files for lost and found Malamutes and those dogs available for adoption. Many breeders would feel encouraged to take back those dogs former owners have returned if, with some assistance from the national rescue organization, they could place the dog in a new home. However, those dogs which were abandoned, those in temporary foster-care situations, do have priority in placements.

The state coordinator also provides information to the national organization newsletter about local puppy-mill activity, and local legislation and policies dealing with the Alaskan Malamute. (As an example, the Albuquerque Animal Shelter holds a Malamute only 24 to 48 hours before destroying it because it cannot be kenneled with other dogs. This policy depends upon the availability of housing.)

226

In those areas where pound seizure is acceptable, the local coordinator will try to encourage the start of a rescue effort, no matter how small, for these are the areas where efforts must be concentrated to save Alaskan Malamutes from a protracted and painful death. (Pound seizure is the taking of a pound or shelter animal by laboratories that act within the sanction of state and local laws.)

Those states which **prohibit or prevent** pound seizure are Connecticut, Hawaii, Maine, Massachussetts, New Hampshire, New Jersey, Pennsylvania, Rhode Island, and Vermont.

States which **require** pound seizure are Iowa, Minnesota, Ohio, Oklahoma, South Dakota, and Utah.

States that **permit** pound seizure are Arizona, Michigan, North Carolina, Tennessee, Virginia, Wisconsin, and the District of Columbia.

The remaining twenty-nine states have no current reference in state law regarding laboratory sales. Generally, the policies are established by cities or counties, which deal directly with the disposition of unclaimed pound animals.

The problem is even more complex, however, in that those states which do prevent pound seizure apply only to those animals which are unclaimed. Dogs and cats that are voluntarily relinquished by their owners are not so protected. Additionally, no state prevents the transfer of animals to laboratories from privately operated shelters.

(The Alaskan Malamute, along with certain other breeds, is a highly desirable experimental laboratory animal due to its high threshold of pain and strong survival instincts.)

AMPL has forms available to interested persons. These may be used as models. These forms have proven invaluable for other breeds' national rescue groups. Included among these forms are waivers of liability for adoptive owners (provided by the Humane Society of the United States. These have allegedly stood in court). Also among the sample forms are adoption applications and forms for foster care providers.

If breeders utilized the basics in these forms *before* selling a puppy, much of the rescue effort being put forth by the AMPL volunteers would prove unnecessary. Copies of these forms are available upon request.

The original committee members of AMPL are Margaret Anderson, Lynn Brandt, Virginia Devaney, and Patricia Paulding. Currently, there are coordinators in the following states: California, Colorado, Connecticut, Georgia, Illinois, New Jersey, New Mexico, Tennessee, Texas, and Washington.

Additional information about AMPL, volunteers, chapters, lost and found dogs, and dogs available for adoption may be obtained by writing to the Alaskan Malamute Protection League, Attention: Virginia Devaney, P.O. Box 170, Cedar Crest, New Mexico 87008.

David Bedford drove his Black Ice three-dog Malamute team to third place among seventeen teams in the three-to-five-dog class at Eagle, Wisconsin. The dogs are Malnorska's Nyack of Black Ice, W.W.P.D., W.T.D., as Wheel; double Lead: Black Ice's Persuasive Force, W.W.P.D., W.T.D. (left), and Black Ice's Shear Force, W.W.P.D., W.T.D. (right). David and Shilon Bedford live in Delano, Minnesota. *Brayer Photography*

228

28

The Alaskan Malamute —All Ways a Working Dog

A̲LWAYS BEING MINDFUL of the breed's purpose is a primary goal of programs promoted by the Alaskan Malamute Club of America. To bring further attention and interest to the versatile Malamutes and their abilities, the Parent Club has established a set of criteria for certification in each field of endeavor for the working Malamute.

WORKING DOG CERTIFICATION REQUIREMENTS

1.0 PURPOSE

1.1 To encourage people to work their Alaskan Malamutes in the pursuits for which they were intended.

1.2 To provide Certification for those Alaskan Malamutes proven in these pursuits.

1.3 To thus encourage the breeding of a better Alaskan Malamute.

2.0 SCOPE

2.1 To establish criteria for Certification of the Working Malamute.

2.2   To establish those specialties for which a Malamute may receive certification.

2.3   To establish the rules for certification.

2.4   To revise the criteria as required to improve the certification program.

2.4.1   The criteria may be modified, amended, corrected, or otherwise changed, or the program may be discontinued upon the recommendation of the majority of the Committee upon approval of the AMCA Board.

2.5   The Working Dog Certification Program shall be self-supporting and thereby not be a burden to the AMCA. Certification charges shall be sufficient to pay for printing and mailing of certificates and any unforeseen costs.

3.0   FIELDS OF CERTIFICATIONS

3.1   Working Team Dog

3.2   Working Lead Dog

3.3   Working Weight Pull Dog

3.4   Working Pack Dog

3.5   Special working dog certification for search and rescue, guide dog, or the like, shall be considered by special application to the Working Dog Awards Committee on an individual basis.

4.0   ELIGIBILITY

4.1   The Alaskan Malamute shall be registered or registerable with a recognized kennel club (AKC, CKC, etc.)

5.0   BASIC REQUIREMENTS

5.1   All races or weight pull events entered shall be open events and must meet requirements in this document.

5.1.1   Open events are those which are not restricted to club members only and are sufficiently advertised so that non-club members may participate for a nominal charge.

5.2   It is the responsibility of the dog owners to make sure that their dogs are sufficiently trained and conditioned that they pose no hazard to the health or welfare of themselves or other dogs participating in the event. Any team proven a hazard to other teams or mushers shall be disqualified from certification. Any driver/handler who displays poor sportsmanship or abuses his dogs shall be disqualified from certification.

5.3   It is the responsibility of the dog owner to obtain and mail all the necessary documents, signatures and otherwise complete all requirements to get their dogs certified by AMCA.

5.4   Dog does not have to run on an all Malamute team.

6.0   CERTIFIED DOGS

6.1   Any dog certified by AMCA shall be privileged to use that title in any AMCA literature.

7.0 PROTESTS

7.1 Any person wishing to protest the eligibility of a dog or dog team, the qualification of an event for certification purposes, or protest any violation of race rules or certification requirements, must do so immediately following the conclusion of the event. The protest may be verbal but must be followed by a written statement to the race marshall or chief judge of the event within 10 days with a copy to the certification committee. The committee shall notify the concerned parties of the protest in order that they may file a rebuttal. It shall be the responsibility of the certification committee to decide whether or not the protest is valid by a 2/3 majority vote.

8.0 DOCUMENTS AND PROCESSING

8.1 Any person found guilty of willingly falsifying* documents in order to certify a dog shall be ineligible for certification.

8.2 The Working Dog Award Committee shall consist of three AMCA members, appointed by the Board of Directors, each from a different geographic location.

8.3 Certification application forms may be obtained by writing to the Working Dog Award Committee Chairperson whose name will be listed in the AMCA Newsletter. The completed form shall be returned to the Committee Chairperson for review.

9.0 OFFICIALS

9.1 Judges, or other necessary officials, may be AMCA members or other persons the Committee recognizes and accepts as having the necessary qualifications. Applications from competitive events must be signed by an event official.

9.2 Officials for approving a sledding or packing excursion shall be impartial persons accepted by the Committee as having the necessary qualifications and integrity. If a club event, the witness may be a club officer or event organizer. If an individual event, the witness may be a park official, forest ranger or similarly qualified person. The mailing address of the official must be provided on the application form.

9.3 DEFINITIONS:

Race Marshall is appointed by and reports to the race giving club, but has complete and full charge and responsibility for the race from the time it starts through to its completion. All other officials report directly to him and are responsible to him in all matters. He has the final word and the power to cancel or stop the race under extenuating circumstances, or weather or trail conditions. Can disqualify or refuse teams at the start, at his discretion. He must be experienced, capable and a responsible expert in the sport of dog racing. He will chair the drivers meeting, officials meeting and protest committee.

---

*Falsifying records may consist of substitution of a dog's name, forging documents or otherwise making false claims to certify a dog.

Time-Recorder is responsible for the recording of the time made by all teams during the race. He may have an assistant known as a recorder. He is responsible to the race marshall. It is his responsibility to use proper and adequate chronographs for this purpose, and be completely familiar with their use. He shall act on the protest committee.

Chief Judge shall report and be responsible to the race marshall. He shall be in charge of the Judges, the Dog Marker and his assistants. He shall deal directly with all drivers and will receive any protests or complaints. He shall be in charge of starting and finish line, and remain at this position during all heats of the race. He will examine teams at the start and finish, and has power to disqualify dogs unfit to run in his opinion.

Trail Judge shall report directly to race marshall and is responsible for laying out, preparation of, and marking the race trail. He should be familiar with the requirements of a race trail suitable for dog teams, and do his utmost to prepare a trail that will not have dangerous corners, road crossings, etc., that can be hazardous to dogs and driver. He is responsible for patrolling the race trail during the race, and placing the trail stewards at locations as may be required.

Protest Committee shall consist of Race Marshall, Chief Judge, Trail Judge, Time-Recorder. To settle all disputes, complaints and protests. To levy all penalties and disqualifications. Decisions of this committee are final and irrevocable.

Spotter or Trail Steward is person located at corner or intersection of trail, responsible for directing teams in corrections and reporting any incorrect occurrence to Trail Judge.

Racer is person participating in a race or races. *Trainer* is person who trains sled dogs for racing, freighting, or weight pull.

10.0 SLEDDING EVENT RULES AND REQUIREMENTS

10.1 Sledding—snow sled or wheeled rig.

10.2 Races shall be held under ISDRA rules plus any amendments created by the officiating club's race rules, as long as they do not change the basic requirements of ISDRA rules.

10.3 The applicant shall pay the costs of entrants plus payment to the AMCA for certification processing.

11.0 WORKING TEAM DOG

A) Vehicle may be snow sled or wheeled rig.
B) Team does not have to be all Malamute.
C) Dog does not have to run on same team each time.
D) Certification may be achieved by any one of the following three methods.

11.1 METHOD 1—RACING OR CROSS COUNTRY

A) Dog must qualify in three different races. The races may be any class. The dog may run in any combination of three races. Minimum number of teams competing is three. Races must be run under ISDRA rules or the rules must have been approved by the Committee. Each heat may count as a race as long as it fulfills the above requirements.

1) The team must complete the race in an acceptable speed as determined by the committee. Under normal conditions this will be 9 MPH for the sprint classes and 7 MPH for freight and cross country races. Under conditions of extreme weather or terrain the committee may accept a slower average time.

2) OR the team must complete the race in the top 30% of the competition.

B) Required distances will be determined by the class in which the dog is running. Required distances will be 1 mile for each dog on the team with a minimum of 3 miles required. The freight class shall be a minimum of 5 miles with a minimum of 50 pounds per dog added to the weight of the sled.

11.2   METHOD 2—RACING

A) Dog must accumulate a minimum of 25 race miles. The dog must have completed the course in all races considered. Races must be a minimum of 5 miles if a freight race. Distances of Method 1 apply.

B) The dog must complete all races in an acceptable amount of time as determined by the Committee.

C) All events must be certified by a race official or an impartial witness.

11.3   METHOD 3—EXCURSION

A) Dog must accumulate a minimum of 40 sledding excursion miles. Dog or dogs must pull sled a minimum of 10 miles per excursion. An impartial witness must sign the form to be sent to the Committee verifying proof of distances and dog or dogs competing.

11.4   METHOD 4—COMBINATION RACING AND EXCURSION

A) One or two 10 mile or longer races may count towards the total of 40 excursion miles.

11.5   ADDENDA

A) Each heat shall be counted as a race for the following reasons:

B) Heats are occasionally run to establish the top teams in each heat. The top teams or team then run in a final heat.

C) Occasionally the first heat is completed, but musher, dogs or equipment may be too damaged to compete in the next heat or heats.

D) A change in weather or other conditions may cause heats to be cancelled.

E) When certifying by accumulation 25 race miles, completing one race of 25 miles or more is qualifying.

WORKING LEAD DOG

A) DOG MUST RUN SINGLE LEAD on a team consisting of 3 dogs minimum.

B) Team requirements are identical to those for working team dog.

C) Dog does not have to lead same team each time to qualify.

WEIGHT PULL DOG

A) A dog must qualify in 4 separate events. Dogs must be weighed before the event.

    1) On natural surfaces such as snow or dirt the weight pulled must equal or exceed 8 times the dog's weight.

    2) On artificial surfaces such as concrete, the weight pulled must equal or exceed 12 times the dog's weight.

B) ISDRA or AMCA rules must be used in qualifying for a weight pull certificate.

PACK DOG

A) Dog must carry an initial weight equal to a minimum of 30% of the dog's weight.

B) Pack trips must be done on natural terrain such as hiking trails or cross country.

C) OPTION 1

Dog must pack a minimum of 30 miles. Each trip must be a minimum of 10 miles per day or an overnight campout with a minimum of 5 miles in and 5 miles out. A minimum of one trip must include an overnight campout.

OPTION 2

Dog must pack a minimum of 40 miles. Each trip must be a minimum of 10 miles per day.

D) Elevation gain may be substituted for mileage in the following manner: 1,000 feet of elevation is equivalent to 1 mile of flat terrain. Elevation gain will be figured as the difference between the highest and lowest points of the trip.

E) Packing requirements shall be spread out over a minimum of 2 trips.

F) An impartial witness must sign the form to be sent to the Committee verifying proof of distances and dog competing.

THE HALL OF WORKING FAME

The purpose of the Hall of Working Fame is to recognize all truly outstanding working dogs of the Alaskan Malamute breed. Such dogs shall have displayed, in their lifetime, the highest standards of working ability, including, but not limited to, sledding, weight-pulling, packing, police work, rescue (avalanche patrol or search and rescue), guide dogs for the blind, and hearing dogs for the deaf.

Eligibility: Open to all registered or registerable Alaskan Malamutes with a recognized registry (AKC, CKC, etc.), that were whelped at least ten years prior to their inclusion in the Hall of Working Fame, or that are deceased. Breeding status such as OFA, ChD, shall have no bearing on the eligibility of a dog for inclusion in the Hall of Working Fame.

Top twenty competitor and weight-pulling dog, Ch. Strawberry Mountain Ice Fall, owner-handler Pat Putman of Strawberry Mountain Kennels, East Wenatchee, Washington.

Northern Lights Kodiak, W.T.D., was only eight months old when this picture was taken along the Lost River. Owners: Mountain Home Alaskans.

Qualifications: Malamutes shall only be included if, during their lifetime, they have demonstrated a consistent excellence of working ability. Each dog shall be individually judged, but the following criteria shall guide the committee in their selection of the Hall of Working Fame dogs:

Weight-pull: Dog shall have made an outstanding record in National Pulls, International Pulls, AMCA Specialty Weight-pulls, or recognized Area Sled Dog Club Weight-pulls. These having been held under the auspices of, or abiding with, the rules established during the period of time in which the dog competed, or later, under the rules of ISDRA or the AMCA. The dog shall have won at least six weight pulls, held at different locations, with a minimum of five other dogs in competition, and shall have pulled on a variety of surfaces.

Sledding: Each dog shall be judged on its individual merit. Dogs, which are considered as candidates for the Hall of Working Fame for sledding, shall be consistent sprint racers, freight racers, or long distance racers over several seasons. The dog shall demonstrate the speed and endurance of an excellent Alaskan Malamute sled dog. Dogs used as members of search services, war, or exploration groups shall be included, if they demonstrated these high qualities.

Packing: Dogs should have been used for other than pleasure trips, and should have demonstrated their packing ability in an extraordinary capacity. (If candidates for the Hall of Working Fame have been used for pleasure trips also, they must have demonstrated their outstanding packing ability over several seasons, and on trips of at least 10 miles in length.)

Other: The working ability of each dog shall be judged on an individual basis, making sure that each individual has demonstrated the highest standard of working competence.

Recognition: All dogs included in the Hall of Working Fame, whose owners are members of the Alaskan Malamute Club of America, shall be entitled to a certificate indicating their dog's inclusion in the Hall of Working Fame. All dogs included in the Hall of Working Fame shall have the privilege of using the title, **HWF,** in any AMCA literature. Dogs shall not be designated as to a specific area of working ability, but simply as a Hall of Working Fame Dog.

THE HALL OF WORKING FAME COMMITTEE

The Hall of Fame Committee shall be appointed by the Board of the Alaskan Malamute Club of America, and shall be made up of three AMCA members (from different geographic regions), with one of these members designated as chairperson.

236

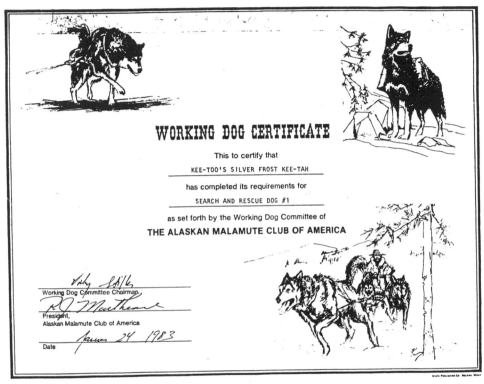

WORKING DOG CERTIFICATE

This to certify that

KEE-TOO'S SILVER FROST KEE-TAH

has completed its requirements for

SEARCH AND RESCUE DOG #1

as set forth by the Working Dog Committee of

THE ALASKAN MALAMUTE CLUB OF AMERICA

Working Dog Committee Chairman

President,
Alaskan Malamute Club of America

Date

This is the certificate awarded to Kee-Too's Silver Frost Kee-Tah, the first dog in the world to be certified as a Search and Rescue Dog. She was trained by Linton Moustakis who, with his wife Kay, owns her.

Responsibilities of the Committee:

1. Shall solicit from all AMCA members and Alaskan Malamute Fanciers, through the AMCA Newsletter and other sources, the names and achievements of Alaskan Malamutes to be considered for the Hall of Working Fame.
2. Shall evaluate each dog recommended for the Hall of Working Fame, and shall choose, each month, a small number of dogs—never to exceed ten—that are of the highest examples of working dogs.
3. Shall, each month, provide to the membership, through the Newsletter, this list of names, and their achievements, which are being considered for inclusion in the Hall of Working Fame. The AMCA membership shall have 90 days in which to register any information concerning the dog, or dogs, which would preclude qualification for this highest working honor.
4. Any controversial dog, nominated by the Committee, which receives negative responses from the members of the AMCA, shall be excluded from the list until such time as the entire paperwork on said dog shall be sent to the Board of Directors of the AMCA. The Board of Directors shall weigh the information and make the final decision.
5. Within 90 days after the names of the dogs have been published in the AMCA Newsletter, the Hall of Working Fame Committee shall certify those dogs, deemed qualified by the Committee and the membership, for inclusion in the Hall of Working Fame.
6. At the next Annual Meeting of the AMCA, these dogs shall be inscribed forever in the Hall of Working Fame.
7. The Committee may continue including dogs in the Hall of Working Fame at the rate of not more than 10 per month, until in the opinion of the Hall of Working Fame Committee and the Board of Directors of the AMCA, all dogs whelped prior to 1970 have been recognized.
8. Thereafter, the Committee will continue to solicit candidates for the Hall of Working Fame from the membership, and may, each year, nominate up to ten dogs, whelped at least 10 years earlier or deceased, to be included in the Hall of Working Fame. The names of these dogs and their accomplishments shall be printed in the Newsletter at least 90 days prior to the Annual Meeting of the AMCA. These dogs may then be included in the Hall of Working Fame at the next Annual Meeting of the AMCA.

Requirements for Nominating Dogs to Be Considered for Inclusion in the Hall of Working Fame

1. The full name of the dog, the date of birth, and the date of death, if deceased.

2. Registration number or litter registration number of dog candidate. If registration numbers are unavailable, due to the age of the dog, the full name of both the dog's dam and sire will be required.
3. The name of the owner of the dog, and the name of the breeder of the dog, if possible.
4. A four generation pedigree for the dog, whenever possible.
5. A record of the dog's accomplishments, together with a letter from a witness or witnesses—such as the race marshall or race official for a Sled Dog Club, an instructor for the guide dogs for the blind, or a search and rescue team leader—verifying these accomplishments.
6. A photograph of the dog, preferably in a working aspect.

THE HALL OF WORKING FAME

Wray of Antartica	Byrd Expedition Dog
Taku of Antartica	Byrd Expedition Dog
Antartica Milt	Byrd Expedition Dog
Antartica Cleo	Byrd Expedition Dog
Dude's Wolf	World War Dog
Dodges Lou	World War Dog
Shadak's Arctic Sonrise, C.D.X.	Packing and all-around Sled Dog ability
Ch. Lorn-Hall's Oogorook	Police work
Coldfoot Princess Panoka, C.D.	Leader dog for the blind
Lady of the Morning Mist, C.D.	Leader dog for the blind
Sno-Pak Kaghi's Tugg	Lead dog
Ch. Traleika of Tundra	Weight puller
Ch. Kodara's El Toro	All-around Sled Dog Ability
Ch. Gripp of Yukon	Lead dog
Ch. Knik of Ro-Ala-Ken	All-around Sled Dog Ability (Motion Pictures)
Ch. Toro of Bras Coupe	All-around Sled Dog Ability
Tuffy Tim-Pat, C.D.	Weight puller
Am./Can. Ch. Igloo Koyuk of Cold-foot, C.D.	Race dog and all-around ability
Am./Can. Ch. Shuyak Caro of Cold-foot, C.D.	Lead dog
Sittiak Anook	Leader dog for the blind
Taaralaste Kiana of Suntrana	Ran and finished the Iditarod
Willowcreek's Sage of White Mountain, C.D.	Race dog and weight puller
Ray's Tuaca (Lobo)	Weight puller

Each of these dogs has many accomplishments, but we have been asked to list only the most outstanding of those.

The two dogs being honored as World War Dogs were chosen as it was certain that they were involved in the work that was done by sled dogs in that war.

An all-male, all–Am./Can. champion team put together by breeder-owner Nancy Russell. All have W.W.P.D., W.T.D. On the left, handled by Jeri Russell El-Dissi, are Storm Kloud's Vvanilla Snoman, C.D., R.O.M.; Storm Kloud's Oomiak, C.D.; on the right, handled by Nancy Russell, are Storm Kloud's Better Than Ever, and Storm Kloud's Ccount on Me, C.D.   *Booth*

Appendix

From great sires and dams come the future of a breed. The Alaskan Malamute Club of America has sought to recognize outstanding producers through the Register of Merit. Dogs and bitches earn the honor of this designation through championship titles earned by their offspring.

To achieve this place of honor, sires must have eight champion offspring and dams must have five.

Am./Can. Ch. Tote-Um's Black Warrior, C.D., R.O.M., and R.O.M.O.B. with two of his pups. The black pup is future Am./Can. Ch. Oopiks's I'm A Warrior Too. Owner is Lorna Muir.

Spawn's Alaska, a great early foundation stud dog. Photographed by Maxwell Riddle at Westminster when he was owned by Hazel F. Wilton.

Ch. Tigara's Torch of Artica, R.O.M., bred and owned by Dorothy Dillingham.

Am./Can. Ch. Atanik's Snopaw I'm Awesome, R.O.M. His owner-handler was Kimberly Meredith of Atanik Kennels, Concord, California.   *Fox & Cook*

244

Ch.	Beowulf's Danska	15
Ch.	T'Domar's Bismarck	14
Ch.	Storm Kloud's Ximious Dream, C.D.	14
Ch.	Shamrock's Kotze Tu B Good	13
Ch.	Williwaw's Sunbear of Targhee	12
Ch.	Storm Kloud's R-Tic Sun	12
Ch.	Kiwaliks Snowbear of Kipnuk	12
Ch.	Kioona's Chibouk of Kaila	12
Ch.	Baronof	12
Ch.	Alyeska Su Son	12
Ch.	Storm Kloud's Echo of Bear	11
Ch.	Atanik's Snopaw I'm Awesome	11
Ch.	Tobe's Tony Baretta	10
Ch.	Storm Kloud's Vvanilla Snowman, C.D.	10
Ch.	Snocre's Sun King of Midway	10
Ch.	Mushateer's Lewis Moon	10
Ch.	Kanangnark's Wildcat	10
Ch.	Glacier's Burbon King, C.D.	10
Ch.	Fleur de Lis El Macho	10
Ch.	Tinut of Fleur de Lis	9
Ch.	Tigara's Karluk of Roy-El	9
Ch.	Sugarbear's Satan of Snoridge	9
Ch.	Spawn's Hot Shot of Roy-El	9
Ch.	Snow Star's Stormy Jack Son	9
Ch.	Sno-Crest's Mukluk	9
Ch.	Sendaishi's Kandu Can-Do	9
Ch.	Nahnook II	9
Ch.	Husky-Pak Erok	9
	Chief Michigamme	9
Ch.	Bigfoot's Field Artillery	9
Ch.	Apache Chief of Husky-Pak	9
Ch.	Vermar's Arclar Terrific Turk	8
Ch.	Tigara's Nordisch Kotze Tu	8
Ch.	T'Domar's Voodoo King	8
Ch.	Shuyak Caro of Cold Foot, C.D.	8
Ch.	Malwood's Dirty Demon	8
Ch.	Kodara Kodiak of Erowah	8
	Highlands N W Black Kong	8
Ch.	Cold Foot Khaibar of Sena-Lak	8
Ch.	Barrenfield's Rocket Torpedo	8
	Aventurero de Korok	8
Ch.	Alcan Past Forgetting	8

Ch.	Arctic Storm of Husky-Pak	8
	Aleutia	8
Ch.	Alcan Mate to Arte	8
Ch.	Wild Wind's Ghost Rider in the Sky	7
Ch.	Sugarbear the Blue Ice Queen	7
Ch.	Storm Kloud's Forever Yours, C.D.	7
Ch.	Mushateer's All for a Dream	7
Ch.	Kutachonauu Kiva of Kachina	7
Ch.	Koldwind's Restless Wind	7
Ch.	Glacier's Tisha Lyng, C.D.	7
	Cobra of Nipigon	7
Ch.	Beowulf's Lynaska Dolly, C.D.	7
Ch.	White Hawk's Tahlequah	6
Ch.	Wenaha's Taneum of Onak, C.D.	6
Ch.	Uyak Indian Inez	6
Ch.	Storm Kloud's Vvanilla Pudding	6
	Sno-Pak Kavik's Oonalik	6
	Siska of Erowah	6
·Ch.	Silver Frost's Kimluk	6
Ch.	Sena-Lak's Thora	6
Ch.	Sabre's Misti Dawn of Snopaw	6
Ch.	Polar-Pak's Foxy Lady	6
Ch.	Malesa's Mischief Maker, C.D.X.	6
Ch.	Kiana of Klondike	6
Ch.	Icefloe's North Star	6
	Glacier Hills Snow Princess	6
	Chilanko's Tishka Doll	6
Ch.	Ca-Jim's Arctic Pride	6
Ch.	Aurora's Kuyana of Windrift	6
	Yukon's Cheyenne Autumn	5
Ch.	Voyageur's Elke	5
Ch.	Vermar's Hurricane Hanna	5
Ch.	Tote-Um's Kooteeyah	5
Ch.	Timberlane's Tuktu of Snocre	5
	Timberlane's Heidi Jane	5
	Strawberries Sable Sparks	5
Ch.	Storm Kloud's Peny of Wild Wind	5
Ch.	Storm Kloud's Hhumble Shaman	5
Ch.	Storm Kloud's Hhell's Angel, C.D.	5
Ch.	Sno Ridge's Mountain Lady	5
Ch.	Sena-Lak's Kiana's Black Witch	5
Ch.	Sena-Lak's Beowulf Tawechi	5
Ch.	Nordic Crystal Storm	5
Ch.	Montak's High Sierra Tundra	5
	Misty Dawn	5
Ch.	Mals-About's Star Song	5
	Malesa's More Mischief	5
Ch.	Lucky Bear of the South Wind	5
	Kotzebue Muffin Chinook	5
Ch.	Knotty Pine's Dark Devil	5
Ch.	Kiwaliks Miacis of Nerak	5
Ch.	Keeley's Magic Moment	5
Ch.	Jingo's Silver Trumpet	5
Ch.	J-Len's Tigress of Kiwalik	5
Ch.	J-Len's Prairie Twister	5
	Husky-Pak Morning Star	5
Ch.	Hug-A-Bear's Karisma Windrift	5
	Far North's Zodiak of Aleutian	5
Ch.	Erowah Roxanne	5
Ch.	Cold Foot's Chevak	5
Ch.	Chena Nenana II	5
Ch.	Ca-Jim's Luv Truck	5
Ch.	Barrenfield's Sunrise	5
	Alcan the Copper Queen	5

Still in good shape at age ten is Am./Can. Ch. Mals-About's Touch of Frost, C.D., R.O.M., the top producing Brood Bitch of all-time. Owner is Pat Fendley. *Randall Williamson*

Ch. Mals-About's Star Song, R.O.M. She is a second-generation R.O.M. produced by Hank and Barbie Corwin of Fairview, Tennessee. Handled by Jim Sawyers. *Noel*

National Specialty in 1986 brought together this great group of brood bitches for judge Ilene Mulry. L. to r. are Am./Can. Ch. Mals-About's Touch of Frost, C.D., R.O.M., handled by Pat Fendley; Ch. Mals-About's Carbon Copy, handled by John L. Roberts; and Ch. Mals-About's Sun Dagger of Alta, handled by Perry Hazelwood. *Booth*

Foundation dam of Poker Flat Kennels is Ch. Malesa's Mischief Maker, R.O.M., C.D.X., R.O.M.O.B. Owner is Robin Haggard, Ivesdale, Illinois.

Ch. Poker Flat's The Soft Parade, C.D., lies in front of her all-champion litter. L. to r. are Ch. Poker Flat's Midnight Toker; Ch. Poker Flat's Nashuba, C.D., W.P.D.; and Ch. Poker Flat's Midnight Cowboy, C.D., W.W.P.D.
Jim Kuenl

Ch. Jingo's Silver Trumpet, R.O.M., whelped a litter of six, of which five won championships and two won R.O.M. honors. She is the daughter of Ch. Husky-Pak Jingo, one of the last of Robert Zoller's great Husky-Pak dams. She is owned by Virginia Devaney of Cedar Crest, New Mexico.   *George Will*

Ch. Storm Kloud's Hhell's Angel, C.D., W.W.P.D., R.O.M., was #1 show bitch from 1982 through 1984. She was bred and owned by Nancy Russell and shown by Jeri Russell.
Shelwyn

Ch. Dorrie's Sitka of North Wind, R.O.M., is the foundation dam of the North Wind and Kanangnark Kennels of Emil and Doris Knorr. She is considered a good example of the crossing of the M'Loot and Kotzebue lines.

Ch. Mushateer's All For a Dream, R.O.M., is owned by John and Laura Swire and was shown by John. The bitch is the dam of seven champions, each of which has produced a champion.
Thacker

Glacier Hills Snow Princess, R.O.M., owned by Val Littfin.

Klein

Glacier Hills Snow Princess R.O.M. (left) is the dam of, from l. to r., Am./Can. Ch. Trilliums' Bull Moose Party and Ch. Trillium's Image of Ruffian, both sired by Ch. Nomarak's Teddi Du-Paumanak; and Yukon King of Trillium and Trillium's Princess Thea, both sired by Ch. Tote-Um's Cinnamon Bear, R.O.M., R.O.M.O.B.

251

Ch. Voyageur's Cougar, R.O.M., bred and owned by Howard and Virginia Devaney. This dog was rated #5 or #6 in the U. S. Top Ten for three years.   *Ludwig*

OBEDIENCE REGISTER OF MERIT

A dog must have a minimum of five offspring which have earned obedience titles in order to fulfill the requirements as an Obedience Register of Merit dog. A bitch must have four. The listing of these animals shows in the first column, the year during which they qualified as an Obedience Register of Merit dog. The second column gives the total number of get which have completed obedience titles, and the last year during which a title was achieved by any offspring. If there is no second-column entry by a dog's name, it is indicative of the fact that the qualifying year and the last year of any get becoming obedience-titled are the same.

OBEDIENCE REGISTER OF MERIT—DOGS

Ch. Aristeed's Frost Shadow	5 1981; 6 1983
Aventurero de Korok	5 1970
Ch. Coldfoot Oonanik, U.D.T.	5 1977
Ch. Glacier's Storm Kloud, C.D.	5 1973; 13 1982
Ch. Inuit's Sweet Lucifer	5 1976; 13 1983
Ch. Maluk of Northern Star, C.D.X.	5 1977; 12 1979
Ch. Sarge's Candy Man of Big Paw	5 1981; 6 1982
Ch. Shuyak Caro of Cold Foot, C.D.	5 1967; 7 1970
Ch. Snopaw's Snoqualmie, C.D.	5 1980; 7 1986
Ch. Strawberry's Clyde All-Mighty, C.D.	5 1987
Ch. Tote-Um's Cinnamon Bear	5 1983; 9 1987

OBEDIENCE REGISTER OF MERIT—BITCHES

Actondale's Kara, C.D.X., T.D.	4 1981; 6 1985
Ch. Beowulf's Lynaska Dolly, C.D.	4 1979
Beowulf Thadja-Kimit, C.D.	4 1975
Ch. Beowulf Thosca of Snow Foot, C.D.X.	4 1973
Ch. Dorry's Sitka of North Wind, R.O.M.	4 1965; 5 1965
Ch. Malesa's Mischief Maker, C.D.X.	4 1978; 5 1983
Ch. Polarpaw's Akela Akamai	4 1981; 6 1983
Ch. Skagway's Get Up 'n Boogie, C.D.	4 1982
Skookum's Paria of Amorak, C.D.	4 1985
Ch. Snow Foot Mushy	4 1966; 5 1970
Ch. Storm Kloud's Forever Yours, C.D.	4 1980
Ch. Storm Kloud's Hhumble Shaman	4 1987; 6 1987
Ch. Storm Kloud's Vvanilla Pudding	4 1987
Ch. Timberlane's Misty Rainbow, C.D.X.	4 1977; 7 1980

Glossary

Alaskan Husky: A breed no longer recognized in the United States by the American Kennel Club (through failure of dogs to be registered since the 1950s), but still recognized by the Canadian Kennel Club. Also, a term commonly used to refer to an Arctic-type crossbred dog (e.g., Alaskan Malamute and Siberian Husky).

Alaskan Malamute Club of America (AMCA): The breed's United States "Parent Club" and a member of the American Kennel Club.

Alaskan Malamute Club of Canada (AMCC): The breed's Canadian "Parent Club" and a member of the Canadian Kennel Club.

alpha personality: Designates the first-position, chief, or highest-ranking animal of dominance in a social hierarchy such as a canid pack.

American Kennel Club (AKC): The governing and registering body of the United States, overseeing the rules and regulations pertaining to registration, dog shows, and field, obedience, and tracking trials. It serves as the registering body for breeds of purebred dogs which it recognizes. As a rule, only parent-breed, all-breed, field, obedience, and tracking clubs may become members of the AKC.

barrel: Rounded rib section.

Best Brace in Show (BBIS): Won by very few braces at an all-breed show. The entry of two dogs has competed at the Breed and Group levels, winning in each category.

Best in Show (BIS): Historically awarded to only a few Alaskan Malamutes, these are dogs which have competed in all-breed shows and who have, through the process of elimination, been selected as the best dog in the show on that date.

Best in Specialty Show (BISS): A synonym for Best of Breed at a Specialty show.

Best of Breed (BOB): The award given to that breed (or variety) representative judged to be the best of the breed at a given show on that date.

Best of Opposite Sex (BOS): The award given to that breed representative deemed the best among the opposite sex (opposite to the sex of the Best of Breed winner) at a given show.

Best of Winners (BW): An award given to the Winners (class) Dog or Bitch, being judged to be the best of either of those two animals at a given show upon that date according to the judge's interpretation of the breed's Standard.

Best Team in Show (BTIS): Same as brace competition, but for an entry of *four* of the same breed and ownership.

Canadian Kennel Club (CKC): The governing and registering body of Canada, overseeing the rules and regulations pertaining to dog shows and field, obedience, and tracking trials. The CKC serves as the registering body for all breeds recognized as purebred by the Club. Individuals as well as clubs may hold membership in the CKC.

Canis familiaris: Any domesticated breed of dog.

Canis lupus: The wolf; there are over three hundred subspecies.

Central Progressive Retinal Atrophy (CPRA): A condition in which a central atrophy of the retina occurs.

Champion (of Record) (Ch.): A prefix used with the name of a dog that has been recorded a Champion by the kennel club of a given country (e.g., AKC, CKC) as a result of having defeated a specified number of dogs in specified competition at a series of licensed or member club shows.

Chondrodysplasia (ChD): Commonly known as "dwarfism." It is a hereditary condition found in Alaskan Malamutes, being produced by a simple recessive gene. Both parents must be carriers for the condition to occur in offspring. Carriers should not be used in a viable breeding program.

close-coupled: Comparatively short from the last rib to the beginning of the hindquarters.

Companion Dog (C.D.): A suffix used with the name of a dog that has been recorded as a Companion Dog by either the AKC or the CKC as a result of having won certain minimum scores (or better) in the Novice classes at a specified number of licensed all-breed shows or member club obedience trials.

Companion Dog Excellent (C.D.X.): A suffix used with the name of a dog that has been recorded a Companion Dog Excellent by either the AKC or the CKC as a result of having won certain minimum scores (or better) in Open Obedience classes at trials under a specified number of judges.

dog brigade: The first northern freight teams were normally composed of three to five dogs, and were known as "dog trains." If more than one dog train was part of a convoy, then the group was known as a "dog brigade" by the early English explorers.

double-lead: Two dogs placed at the front of a team, performing in unison to the driver's signals. Double-lead is also used as a method for training a new lead dog and easing the load when traveling across virgin snow.

double-tandem: This is currently the most popular method of hitch for a dog team. While there may be either one or two dogs in lead, the following team dogs are hitched by brace. The positions are normally point, swing (first, second, etc.) and wheel dogs. (Also known as "gang-hitch.")

Hall of Working Fame (HWF): An award for those special dogs which have performed outstandingly.

Hall of Working Fame Committee (HWFC): Established by the Alaskan Malamute Club of America. The committee set up and continues to regulate the qualifications required by a registered (or registerable) Alaskan Malamute to be awarded the coveted working-dog title of HWF.

High in Trial (HIT): Awarded to that dog which scores the highest number of points in an obedience trial. A perfect score is 200. All dogs begin their obedience exercises with perfect scores. Whole or half points are deducted for flaws in the execution of an exercise. Three Alaskan Malamutes are known to have achieved the distinct honor of having won a High in Trial at an all-breed show.

Hip Dysplasia: A malformation of the acetabulum and/or the head of the femur; may include a thickening of the neck of the femur. The condition can be caused virally, congenitally, or by trauma. Early arthritic changes can occur in the joint as a result of hip dysplasia. Mild cases may go unnoticed except by radiographic evaluation. The most severe cases are pronounced and require surgical intervention for the animal to live a near-normal life. (See OFA.)

Hypothyroidism: A condition manifested by a low metabolic rate (among other clinical signs). It is a condition that is determined by a veterinarian. Many Alaskan Malamutes are prone to hypothyroidism from as early as eighteen months onward. Treatment is ongoing and effective when detected early, before irreversible changes occur in the animal.

International Sled Dog Racing Association (ISDRA): ISDRA recognizes gold, silver, and bronze medal winners (first through third placements) annually in each weight division, awarded to the top three dogs per division which have accumulated the most points from dogs defeated in the best of their four pulls for that season.

International Weight Pull Association (IWPA): The criteria of recognition is the same as that of ISDRA.

Obedience Trial Champion (OTCH): A title which has been awarded to two known Alaskan Malamutes for their advanced work and outstanding performances in the field of obedience trials.

Orthopedic Foundation for Animals, Inc. (OFA): A body of veterinarians that evaluates the hips and elbows, providing consultations for radiographs, and certifying those animals whose X-rays show them to be free of joint disease.

Parent Club: The national club for the breed. The listing with the name and address of the secretary can be obtained from the American Kennel Club, 51 Madison Avenue, New York, NY 10010.

point dogs: The first pair of dogs hitched in a team, behind the leader.

Progressive Retinal Atrophy (PRA): A hereditary condition involving a progressively diminishing pupillary response to light. Cataracts may or may not be present with this condition. Transmission is by an autosomal recessive factor. Dogs with this condition should not be bred.

Register of Merit (R.O.M.): A suffix awarded to those dogs whose progeny have met the criteria as established by the Register of Merit Committee of the Alaskan Malamute Club of America. Males must have sired a minimum of eight progeny which have earned their championships. Females must have whelped a minimum of five progeny which have earned their championships.

Register of Merit Obedience (R.O.M.O.B.): A suffix awarded to those Alaskan Malamutes whose progeny have met the criteria established by the Register of Merit Obedience Committee of the Alaskan Malamute Club of America. Dogs must have sired at least five progeny which have earned obedience titles. Dams must have whelped no less than four offspring which have earned obedience titles.

Shock: A condition of acute peripheral circulatory failure due to derangement of circulatory control or loss of circulating fluid and brought about by injury. It is marked by pallor of the mucous membranes, decreased blood pressure, feeble, rapid pulse, decreased respiration, restlessness, anxiety, and sometimes unconsciousness.

spreader bar: A bar used to keep the freighting harness straps apart, preventing them from rubbing the dogs' flanks. It also helps to equalize the load being pulled.

swing dogs: The dogs hitched into a team behind the point dogs and in front of the steer dogs. There may be any number of pairs of swing dogs (first, second, third, etc.) in a large team.

Targhee hound: A breed of dog commonly used in sled dog racing, resulting originally from crossing Irish Setters and Staghounds.

Temperament Test (T.T.): A relatively new form of trial, one not under AKC auspices. The dog and handler move through an established obstacle course of events which may be encountered in daily life. A qualifying score at one trial allows a dog to add the suffix T.T. to its name. Fewer than a dozen Alaskan Malamutes have earned this title.

Tracking Dog (T.D.): A suffix used with the name of a dog that has been recorded a Tracking Dog as the result of having passed a single AKC (or CKC) Licensed or Member club tracking test. The title may be combined with the U.D. title and shown as a U.D.T. suffix to a dog's name.

Tracking Dog Excellent (T.D.X.): A suffix used with the name of a dog that has been recorded a Tracking Dog Excellent as the result of having passed a single AKC-licensed or member club Tracking Dog Excellent test. The title may be combined with the U.D. title and shown as a U.D.T.X. suffix to a dog's name.

Utility Dog (U.D.): A suffix used with the name of a dog that has been recorded a Utility Dog by the AKC (or CKC) as the result of having won certain minimum (or better) scores in Utility classes at three AKC- (or CKC-) Licensed or Member club obedience trials. The title may be combined with the T.D. or T.D.X. title and the dog shown as a U.D.T. or U.D.T.X.

withers: The highest point of the shoulders, immediately behind the neck.

Working Lead Dog (W.L.D.): A title earned by a registered or registerable Alaskan Malamute which has met the qualifications for that category established by the Working Dog Committee of the Alaskan Malamute Club of America.

Working Lead Dog Excellent (W.L.D.X.): A title earned by those few registered or registerable Alaskan Malamutes which have met the criteria established by the Working Dog Excellent Committee of the Alaskan Malamute Club of America.

Working Pack Dog (W.P.D.): A title earned by a registered or registerable Alaskan Malamute which has met the criteria for that category as established by the Working Dog Committee of the Alaskan Malamute Club of America.

Working Pack Dog Excellent (W.P.D.X.): A pack dog title earned by a registered or registerable Alaskan Malamute which has met the qualifications as set forth by the Working Dog Excellent Committee of the Alaskan Malamute Club of America.

Working Team Dog (W.T.D.): A title earned by a registered or registerable Alaskan Malamute which has met the qualifications for that category as established by the Working Dog Committee of the Alaskan Malamute Club of America.

Working Team Dog Excellent (W.T.D.X.): A sled-team dog title earned by a registered or registerable Alaskan Malamute that has met the qualifications as set forth by the Working Dog Excellent Committee of the Alaskan Malamute Club of America.

Working Weight-Pull Dog (W.W.P.D.): A title earned by a registered or registerable Alaskan Malamute which has met the criteria established for that category by the Working Dog Committee of the Alaskan Malamute Club of America.

Working Weight-Pull Dog Excellent (W.W.P.D.X.): A weight-pull dog title earned by a registered or registerable Alaskan Malamute that has met the qualifications as set forth by the Working Dog Excellent Committee of the Alaskan Malamute Club of America.